▶

Writing for the World Wide Web

Victor J. Vitanza

University of Texas at Arlington

Allyn and Bacon

Boston • London • Toronto • Sydney • Tokyo • Singapore

Vice President, Humanities: Joseph Opiela
Production Coordinator: Susan Brown
Editorial-Production Service: Matrix Productions Inc.
Cover Administrator: Brian Gogolin
Composition Buyer: Linda Cox
Manufacturing Buyer: Suzanne Lareau

Library of Congress Cataloging-in-Publication Data

Vitanza, Victor J.
    Writing for the World Wide Web / Victor J. Vitanza.
      p.   cm.
    Includes index.
    ISBN 0-205-26693-2
    1. Web sites—Design.   2. Interactive multimedia—Authorship.
    3. World Wide Web (Information retrieval system)   4. HTML (Document
    markup language)   5. English language—Rhetoric.   6. Report writing.
    I. Title.
    TK5105.888.V57   1997
    808′.066005—dc21   97-27601
                                                                           CIP

The World Wide Web is a fast-changing medium. Between the time Web site
information is gathered and the time it is published, it is not unusual for some
sites to have closed or moved. The URLs listed herein were accurate at the time
of printing.

Credits appear on p. 236

Printed in the United States of America

10   9   8   7   6   5   4   3   2   02   01   00   99   98

Contents

The Net [and World Wide Web] is not a place for "professionals" to publish and the masses to merely download. Online, everyone is becoming an artist; everyone is a creator. The network is providing new opportunities for self expression, and demands a new kind of artist: the artistic instigator, someone who inspires other people to be creative by setting a positive example with their own work, and providing others with tools, context, and support. That support can be technical, aesthetic, or emotional—encouraging others to believe in their own capabilities and take the risk of trying to make something personally meaningful.

Cyberspace is not Disneyland. It's not a place to wait on line to see the virtual Pirates of the Caribbean. It's a place to build your own pirates, your own Caribbean, your own self portrait, your family history, your animation demo, your thoughtful essay, your silly poem. Online, it's true you can download paintings from the Louvre—but much more interesting is the fact that you can upload your own. Or better yet, inspire others to do so.

—Amy Bruckman

▶

Preface
to Students (and Facilitators)

Here is a rather FORMAL statement of what my intentions were in writing this book: The general purpose of this book is:

To introduce you (students) to "writing" for the world wide web. The book *is an introductory book* and is meant for those of you in English and Communications courses but can be used, in general, by others of you in the Humanities and other academic areas.

But exactly what does "writing" mean in the title *Writing for the World Wide Web?*

What I concentrate on in this book is instructing you in the overall development of Web sites and spend less time on the kind of instruction that you would normally expect to find in a traditional textbook on writing. But do not be mistaken: Being able to write clearly and to get ideas across quickly are exceptionally important. And they are no less, if not downright more, important on the WWW. You definitely will want to use, along with this book, a writing handbook so that you can get instructions on mechanics (spelling, punctuation, grammar). Also, you will want to use the various links to be found at Ted Nellen's collection on the Writing Process (http://mbhs.bergtraum.k12.ny.us/writing.html), which includes everything that you could ever imagine.

These elements—I cannot stress enough—are extremely important. No matter how much effort you put into the design of a webpage, no matter how many great-looking graphics you have, a poorly constructed sentence or phrase, or misspelled words or the ineffective use of punctuation will annoy many people who visit your website.

You need to understand, however, that besides writing for print on paper, which is exclusively the kind of instruction that you get in a writing handbook, you will have to learn *how to write for the Web*. Therefore, I see it as my task to suggest to you intermittently—when and where appropriate, and always in context—*how* to write specifically for the different and evolving genres that you will find on the Web. "Writing" for the Web, in most cases, requires a clipped (highly abbreviated) style. Moreover, "writing" for the Web requires some knowledge of design and graphics to make "writing" for the Web more acceptable and easier to read. (What is easy to read in print is not necessarily easy to read on a monitor.) Further, writing for the Web requires not only knowledge of the English language or your native language, but also requires a basic understanding and knowledge of Hypertext Markup Language (HTML), which is the universal language, or code, that determines the disposition of words, images, or links on a Web page.

Besides learning about the mechanics of constructing Web pages, you also learn in *Writing for the World Wide Web* how to revise a web page in terms of re-visioning (re-seeing) it. I take you through several revisions, for example, of a personal home page and suggest to you how to connect your other web writings to your page.

All of these many and various aspects, then, are what I mean by "writing" for the WWW. (For a continuing answer to the question concerning writing, read the Introduction to this book.)

The other, more specific purposes are:

- To describe and establish for you a series of templates for personal home pages (expressive writing), and for the electronic essay, informational Web sites, and collaborative sites (expository and persuasive writing), and, in passing, to introduce you to experimental writing for the Web (aesthetic, creative writing).
- To suggest to you ways of thinking about discovering and developing a sense of style for your work on the Web.
- To instruct you in the logic of computer directories and how to transfer files to a server.
- To provide you with the necessary Web resources (e.g., updates on browsers, information on hexidecimal [color] codes, places to find graphics in the public domain) that you will need to be successful.
- To introduce you to the problems of copyright infringement in respect to both text and graphics, multimedia.
- To provide you with a handy checklist for revision and for corrections.
- To point you to more sophisticated software and technology that will have an impact on writing and designing for the WWW.

You are expected to create an HTML document/file by typing in each of the examples and thereby creating a repertoire of templates. The typing of the HTML puts you in the position of working through each section of the code, and of course puts you in the position of having to find and correct your typos, just as you would have to find your errors and typos in an essay for print. Once the templates are stored in hard disks or on various floppy disks, then you can begin to work from them, testing them, filling them with your own content and graphics, modifying them altogether as you learn more about HTML and you envision *what* and *how* it is that you want to communicate. You are also encouraged to surf and study the Web itself—your other textbook—looking for sites that also can be used for templates.

Since this book about the Web is *a book,* it has its limitations. Therefore, there is a website that updates and supplements this book. Visit *http://www.abacon.com/*

Now here is my more INFORMAL set of intentions for writing this book:

Direct your eye right inward, and you'll find
A thousand regions in your mind
Yet undiscovered. Travel them, and be
Expert in home-cosmography.

Thoreau, *Walden*

The purpose—I want to write, instead, 'porpoise', but my editor will never let me get away with such a silly reference—so the purpose of this book is

- To get you (students) to enjoy—to have fun!—writing for the WWW, and to figure out who you might be out on the Web.
- To get you to hear what I am saying, namely, "Go Web, Young Men and Women; Go Web." The West is closed, and outer space is too far. As Richard Rodriguez says: "See how the metaphor of the West [California, the Edge] dissolves into foam at my feet." And Congress continues to say No to funding the exploration of outer space. So venture into Cyberspace! And be one of its pioneers. Be not an expert but, as Amy Bruckman suggests, "the artistic instigator" in home-cyberography.
- And finally, to invite you to feel comfortable in both writing with ink for print and with pixels for the Web. To get you to become an *amphibian.* To grow webbed feet. These, indeed, are silly metaphors that I use, but they illustrate unforgettably the necessity for you to live in two radically different cultural environments—on paper and on monitors. To get you to take as many steps as you can to walk out of the water onto the shore

and stay as long as you can. And then, after returning to the water, to return as soon as you can to the shore and then beyond. Or to invite you at least to be a porpoise, lifting yourself out of your everyday element, arching yourself up and away before diving back into your so-called natural environment. The motive for being a porpoise would not be to take an intermediary step to altogether leave the water, but to live and dwell in both print and the WWW in the most successful way that you can.

In any case, Make VVaves.

And let me hear from you:

VVitanza@aol.com

Acknowledgments and Credits

I would like to thank Collin G. Brooke, Matthew A. Levy, David M. Rieder, Alan P. Taylor, and of course David M. Vitanza for their technical assistance with this book. Also, I am appreciative of the help given me by Jeff Galin on matters of copyright issues and Barry W. Pase, Barry's Clip Art (http://www.barrysclipart.com) and Gioacchino La Vecchia, Icon Browser (http://www.cli.di.unipi.it/iconbrowser/icons.html) on matters of graphics in the public domain.

I would especially like to thank my wife, Toni, and my youngest son, Roman, for their patience through out the summer of my writing this book. Without their approval and understanding, I would not have been able to take up yet another summer with writing a book. Next summer is theirs!

Thanks to the following people for their reviews of the manuscript: Ray Dumont, University of Massachusetts, Dartmouth; Marcia Peoples Halio, University of Delaware; Christine Hult, Utah State University; and Ed Klonoski, University of Hartford.

And I would also like to thank Joe Opiela (my editor), Kate Tolini, and all the folks at Allyn & Bacon who take care of the server where our webfiles for updating this book reside.

In designing the websites in this book, I used a number of graphics from public domain sites and designed generic graphics or took photographs myself. Here is an accounting of the various graphics:

Fig. 10–12, eye, Icon Browser
(*http://www.cli.di.unipi.it/iconbrowser/icons.html*).

Fig. 13, 17, eye, personal photo, taken at Ft. Worth Zoo.

Fig. 14, 17, eye wink, Dick Collier (done for hire)

Fig. 21, arrows, Icon Browser; buttons, Allyn & Bacon

Fig. 30, a cool guy, eyeguy, critic, blade, running man, surfer—all from Icon Browser. Bob, Barry's Clip Art (*http://www.barrysclipart.com*). Nerd (GifAnimation), MicroMovie MiniMultiplex (*http://www.teleport.com/~cooler/ MMMM/index.html*). Alphabetic blocks and Cybermonster, homemade.

Fig. 31, man with money, Barry's Clip Art

Fig. 33, video and sound icons, Icon Browser. Allyn and Bacon Icons, from A&B (*http://www.abacon.com/*).

Fig. 42, tomatoes in bunch and single, personal photo.

Fig. 43, musical note (GifAnimation), MicroMovie MiniMultiplex. Return button, Icon Broswer.

Fig. 44–45, eyeguys, Icon Browser.

Fig. 45, Zine logo with eyes, personal design. I wanna be electricity, Matthew Levy (with permission). Electricity button, Icon Browser.

Fig. 48, crackers, personal photo.

Fig. 49, I love my tattoo, personal design.

Fig. 69, Nervous Text, Java (*http://java.sun.com/applets/applets.html*).

—Victor J. Vitanza

▶

Introduction: Orality, Literacy, and Electronic Discourse

For the Students: The Purpose of this book, as the title states, is to introduce you to Writing for the World Wide Web (WWW). Writing a speech that you or someone else is going to deliver and writing an essay that you are going to submit to your teacher for a grade are both very different tasks from one another. Writing for the WWW is just as different. You might ask, "How could this be the case? After all, is not writing just writing?" My answer to that question has got to be "No!" Why? Because . . .

Researchers have learned by studying both experienced and inexperienced writers that success or failure is greatly dependent on whether or not writers are aware of the *constraints* and *conventions* of the genre in which they want to speak and write and whether or not they can execute them well.

By constraints, I mean the limitations that are placed on both the writer and the audience. For example, whereas writing for print can be reread if not understood, writing presented orally can pass on by, at times, without being clearly heard. Whereas discourse in print, with the author not present, cannot at times be understood, no matter how many times we reread it, discourse that is presented orally, with the speaker present, can similarly not be understood or in passing heard but is open to being clarified if a member of the audience asks a question. Whether the author/speaker is present or absent is of major importance. (The speaker's presence, however, is not necessarily a solution to the problem that the audience might be having with the aim or meaning of a statement. The author is not considered by a lot of people today to be the final authority for what was said. In other words, it is difficult to defend the proposition today that the author means what s/he says; and says precisely what s/he means. And yet, we still in many ways hold on to the possibility of asking the author for a clarification if we wish one.)

By conventions, I mean the commonly accepted genres of communicating (or kinds of discourse) for different purposes and media. Listeners and Readers have certain expectations, given their understanding of the purpose of the communication, that they desire to be fulfilled. For example, if you want to appeal a grade you received in a class, there is a time-honored way of formulating your request to be heard and way of linking together good reasons for the request to be granted. You have to know what will and will not count as an argument and what will be compelling enough to influence your audience to grant what action you want them to take. There are numerous conventions for all kinds of writing to be delivered orally or put in print. And there are, of course, even conventions for being unconventional.

What you will read about in this book are some of the evolving conventions of writing for the WWW. Yes, though the WWW is a fairly new medium, it is possible at this point in time to begin thinking about conventions. This does not mean, however, that they will be set and will not change. What the Web is all about *is* change. And yet, there are some basic principles of communication, even in electronic discourse, that are not going to change that rapidly, if change at all. You have heard the adage that the more that things change, the more that they stay the same? There is reason to believe this statement to be the case. There are constants in human communication. But at the same time, there are equally good reasons to believe that the electronic environment of cyberspace itself is causing us to rethink and restructure what will count as successful communication there. The technology and its constraints are demanding the evolution of newer, appropriate conventions, with which we will have to be familiar, if we are to live successfully in virtual communities. Already, for some of you, whether you know it or not, the WWW is *the* medium for your future livelihood. It will be the other place where you will also be a citizen ("netizen"). In general, it is the place for your personal and professional identity in cyberspace; in particular, it is the medium for presenting yourself to prospective employers and to others on the Web who might want to conduct business or associate themselves (link up) with you. You might at present be proficient with electronic mail, but building a virtual home or business on the Web is a great deal more complicated.

Let's recoup and slightly reformulate and elaborate. What I have suggested thus far in passing is that there are constraints on and conventions for

- speech (oral discourse on sound waves), for
- writing (printed discourse on paper), and for
- electronic discourse/WWW (magnetized pixels on black and white or colored monitors).

We know from experience and study that if someone writes a speech that has very complicated sentences, that are not necessarily broken up into parallel repetitive structures, but that are labyrinthine in structure, twisting and turning while exploring different avenues of thought, the audience will most likely be at a loss to follow what is being said. If, however, such writing is done for print, it might be easier to follow, though for some people still difficult to process. It might be easier to follow because the readers can usually reread what they only partially understood. (Though the previous three sentences were not written for a speech, you might have found yourself having to reread them in order to get through them. They are purposefully written as they are so as to illustrate my point of what is acceptable in writing for oral delivery and for print.)

Writing that attempts to inform or persuade an audience has got to be relatively easy for readers to process. There is a general rule of thumb that an average listener or even a reader can process only 7 + or − 2 bits of information at one time. So writers either intuitively or experientially have come to understand that they must chunk and package their information in certain ways. And even repeat and summarize what has been said before going on to the next point in order to be successful. And yet, writing that attempts to be literary or experimental does not necessarily have to be easy to follow. Such writing presents puzzles or mysteries for the reader to solve or presents strings of words to learn to appreciate. Often the reader is expected to reread what has been written. And to study it. Ponder it. The way that you might look or stare at a painting in a museum. A writer who wants to communicate information but presents it ineffectively, however, should never hide under the pretense of being an innovator. Writing in an innovative style requires great skill and command of a language and it requires also to understand when to abandon oneself to the flow of language. This book, though it will touch on innovative writing for the WWW, is not a book about what is normally called "creative writing." It is a book that will concentrate on the basic, yet evolving, conventions of writing electronic discourse. What will complicate matters—and bears repeating here—is that the basic conventions are very unconventional when compared with the conventions of speaking and writing. And therein lies the problem that we have to ponder and solve if we are to be successful.

When writing for the WWW, writers tend to compose with very few words because they rely more on icons (images, pictures, graphics) as a means of communicating or guiding the reader, who for the most part just clicks from section (or file) to section. If you were to write for the WWW the way that you write a lengthy essay or report for your teacher—say, ten-typed pages—you would probably altogether lose your audience, who would just click you out of sight. And go elsewhere. I am not suggesting, however, that you should not have ten pages of type; I am suggesting, as you will see eventually in the discussion of this book, that there are conventional ways of presenting even that amount of text, making it easier for your readers to sift through it all. A chunk at a time. But beware, for in my making this statement, I have taken leave of what some people believe about what should or should not be an acceptable practice on the WWW. Many believe deeply in the motto: "Fewer words, more images." And many believe that everything (each page or file) is to fit on the monitor (after every click) without the reader of a page having to scroll down at all. The average size of a monitor is about 14–15" measured diagonally, and therefore that physical constraint is generally considered to be your target size. To this issue of words versus images and size of screen, we will perpetually return.

Electronic discourse . . . is what you will be studying and practicing in this book. So from time to time remind yourself: Electronic discourse is not *oral discourse* and is not *printed discourse*. It is (becoming) *something else.* Your success as a communicator on the WWW will in great part, therefore, be based on your understanding the differences among these three technologies and media.

And yet, being able to understand and to practice the differences among oral, printed, and electronic discourses is not—nor will it ever be—enough to know; for electronic discourse often incorporates oral and printed discourses. Electronic discourse is an olio of technologies and media including words, speech and music, and graphics and video. It's a lot like operas, classical or rock, with all of the elements of words, speech, music, graphics, props, etc. It will become more and more like MTV, but interactive. In learning to write for the WWW, you will have to learn eventually how to mix all three forms of discourse in terms of multimedia, though we will concentrate more so on words and graphics in what is called *hypertext* (a format, literally, of extended-words that may or may not be always logically, but figuratively, connected). You, therefore, will be doing more than is suggested in the foregoing by the word *writing;* we might better characterize, instead, what you will be learning and doing as *composing.* Here is what the *American Heritage Dictionary* variously has to say about the word *composing:*

> —*v. tr.* **1.** To make up the constituent parts of; constitute or form. . . .
> **2.** To make or create by putting together parts or elements. **3.** To create or produce (a literary or musical piece). **4.** To make (one's mind or body) calm or tranquil; quiet: *compose yourself and deal with the problems.* **5.** To settle or adjust; reconcile: *composed their differences.* **6.** To arrange aesthetically or artistically. **7.** *Printing.* To arrange or set (type or matter to be printed).—*intr.* **1.** To create literary or musical pieces. **2.** Printing. To set type.

You will be shown how to perform every one of these tasks. (For example, you will be *setting type* when you put in hypertext markup language [HTML] for the fonts and their sizes and colors.) And you will be invited to improve on these tasks.

* * *

For the Students and Facilitators: What and especially *how* I have written—composed—the foregoing statement is purposefully rendered to illustrate a point. I myself find it rather dull and bland, primarily because of the tone, which, at times, projects a voice, or attitude, of seriousness and pedantry. (Notice the jarring contrast between the opening full-page quote from Amy Bruckman and what follows in the first section of the "professional" preface. And notice the differences in the formal and informal sections of the Preface to this book.) The foregoing part of this introduction is not written, as I would normally write, in a different style for my particular audience: Students. And yet, as I said, it is purposefully written in this manner. Why? So that I might illustrate a point, namely, that I—and you—can take a piece of prose that is extended over a series of pages in print and *recompose* it for the medium of the WWW and turn bland expository prose into a high-energy presentation. In that way I—and you—can be as Bruckman suggests "artistic instigators." Or so I would think so. This is a very tricky thing to attempt, but attempt I—we—*must*, because as I will explain and illustrate through out this book, the medium of electronic discourse is very, very different—so very different—from printed discourse that a piece of clear, successful exposition in print, say, in an encyclopedia, can be an absolute failure on the Web if simply presented there as in print; or that your essay assignment in print that received, let's say an "A," can be an absolute failure as electronic discourse on a website. As Marshall McLuhan said: The medium is the massage. Or as I would rephrase: The container shapes the content of the message.

By the time you get this book, my publisher and I will have established a website on which there will be supplementary and complementary files with links to each section of the printed book. (In this way, we can constantly update the site and keep in touch with you.) At that site, I will also include a file/link to this Introduction but *as recomposed* in a hypertext format and in part a multimedia format, so that you might see the difference between the print version here and a multimedia version of the "same" Introduction on the Web, and perhaps might even see it as being more palatable. (I will limit what I do in terms of markup language [HTML] to the codes and techniques given in the book.) It may very well be, however, that if you are the kind of person who prefers words in print alone and in a regular font size with black ink on white paper, it will not matter at all what I—

or anyone else—will or could have done to this Introduction in the electronic medium that we are about to study. I have many friends who are consistent in preferring a story told in print rather than presented in film, and who have never enjoyed a novel that has been made into a film. (As if the two genres are even comparable!)

Should I rewrite this introduction and include a second—at least, for me—more exciting, high-energy draft in this book? Why should I? The purpose of the book is not to compare the differences between what I believe to be "good" and "bad" writing, or bland and highly rhythmic, perhaps punk, prose in print for students, nor is the purpose to illustrate what I personally or in conjunction with my colleagues consider in general to be "good" or "bad" writing for print. Should I place a better draft of this introduction on the website for this book instead of here in the book? Why?, so that it can sit there and, in the eyes of people who are familiar with and sensitive to appreciating the genre(s) of the WWW, just look worse, or look like an unsuccessful fish out of water? I have the rest of the book to write in print. Why double up here, when I can double up this introduction by way of the very medium I am attempting to invite you to learn and to use?

Really, What's more important? Writing for print or for an electronic environment? To be sure, this is a question that we in academia and in the popular press are wrestling with. Right now, as will continue to be the case, writing/composing electronic discourse is seen as supplementary, not as primary. In other words, it is generally assumed that it is more necessary (hence, more important) to be able to write following the conventions of print. Given where we are right now, I do agree. Given where we will be, however, I agree *and* I disagree. Writing/composing for the Web and any future technology that lies beyond the WWW, wherever and whatever that might be, is equally, if not in some ways more, important than writing the academic essay for print. Therefore, we (students and facilitators) must learn to write and to teach for the present *and* for the future. As Michael Joyce says, we must be "of two minds." As I would interpret that to mean: We must firmly place one writing hand on paper and boldly move one typing hand in(to) the future.

These are, no doubt about it, heavy and quarrelsome questions and issues and will remain so for a long time. When in our long academic history we moved from an oral culture to a print culture, there were and still are today similar disagreements. Battles! And many are political. McLuhan, for instance, writes: "Today's child is growing up absurd, because he lives in two worlds, and neither of them inclines him to grow up. Growing up—that is our new work, and it is *total*. Mere instruction will not suffice" (18; McLuhan's emphasis). I am not here interested in attempting to resolve this issue of separate tasks or totality; it is irresolvable by me or us and will either be solved or just dissolved in time and space. As time and space themselves are refigured or dissolved. As I stated, these are heady questions and topics, which I will set aside; for I am more interested, instead, in introducing this new medium to you, students, so that you might, for the time being, not only understand it and practice it and introduce others to it, but more specifically so that you might come to understand that what counts as a good speech, as a good theme/essay, as a good webpage can be radically different from each other. And that your best be skillful and successful at communicating in all three media. Living, working, and playing in all three and in any additional media. Paradoxically, we (as students and facilitators) must learn and invite others to be, as I said in the preface, *amphibians.* On our way out of the "absurd" world we find ourselves in, perhaps to the global (total) village and, yes, back again to the absurd, at least, for a while. Finding ourselves to be sojourners in both.

There's something new on the Web that you might enjoy. It's called "The Main Quad: A Global Community for College Students." Visit *http://www. mainquad.com/.* You might want to enroll.

McLuhan, Marshall, and Quentin Fiore. *The Medium is the Massage: An Inventory of Effects.* NY: Bantam, 1967.

▶ 1

First Questions and Concerns

What Is the World Wide Web (WWW, W3, the Web)?

Why Should a Student of the Humanities Know About the WWW?
> *Why Should Students of the Humanities—presumably, you yourself—Know How to Write for the WWW?*

What Should a Student Know?

What Are the Languages of the WWW?

What Are the Conventions of a Web Site or Home Page?

How to Access Web Space to Begin Writing and Publishing

References (Books and Web Sites)

Let's begin with a few basic questions, which I will only briefly and tentatively answer, so as to establish a further context for what follows as the purpose of the book. You will find numerous other and more lengthy answers to these questions in a variety of books (both how-to manuals and commentaries on the Internet and the World Wide Web) and, of course, you will find many answers out on the Web itself. (I will give the Uniform Resource Locators, URLs, or addresses to sites, from time to time.) Our first, rather obvious question is . . .

WHAT IS THE WORLD WIDE WEB (WWW, W3, THE WEB)?

There are lots of ways to answer this question. One way is that the Web is part of the Internet (the Net). So we must have some understanding of what the Net is.

It is tempting to say that the *Net* is millions of wires and cable encircling the earth. It certainly is that, but a great deal more. Originally, in the United States the Net was constructed and used by the Federal Government. It was called *ARPAnet* (American Advanced Research Projects Agency). It is one of the earliest computer networks, developed by the Department of Defense to connect researchers. It essentially established, in part, an e-mail system so that researchers could communicate and share information. Eventually, the Net was turned over to the private sector, and now is potentially available to all of us. We send each other millions of messages daily from all parts of the world. But as I said it is more than a bunch of cables. For the Net to work, there must be a set of conventions in terms of technology (hardware) and computer programs, codes and languages (software), and most important, the willingness of everyone on the Net (sometimes called Netizens) to work together in a cooperative manner. The Internet is perhaps the world's largest consortium. (This is greatly oversimplified but it gets the general idea across.)

The *Web* was developed at the European Center for Nuclear Research (CERN) in Geneva. Its purpose was and is today to allow for the means of linking specific nuclear research documents among different locations where research is being conducted. With the opening up of the Web to everyone and with the building of more nodes, connecting and strengthening the Web around the world, it has become perhaps the world's "library." Everyone— from nuclear scientist doing research to amateur "scientist" tinkering, from commercial enterprises touting their goods to the person next door or you yourself with your home page—can use and be reached on the Web.

What the Web does, as part of the Net, then, is to allow for the linking of documents (files) stored in servers around the world. The documents are connected by way of hypertext *links* (hot links, hyperlinks) from server to server. (A server is a computer that is connected to the Internet, stores your files, and has Web-server software that allows for your files to be retrieved and read by others. In many ways, a server is like a local library.) In order to read these documents on your individual computer, you must have a browser or a client program—such as Lynx, Mosaic, or Netscape Naviga- tor—that reads the language, or format codes, used to construct the docu- ments. (The language that is used is called HTML, which I will explain later.) A document that you see displayed on your monitor will most likely have a visible link, that is, an underlined statement such as *About the WWW* (see Fig- ure 1, which is the Web page for the World Wide Web Consortium, W3C).

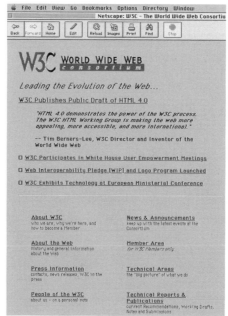

FIGURE 1

When you click on this underlined phrase or single word or image, the file you are reading vanishes while another is loaded and displayed on your monitor. The various links allow a user to move from document to apparently related document no matter where documents are stored in various servers on the Web around the world. Theoretically, all documents in the world that are in servers and that are accessible by way of a "browser" are *linked*. In a way, as Marshall McLuhan might suggest, the Web is "a global village, [a potential] simultaneous happening."

To continue with the analogy that I started earlier: All the local libraries (servers) in the world are linked to the Web (the world's library) so that we can read everything we want to read. When you go to your local library—whether a municipal or university library—you can use that library's online public access catalog to find out what is in that particular library and whether or not it is currently available or checked out. Moreover, if it is not available in your library, you can find out its status in other nearby libraries. These computers simply provide a catalog of what is available; you can't actually read the books or articles that are catalogued online. Similarly, when you boot up and get on line to go to the WWW, the world's library, you can find out what is out there, and in many cases actually read it from your own computer or print it out to read on paper. For example, let's say you are looking for a copy of Thoreau's *Walden* in your library and want to know if it is on the shelf. In order to read *Walden*, you must either check it out or read it in the library. However, if you go out on the Web and use one of the search engines and query the whereabouts of *Walden*, there is a high probability that you will find an electronic copy that you can actually print out and read.

The contents of the worldwide library are changing every second of the day with more and more being added.

One thing you need to keep in mind, however, is that although everything on the Web is potentially linked and readable, you will not necessarily be able to read everything placed into servers. Some files are locked and not accessible except to certain people with special access; some files, as you will immediately discover, have been reassigned new Uniform Resource Locators (URLs), while others have been deleted from the library altogether. (On the WWW, there is no system such as the Library of Congress cataloguing system for books in a library, but there are basic, uniform ways of locating files in a server so that they might be retrieved.) If files are moved or assigned to another directory in a server, usually the author will have a forwarding link to the new site. In many cases, however, you will get the infamous 404 message, which means the file is either no longer available or has been moved to another directory or to another server altogether and without a forwarding address. So goes the Web, like so many things in a state of perpetual change. And nothing changes more than the Web.

WHY SHOULD A STUDENT OF THE HUMANITIES KNOW ABOUT THE WWW?

There are also many answers to this question. One is simply that students need to know about the Web for the same reason they need to know about a library: to do research. People often disagree with this answer by arguing that there is so much junk on the Web and that it is nothing like a good research library. In many ways this is true. However, libraries around the world are online, and to get access to their holdings and other valuable information, you have to know about the Web and how to navigate it. Moreover, every day more and more valuable information and resources are being placed on the Web. It's true that the Web is not a substitute for a library. But the day will come when it will be the world's library. And that day is quickly approaching. There will always be junk on the Web, just as there is junk to be found everywhere. And yet, what is considered junk by one person is of great value to another. The question of who is to arbitrate between junk and valuable information is being seriously questioned today, even within professional fields.

Why Should Students of the Humanities—presumably, you yourself—Know How to Write for the WWW?

Again there are several good reasons, but not necessarily all would be satisfactory for you. Among all the possible answers, I will give two in depth. As we proceed through the book, you will be able to see that the number of good answers to this question are limited only by our imagination.

Establishing your own website or home page

Let's begin thinking about this question in terms of a very practical answer. Knowledge in theory and especially in practice of a new technology is generally interpreted in favorable ways by people around you, especially prospective employers. This is the case even for people—perhaps, especially for people—in the *Humanities*. It is extremely important that you know how to speak, read, and write effectively in a number of different ways for different occasions. Knowing more than one language also improves your chances of getting the kind of position you want. In a single word, the more you know about a variety of things, the more competitive you are. Ways of being more competitive today also include knowing how to write (to compose) effectively for the WWW.

Let's get more specific with this practical answer. A purpose for getting an education is to get the right credentials for the profession or job in which you want to express yourself, to contribute to society, and to make your livelihood. When you are applying for positions in your field or profession, you will most likely be asked to submit a resume or curriculum vitae (CV). (It is now becoming common at particular schools for many students—undergraduate as well as graduate—to establish a home page and post a link from it to their resume. In fact, their home page may very well be nothing but their resume, which is constantly updated.) When filling out an application, you could simply add, to your advantage, a statement giving the URL to your Web page. Sometimes, however, you will even be asked to give, along with your fax number and e-mail address, the URL for your page, that is, if you have one. (A prospective employer may possibly see your home page on the Web as an indication of your value to them.) At present, many universities or prospective employers are giving students and recent graduates the opportunity to apply for attending school or for a position right on the school's or company's web site. Often, they will ask you whether or not you have a home page since you are accessing theirs to apply.

Can you afford in today's overly competitive market not to have a Web page? Many universities and companies know that they themselves cannot afford to be without one. Those searching for schools to attend or companies to apply to should study very carefully the Web pages they find. A prospective employer may even ask questions that you can answer only with an intimate knowledge of their Web site. It used to be that you had to have only an impressive resume. Just as many schools and employers have demanded for a long time now that you have a personal computer or at least know how to use one effectively, many are now expecting you to have a home page and to know how to write for the Web. It is one thing to have someone put out a Web site for you, and quite another to know *how* to do it for yourself. The number of people expecting you to have knowledge of this technology surrounding the WWW will continue to grow. You can learn it quickly and be effective in using it because the basics of writing for the Web are so very easy to learn.

Publishing Your Work

This would include things besides, but supplementary and complementary to, your basic resume. If you decide to have a Web site, given the reasons that I summarized in the first series of answers, you should know how to present your work effectively, just as we all assume that you would need to know how to do so on paper. I strongly suspect that prospective employers can tell a great deal more about you simply by the way you formulate your home page and display your work than they can from your application and work on paper. There are most likely more ways that you can go wrong and lose your acceptance by others if your Web page application is poorly constructed for the intended purpose. For this reason, you might very well want to surrender to the old way of sending in a packet of paper! And yet, I would not encourage you to do this. I encourage my students to do both a paper application and an electronic one. There are some instances of work that cannot easily be sent in on paper without greatly diminishing the effectiveness of particular kinds of collaborative projects. Therefore, while you snail-mail (i.e., conventionally, through the U.S. postal service) your application directly to the company or university, you make available the electronic version of your application on your Web page. If the latter is not looked at, it will be available in any case. Keep in mind, however, that it will eventually be looked at by a prospective employer.

Since I will be showing you how to develop such projects in this book, let's take a summary look at what would be appropriate on a Web page. Remember that what you place on your home page would be part of your application.

One thing we are learning about the environment of electronic discourse is that it allows for collaborative work and for more interactive exchanges with people who are reading your work. I mention collaboration and interaction because more and more students and faculty in the Humanities, and for some time now employers and employees in corporations and businesses, have placed high value on and engage in collaborative work. There is a high probability—given of course your teachers' views about learning and practicing academic work—that you will be asked to do collaborative work, along with your individual work. It is true that at present it is generally considered more important to work as an individual and to publish academic articles in print journals, but this over emphasis on individual work is changing for those of us in the Humanities primarily because of electronic environments.

There are some very good reasons for publishing on the Web and not on paper, and there are some time-honored reasons, accepted by even the most traditional and conservative teachers, to work in a collaborative manner. For example, let's say that someone wants to establish a glossary of terms, either for a class or department or for any other interested person (a relatively brief project) or is more ambitious and wants to publish an encyclopedia (a gigantic project) for a specialized field. When such a project is conducted among scholars and students with the common intention of publishing it in print, there are all kinds of pitfalls: terms can be left out, information cannot be updated until later editions, which can be very expensive, and the information cannot be readily responded to by others in the field. To be sure, someone can and often does review and contribute to the work, but only in passing, and then it takes a long time to get the review in print and then disseminated. Let's face it: As soon as it is published, it may very likely be obsolete. This book, like all books, is a case in point. Knowledge grows, while the pulp version of its representation just sits before us. That's why my publisher and I have agreed to make available a book Web site to correct and continuously update this book.

The technology available for the Web is getting so sophisticated that it is possible for someone—let's say a scholar in the field—to add to the document by way of CGI script forms that would be part of the project itself. (These forms are exactly like all forms that ask questions and give you space to answer them.) If a term is missing that should be dealt with, it can be assigned to the appropriate person or persons, who can work on it. When completed, the new document can then be added as a link to the larger work. (This is such a simple task in contrast to preparing a new edition.) This addition/submission could be controlled by the editorial board, if so wished. Also, access to the information by people around the world is going to increase greatly. Therefore, there are all kinds of reasons for accepting this kind of electronic publication and work. If you have the opportunity to work on this kind of project with your classmates, you can place it on your Web site and be very specific about what part or parts you contributed to the overall project. (Parts are often signed.) Lest we forget, there is the paradox of people wanting to know what you yourself contributed to a collaborative project!

As we proceed and as later browse our way to the Web site, or Web book, for this book in print (which in itself is a paradoxical combination), you will find ample examples of how to develop this kind of collaborative work and make it effective.

WHAT SHOULD A STUDENT KNOW?

As I have partially answered this question already in the Preface and in dealing with the previous questions, you will need to know the *basic conventions* of electronic discourse and how to elaborate on them, and the conventions for being unconventional, if you so wish to risk being unconventional. But a caveat: It is a lot easier for me to be unconventional on my Web site and be successful at it than you on yours. Time and reputation count. If you attempt to just mimic someone, you may be open to the charge that you are not being yourself . . . *whoever* you are in Cyberspace.

What exactly are the *conventions*? Well, here are a few things you need to know. Recall that I said that the Net and the Web required a great deal of cooperation and that it begins with hardware and software. It is important to know:

- How to get access to a computer, the right software and hardware, and a server
- How to write (format) using the conventional language of the Web—Hypertext Markup Language (HTML)—and how to set up basic multimedia pages
- How to develop Web pages with a number of documents/files according to basic layout conventions
- How to format each document, link them all, and if you have direct access to a server, how to place each document in a server and maintain the Web site
- How to use and where to find additional information on the WWW, and how to use such helper applications as PhotoShop and video and audio applications
- How to ask for help from others and to give it freely when someone asks you. (There is the ethic of helping other people which, if not already a part of your value system, you should develop.)

There's more, but this will give you some impression of what you have to know.

WHAT ARE THE LANGUAGES OF THE WWW?

The primary language of the Web is called Hypertext Markup Language (HTML), which is not computer programming, but a markup language, or a set of logical *tags*. The purpose of these tags is to tell your browser program (e.g., Mosaic or Netscape) how to read the layout of the page. These tags are placed in angled brackets <> so that they will not be visible on the screen. Again, their purpose is to tell the browser how to make visible what language will be projected on the monitor. There are tags *for the entire layout of the page,* which includes the title for the index page and subsequent pages, the title or headings on the separate documents, the body of the document, etc. For example, the tags for the title of a document or file are

<Title>You place your Title here</Title>

Another example: the tags for headings in a document are

<H1>Your Heading</H1>

Note how a tag opens up the form and then how a tag terminates the command with the slash </>.

The browser will read these tags in such a way as to place the text within the tags—as in the case of the *title* of the document or file—at the very top of the browser program, just as the Save or Save as function in a word processing program performs the same task. The difference between the browser program and a word processing program, however, is that one reads the tags/codes that you supply, whereas the other supplies the codes for you when you click on the appropriate icons or pull down the right menu item. For example, I use a word processing program, that allows me to type in a heading such as "Hypertext Markup Language" and highlight it (or the title of my paper, but not necessarily my document or file) and then go to the menu or rule and pull down the font size to 14 pt and click on B for bold. The results will be

Hypertext Markup Language

In order to center this heading, I did not type in the code <center>Hypertext Markup Language</center> but simply highlighted the phrase and clicked on an icon that signifies the centering of the text. Again, when I clicked, the program inserted the code, which is invisible on the screen.

There are numerous other tags, but really only a few that you will use time and again. There are tags for:

- Establishing and anchoring links to other documents or files
- Alignment and size
- Backgrounds, colors, images, etc.

Is this beginning to sound too difficult because, perhaps, you would rather just click on icons or pull down menu items and send a command? If so, there are today several HTML editing programs that allow you to avoid learning codes, but what we are going to learn here is so easy, I don't think it's necessary to purchase or even use them. There are a few programs that are free, but you get what you pay for, right? My assumption here is that you might want to know how the markup language works and to be able to manipulate it so that your Web page does not come out looking as if it were formulated on an assembly line. Once you learn the basics, you can then learn how to do things that editing programs most likely cannot yet do for you—and may never be able to do.

There are other markup languages such as Standard Generalized Markup Language (SGML) and Virtual Reality Modeling Language (VRML). We will not be concerned with these languages here. Also, there are other languages used now that are really programming languages such as CGI (Common Gateway Interface) Scripts and JAVA, which is a programming language that can be difficult to learn, though we will examine it briefly in relation to **applets** in Chapter 10.

You now know that a conventional language must be used. Once we know the basics of the *language,* there are other basics to cover.

WHAT ARE THE CONVENTIONS OF A WEB SITE OR HOME PAGE?

While the previous set of conventions in terms of HTML and its various tags are invisible on the screen, another set of conventions determine how you should use these invisible tags to establish a general format for what will be visible on your first page and subsequent pages. In no time at all, graphic de-signers of Web pages have arrived at conventions for chunking information, which include:

- Links (as text and/or graphics, at the top and/or bottom of the page) to navigate from place to place
- A Title (as text and/or graphic) that will identify the site
- The main body or content of the page
- Signatures (as name and e-mail address of the person who maintains the site, the dates of establishment and last modification, etc.)
- Repetition of links to navigate

These conventions will be discussed in greater detail, with ways of modify-ing them, when we look at a variety of different first pages.

HOW TO ACCESS WEB SPACE TO BEGIN WRITING AND PUBLISHING

Perhaps all of the talk up to this point has assumed the impossible! Perhaps there is a problem: If you can't get access to the Web, then in reading this book you will have gained information that you cannot use. Generally, ac-cess is not a problem if you are at a school or university that has the tech-nology you need—and more and more have computer labs for the teaching of writing. This allows and encourages you to use the technology for the purposes discussed here. Most likely you will be using this book as a textbook in a class, and therefore will have access to the most conventional hardware and software. If you have your own computer and the necessary hardware and software but are not in a class that is concerned with writing on and for the WWW, and you have the financial means of obtaining a *PPP account* from what is called a *provider* in your local area, then you can pay for access to e-mail and a Web site and start practicing what is discussed in this book and getting out on the Web. If you don't have the financial means, perhaps you can find someone or some agency that will let you use their equipment and their access account. Don't despair, for I believe that access to this technology will eventually be as widespread as television sets are today.

I have more to say about access to the WWW in Chapter 4. But first, we need to get some idea of what the basic codes, or tags, are that will allow you to write for the WWW, which is the subject of the next chapter.

REFERENCES (BOOKS AND WEB SITES)

Here are some books that you might like to read about the World Wide Web and associated issues and some Web sites that you might like to visit and study:

History of the Internet: gopher://gopher.isoc.org/11/internet/history

Lanham, Richard A. *The Electronic Word.* Chicago: The University of Chicago Press, 1993.

Mitchell, William J. *City of Bits: Space, Place, and the Infobahn.* Cambridge: MIT Press, 1995.

Negroponte, Nicholas. *Being Digital.* New York: Alfred A. Knopf, 1995.

Rheingold, Howard. *Virtual Reality.* New York: Simon & Schuster, 1991.

Turkle, Sherry. *Life on the Screen: Identity in the Age of the Internet.* New York: Simon & Schuster, 1995.

Thoreau, Henry David. *Walden.* A virtual copy can be found at a University of Maryland site: http://www.inform.umd.edu:8080/EdRes/ReadingRoom/HistoryPhilosophy/OnWaldenPond. See if you can find virtual copies of any of the books mentioned here. Go to one of the search engines, say, AltaVista (http://altavista.digital.com/) and type in the last name of the author and the short title of the book and see what you get.

Web (loads of info): http://www.yahoo.com/Computers/World_Wide_Web/

Wiggins, Richard. "How the Internet Works." *Internet World* (October 1996): 54–60.

Woolley, Benjamin. *Virtual Worlds.* New York: Penguin, 1992.

WWW Frequently Asked Questions (FAQ) http://sunsite.unc.edu/boutell/faq/www_faq.html

W3, the Project http://www.w3.org/pub/WWW/TheProject.html

► 2

The Elements of Hyperstyle:

A General Guide to Hypertext Markup Language (HTML)

Preliminaries

Hypertext Markup Language (HTML)
> *Page Construction: HTML, Head, Body (Background, Color and Graphic), Invisible Comment Tags, Visible Blocks of Text (Signature), End of Body*
> *Headings and Font Size*
> *Text Blocks: Paragraphs, Preformatted Text, and Block Quotations*
> *Text Style: Italics, Emphasis, Bold, Code*
> *Lists: Bulleted, Numbered/Ordered, Definition*
> *Menus (Vertical and Horizontal) and Signatures*
> *Links: Textual, Absolute, and Relative*
> *Destination Markers and Jump Links*
> *Pictures/Graphics (JPEGs/GIFs), Tagging and Linking, Aligning Text Blocks/Graphics, and Resizing*
> *Rules, Bars, Balls, Buttons, Backgrounds/Tiling, Color Codes*
> *Tables*
> *Special Characters*

Comments and Suggestions
> *Templates*
> *Differences Among Browsers*
> *Making Web Sites Accessible for Sight- and Hearing-impaired*
> *Netscape: Obtaining a Copy*

Web Site Resources
> *HTML Web Sites*
> *Color, RGB, Hexadecimal Codes*
> *Update on Changes in Browsers (Netscape Navigator, Netscape*
> *Explorer)*

PRELIMINARIES

We are now going to begin—as the title of this chapter suggests—introducing in detail the various individual elements or tags of Hypertext Markup Language (HTML). You will intermittently return to this chapter, refreshing your memory, as you would return to any basic how-to section in a book. As we proceed into later chapters, in which I give detailed step-by-step approaches to constructing a variety of Web sites, we will begin to bring these various elements together, and I will suggest alternative ways of using them. Read through these sections carefully, absorbing as much as you can and familiarizing yourself with what is possible in terms of basic tags. Remember that you acquire knowledge of these elements by using them repeatedly. There is no substitute for *doing*.

You can find much of this kind of information on the Web. I supply it here so that you might have it handy in book form when you are away from your computer and the Web itself. At times, you will want to access particular Web sites to get additional information and updates. *I have tried to select tags that work with both Netscape Navigator 2.01 and Netscape Explorer 2.01 and have generally avoided tags that are specific to one operating system.* (Tags for version 3+ are available on the Web.) Therefore, understand that there are many more tags than are given here. (At the end of this chapter and at the Web site, you will find a number of valuable URLs for additional information.)

The first very important thing that you must remember is that when you are constructing a page with these elements, you should save it all in Text Only, or what is also called *ascii*. You do not want to construct a page in any other format, because then all the invisible tags that allow for your word-processing program to configure the page and text for you will be put out on a Web site; most likely, however, you will never get them uploaded because the server will reject the file. And then, you are going to be sitting there wondering, "What went wrong?!*&¢@#$" Just remember: If you do use your word-processing program, all you have to do is to go to *save as* and then select *text only*. (There are other options concerning this issue that will be discussed later. All you need to know now is that you will be writing visible code, HTML, and you don't want any invisible code anywhere in your file. What you can't see can hurt you!)

The second thing you need to know is that the document (file) needs to have the suffix .html or .htm, for example, file1.html or file2.htm. Once these two steps are done, you will have a (new) file that you can upload.

HYPERTEXT MARKUP LANGUAGE (HTML)

Page Construction: HTML Head, Body (Background, Color and Graphic), Invisible Comment Tags, Visible Blocks of Text (Signature), End of Body

I introduced this basic convention earlier; now we will look at it in greater detail. One thing you will discover is that it is not really necessary to use all of these tags; a number of browsers, especially Mosaic and Netscape, will read a document (file) without some of them. For example, I very seldom use the tag <HTML> at the beginning of a document, but it is good policy and style to include all of them if for no other reason than to minimize the probability of a browser's propensity for making a reading mistake or a browser's needing all the tags. And then there's always your instructor who might insist on your using all of them! It's silly to have to say these things, because I seldom myself follow what I am saying here; but I do know that these elements are expected by many people, and there are some good reasons for them.

Page construction—every page, not just the first—*at the level of tags,* and therefore invisible on the page, is usually chunked into these major *categories,* which are then closed in a nested manner at this *macrolevel:* HTML, Head (which includes Title of the Netscape page), and Body. Vertically, which is the way that you would set up tags, these particular tags will look like this:

```
<HTML>
        <HEAD>
                <TITLE>
                </TITLE>
        </HEAD>
        <BODY>
```

(Content of page: Here, you have several possible tags and text, everything from the title of the page to the signature.)

```
        </BODY>
        </HTML>
```

What you have to remember and understand here is that when these chunks of tags are put into angled brackets <HTML> or <TITLE>, they are not visible on your monitor. They are read as commands but screened out by the program browser. What is visible is all of the effects of the tags (e.g., spacing and color) and text. (I recommend that you make a template in a Text Only file and keep it on your hard disk so you can constantly reuse it. I have a folder on my desktop at all times filled with templates for various purposes.)

It is considered by some to be good practice to put in *invisible comment tags* so that you can identify what the project is for, and what the chunks of information are beyond what the standard tags announce. You can construct invisible comment tags by putting your comments in angled brackets with a preceding exclamation point: `<!----here, I want to put a table with three rows--->`. So what this amounts to is a note to yourself. The exclamation point stops the browser program from reading anything in the angled brackets as code. Your comments can be more elaborate and formal. Here is an example of these tags with more elaboration:

```
<HTML>
<!--author: Victor J. Vitanza----------------------------------->
<!--date created: 8 June 96. last modified: 9 June 96------>
<!--document name: Chapter 2/The Elements of Hyperstyle---->
<!--purpose: example/Writing for the WWW------------------->
<HEAD>
<TITLE>
Chapter 2, Writing for the WWW
</TITLE>
</HEAD>
<BODY>
```

(Content of page: Here, you have several possible tags and text including a signature, which could be either at the top, bottom, or both.)

```
</BODY>
</HTML>
```

Now, at this point you might wonder why this information is included since it should, after all, be part of the signature at the bottom of the page. You have to remember that files are constructed on a disk (floppy or hard drive), and that while they are being constructed you (and others, if you are collaborating) will need this kind of information before it is uploaded. Also remember that files are loaded and then often downloaded and stored. So you need this information for any number of situations and occasions. And obviously, you can put other kinds of information in this special format that would never be included as visible on the page. Before leaving this section, make a template from the above code; that way, you will have the basic format with and without the invisible comment tags.

Headings and Font Size

You will *not* use Headings for determining the font size of the title for the page—displayed at the top of the browser on, say, the Netscape frame—but you will use Headings for determining the font size of the "title" *in* the page of the frame, and especially for sections and subsections. You will use font size commands throughout the text to vary the sizes of fonts in general.

There are six sizes for Headings:

```
<H1>Heading Level 1</H1>
<H2>Heading Level 2</H2>
<H3>Heading Level 3</H3>
<H4>Heading Level 4</H4>
<H5>Heading Level 5</H5>
<H6>Heading Level 6</H6>
```

If you have a typo or don't close these tags correctly with, for example, the right size number or the slash, the browser will continue to read everything that follows in terms of the heading size. It can look rather stupid! Be sure to proofread the tags very carefully and test them before you put them into the server. *How do you test them?* Let's stop the discussion and illustrate this point because you will want to test and see how these work as we go along.

First you need a browser program. I recommend Netscape 2+ for both Macs and PCs, which will most likely be provided by your university. (If not, see the section at the close of this chapter for the URL and instructions for obtaining a copy of Netscape.) Click on Netscape, whether it is in the server or on your hard disk at home. If it is in the latter, you do not have to be connected by way of a PPP account. Remember: We are just going to use the browser to test our files, so we do not need to be online. If you activate Netscape and you are not online, the browser will look for a connection and not find one and will tell you so. What you do is tell it not to worry, by clicking on the appropriate place in the dialogue box. You might also have to click on the Stop button at the top right side. Once the program is stable, you then go to the File menu and pull it down to Open File. (Depending on the system you are using, a Mac or a PC, you will have to go about finding the file in different ways, just as you would if you were attempting to load any file from your desktop or your hard drive or Document folder or in Drive A, B, C, etc. You should already know how to do this. If not, it would be best for you to check the manual that accompanied your system software.) After you have found the file, call it up.

A shorter method to use—if you are using a Mac—is to drag and drop the file onto the Netscape window and it will automatically open. Macs have had this drag-and-drop feature for some time now, and other operating systems are getting it as well.

Whether by way of Open File or drag and drop, what you will see as the browser uploads the file on your monitor is what you will see as if the document (file) were out in a server on a Web tree.

As an experiment, let's take what we have learned thus far and have Netscape read this code. Remember that it must be in Text Only, ascii, and the document (file) name must have the suffix .html or .htm. Simply call up the file or drag and drop it on Netscape.

```
<HTML>
<!--author: Victor J. Vitanza---------------------------------->
<!--date created: 8 June 96. last modified: 9 June 96------>
<!--document name: Chapter 2/Update for Web-------------->
<!--purpose: Writing for the WWW--------------------------->
<HEAD>
<TITLE>
Chapter 2, Writing for the WWW
</TITLE>
</HEAD>
<BODY>
<H1>Chapter 2, Writing for the WWW</H1>
<H2>Chapter 2, Writing for the WWW</H2>
<H3>Chapter 2, Writing for the WWW</H3>
<H4>Chapter 2, Writing for the WWW</H4>
<H5>Chapter 2, Writing for the WWW</H5>
<H6>Chapter 2, Writing for the WWW</H6>
</BODY>
</HTML>
```

Now let's return to our discussion of font size. Besides headings, there are other ways to determine size. They go like this:

```
<FONT SIZE=+1>FONT SIZE 1</FONT>
```

Or you can vary them:

```
<FONT SIZE=+3>F</font>ont <FONT SIZE=+3>S</FONT>ize
```

Or getting a little fancier, you can code them variously as:

```
<FONT SIZE=+3>F</font><FONT SIZE=+4>o</FONT>n<FONT
   SIZE=+2>t</FONT> <FONT SIZE=+9>S</FONT>i<FONT
     SIZE=+3>z</FONT><FONT SIZE=+12>e</FONT>
```

And what does this look like on Netscape? I will add them to the previous code (Figure 2).

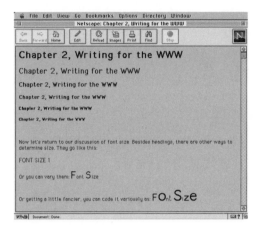

FIGURE 2

You may be aware, just by glancing at what is shown, that there are some additional codes hidden in this image to make happen what happens in it. *How would you find out what those codes are?* It's very simple! If you, just like anyone else, are using Netscape and you want to know how someone coded a document (file) so that you can learn how to do it the same way, all you do is go to the View menu and pull down Document Source. You will eventually see a file in Text Only on your screen giving you the codes. (By the way, this is not considered stealing or plagiarism. We all use the same code. If anything, you might be learning someone's particular style, especially if it is wildly different from other people's general style of tagging. But we have not reached that point in our discussion of examples yet. When you do use someone's special mixture of codes, for example, colors, you might state on your Web page that you have learned from the person. This is not a necessity; it is a matter courtesy and a showing of respect for someone's work. And it is really not necessary either to e-mail them and ask if you can be influenced by them, unless you wish. We will return to this issue of borrowing because there is a definite limit of what you can use from these source codes without violating copyright codes.)

Text Blocks: Paragraphs, Preformatted Text, and Block Quotations

The tags here with respect to these formats, like the previous ones, also are fairly simple. Let's say that you want to place *paragraph breaks* between or among paragraphs. To accomplish that, use the code <P> to signal to the browser to make space for a new paragraph. Very often you will see at the end of a paragraph something like this: </P>. This serves absolutely no purpose at all, other than to waste your time typing; and yet, you will find it—and perhaps for good reason—because it visually reminds us that the paragraph has come to an end.

One thing you need to know is that it does not really matter how much space there is between words or paragraphs or graphics when you are in Text Only and then upload the file to a server. The available browsers do not read the space on your page; they read tags/code. Therefore, it might be helpful to someone who has a lot of words on a page to put in </P> to signal the end of a paragraph. But since I am fairly neat when constructing documents/files, I don't need as many visual clues.

Besides paragraph breaks there are just plain *breaks*, which are coded as <BR>. You need to show breaks to arrange, for example, words and their sequence on a line, which is important in headings or on the page Titles and Sections or in narrow spaces in boxes (i.e., tables). Breaks are automatic in some coding such as tags for headings, lists, or preformatting.

A while ago I said that browsers do not read the actual spacing that you might have on a page but the tags/code. But what if you wanted to have the browser automatically read more than one space between words? HTML allows for extra or irregular spacing by using the tag for *preformatted* text. (See Figure 3.) If you want to accomplish a different feel from a mechanical look of regularity in spacing, all you have to do is use the tag <PRE>

```
    and                     then        you could
lea   v eeeeee  e   e       ee
   big   G  A       Pssssss s s   s     s      s        SSSSSSS
                like
T                H              I           S.
                                     and still use some more
silly spacing like t    h     i     s    !!!!!!!!     </PRE>.
```

If you want to indent a *block quote*, however—which I see as the opposite of the possibilities of a preformatted text—you could tag such a quote with <blockquote>YOUR QUOTE here</blockquote>. Does it have to be a quote? Of course not! But you should make sure that it does not appear to be read as a quote. Always establish a context for the words you are including on a page.

Now, let me give you an example. Suppose I do it this way in code, combining all of the above:

```
<HTML>
<!--author: Victor J. Vitanza------------------------------->
<!--date created: 8 June 96. Last modified: 9 June 96------>
<!--document name: Chapter 2/Update for Web--------------->
<!--purpose: Writing for the WWW------------------------->
```

```
<HEAD>
<TITLE>
Chapter 2, Writing for the WWW
</TITLE>
</HEAD>
<BODY>
<P><P><BR><BR>


<H3>Examples of Blocks of Text</H3><P><P><BR>
```

Here are some examples <P> of what will happen with the
same example of discourse <BR> when tagged as preformat and
as blockquote, <P> and what will happen within the brief
introduction (like this one) to these examples <BR> when
tagged for both paragraphs and breaks:

```
<P><P><BR>
<PRE>
<font size+2>H</font>ere's what happens with preformat
    tags:<P><P>
 and                    then           you could
lea      v eeeeeee e   e    ee
      big         G        A       Pssssss s s   s    s     s


SSSSSSSSSSSSSS     like
T             H              I           S.
              and still use some more


silly spacing like


t        h     i        s



                     !!!!!!!!!
</PRE>.
<P><P><BR>
<font size=+4>H</font>ere's what happens with blockquote
    tags:<P><P>
<Blockquote>
 and                    then           you could
lea      v eeeeeee e   e    ee
```

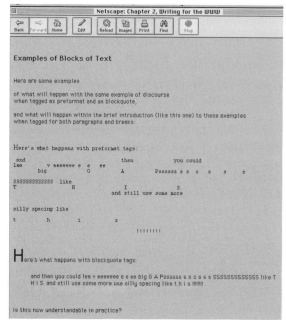

FIGURE 3

```
      big        G       A         Pssssss s s   s     s     s     s

SSSSSSSSSSSSS      like
T             H              I              S.
                   and still use some more

silly spacing like

t       h       i       s

              !!!!!!!!!                            .
</blockquote>
<P><P><BR><BR>
Is this now understandable in practice?
</BODY>
</HTML>
```

One thing that the above set of tags should illustrate for you is that the number of spaces between letters and words are all reduced to as if there were but one space, unless there is a preformat code for the browser to read. (You can see what this all looks like in Figure 3.) If you look very carefully you might notice that when the tag of preformat is used the font in Netscape changes to Courier. So you should keep that in mind when using it.

Text Style: *Italics, Emphasis, Bold, Code*

Italics is tagged as `<I>Italics</I>`. You can substitute the tag `<CITE>Cite </CITE>` You can substitute the tags `<EM>Emphasis</EM>` or `<CITE>Cite </CITE>`.

Bold is tagged as `<B>Bold<B>`. You can substitute the tag `<STRONG>Strong </STRONG>`, if you want to do all the extra typing!

Code is tagged as `<CODE>Code</CODE>`. (This tag is often used to represent text of a computer program. It creates fixed-width font.) You can substitute the tag `<KBD>Keyboard</KBD>`.

Let's put them to use:

```
<font size=+2>
<B>This is easy, easy, easy; let's illustrate it like
    this:</B><P>
This is <I>easy ... Italics can be very difficult to
    read;</I><P>
<EM>easy ... Emphasis</EM> (same as italics);<P>
<CITE>easy ... Cite</CITE> (same as italics);<P>
<B>easy ... Bold;</B><P>
<STRONG>easy ... Strong</STRONG> (same as bold); <P>
<CODE>easy ... Code</CODE>.<P><BR>
<\FONT>
```

```
When all this is in paragraph form, it can look as it looks
here. This is <I>easy ... Italics can be very difficult to
read</I>; <EM>easy ... Emphasis</EM> (same as italics);
<B>easy</B> ... Bold; <STRONG>easy ... Strong</STRONG> (same
as bold); <CODE>easy ... Code</CODE>.<P>
```

```
<I>Look </I>at <I>what </I>happens <I>when </I>normal
<I>type </I>and <I>italics </I>are <I>staggered </I>in
<I>this </I>manner<I>!</I><P>
```

```
This may be very easy, but there are <B>two complica-
tions</B>: All browsers (Netscape, CyberDog, Mosaic, etc.)
do not read the tags in the same way. Moreover, the <I>op-
tion on many browsers of selecting</I> the font that the
text on Web pages is to be displayed in on an individual
monitor <EM>slightly</EM> undercuts these settings. If you
have studied the various differences in how <B>BOLD</B> can
get displayed in various fonts, then, you can understand
that BOLD is not <CODE>just bold</CODE> for it can be a
narrow bold, a faded fold, a thick <B>bold</B>, etc.<P>
```

When read by Netscape Navigator 2.01+, we get the results we see in Figure 4. Note that I resized the fonts in the first seven lines for the monitor version.

There is a tag for underlining, but you should not use it since underlined words are impossible to distinguish from linked words. However, if your purpose is to be mischievous or to confuse people, then use it.

Lists: Bulleted, Numbered/Ordered, Definition

Now the codes are going to get just a little more difficult, though very formulaic and therefore memorable. Lists are generally started with one of these three tags:

<UL>   (for unordered list), this is called unordered because the tag does not automatically list numbers;

<OL>   (ordered, numbered list); or

<DL>   (definition list)

There are several different kinds of lists. There is the generic Bulleted list, which is coded:

```
<UL>
<LI>item one
<LI>item two
<LI>item three
</UL>
```

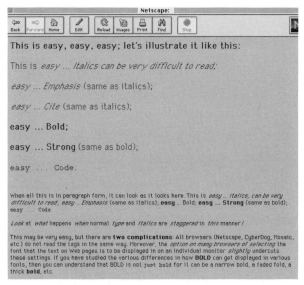

FIGURE 4

Then the double/triple-tiered or nested bulleted list:

```
<UL>
<LI>item one
<LI>item two
<LI>item three
<UL>
<LI>item a
<LI>item b
<UL>
<LI>item 1.
<LI>item 2.
</UL>
</UL>
</UL>
```

Note that in both the preceding and following codes no tag is necessary for a break in a line <BR>. (See Figure 5.) If, however, you want to put more space between lines, you can add break <BR> and paragraph <P> tags.

The second kind of list is the *ordered/numbered* list:

```
<OL>
<LI>item one
<LI>item two
<LI>item three
</OL>
```

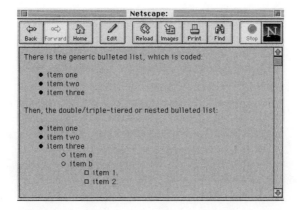

FIGURE 5

Then, the double/triple-tiered ordered list:

```
<OL>
<LI>item one
<LI>item two
<LI>item three
<OL>
<LI>item a
<LI>item b
<OL>
<LI>item 1.
<LI>item 2.
</OL>
</OL>
</OL>
```

As you can see, the only difference here is in code: The `<UL>` is simply replaced with `<OL>`, which gives us the set of relationships in Figure 6.

The third kind is the *definition list* `<DL>`, which is composed of two parts, namely, the Thing being defined `<DT>` and the Definition `<DD>`. (See Figure 7.)

```
<DL>
<DT> Bulleted list
<DD> A Simple list that can be nested from a solid bullet
to an empty bullet to a square bullet and usually nested no
more than three times
<DT> Ordered/Numbered list
```

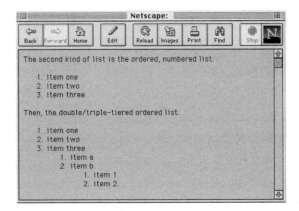

FIGURE 6

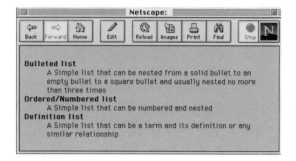

FIGURE 7

```
<DD> A Simple list that can be numbered and nested
<DT> Definition list
<DD> A Simple list that can be a term and its definition or
any similar relationship
</DL>
```

Menus (Vertical and Horizontal) and Signatures

Menus are a list of items that usually serve as links to sections, or files of the Web page. In print terms, they are like chapters or sections of chapters. There are many different kinds of menus, but the two basic ones are: the Vertical menu, which is a simple list. (I will not give an example since any of the lists in the previous section serve as examples) and the Horizontal menu, which can look like this in brackets:

```
[item one] [item two] [item three] [item four]
```

Or you will see it represented as:

```
|| item one || item two || item three || item four ||
```

or as:

```
&#167; item one &#167; item two &#167; item three &#167;
item four &#167;
```

which is composed of a tag for *ISO-Latin-I code*, which we will take a look at later. The particular tag *§* is for "§." Notice that I did not use angled brackets <> with these codes.

As before, you will find Signatures at the top or bottom of the page. The latter is usually the choice. Generally they include the following information in a variety of configurations, but the most common is:

```
Author: Victor J. Vitanza VVitanza@AOL.COM<BR>
List established: 6 June 1996; Last updated: 13 June 1996<BR>
Copyright 1996 Allyn&Bacon<BR>
```

Instead of graphically simulating what these will look like on Netscape, let's go on to the next item, links, and how they are tagged. I will use the above text, all of which normally have hyperlinks, as examples.

Links: Textual, Absolute, and Relative

For a word or phrase (or more) to be hyperlinked to another document or file, either in the local server where you keep your documents or in a server on the other side of the world, it is necessary to designate the Uniform Resource Locator (URL) as part of your code. The tags that will surround a piece of text or a graphic are

```
<A HREF=> and </A>
```

The full address in double quotes will follow the equals <=> sign, and a name (Allyn&Bacon) will be included for the visible link, which is anchored by the tag </A>:

```
<A HREF="http://www.abacon.com/">Allyn&Bacon</A>
```

(I am putting in only one link with its URL in the following examples; the principle is the same for each additional link.) It will look like this in a vertical list:

```
<UL>
<LI> <A HREF="http://www.abacon.com/">Allyn&Bacon</A>
<LI> <A HREF="http://www.abacon.com/cyber/public_html/
    Ch01.html">CyberReader,
Ch. 1</A>
<LI><A HREF="http://www.abacon.com/cyber/public_html/
    Ch02.html">CyberReader,
Ch. 2</A>
<LI> Etc.
</UL>
```

A horizontal list will look like this:

```
[<A HREF="http://www.abacon.com/">Allyn&Bacon</A>] [item
two] [item three] [item four]
```

or:

```
|| <A HREF="http://www.abacon.com/cyber/public_html/
Ch01.html">CyberReader, Ch.1</A> || item two || item
three || item four ||
```

or:

```
&#167; <A HREF="http://www.abacon.com/cyber/public_html/
Ch02.html">CyberReader, Ch.2</A> &#167; item two &#167; item
three &#167; item four &#167;
```

A Signature with an e-mail address as well as a URL will look like this, but with a minor change in the tag to signify an e-mail link to the browser:

```
Author: Victor J. Vitanza <A HREF="MAILTO:VVitanza@AOL.COM">
    VVitanza@AOL.COM</A><BR>
List established: 6 June 1996; Last updated: 13 June 1996<BR>
Copyright 1996 <A HREF="http://www.abacon.com/">Allyn&Bacon
    </A><BR>
```

Let us recall that when a section of text is a link—because of the tags <A HREF=> and </A>—it is represented by the browser as <u>underlined</u>. (For the vertical and horizontal lists and links as well as the Signature, see Figure 8.) When you click on the link of a text, you go elsewhere, presuming that the URL has a file at the other end to load up. You will find intermittently that files are removed from servers or moved to other directories and the URL/link on a page is no longer any good.

Caveat

While the tags and codes are not case-sensitive (uppercase/lowercase), *HTML*, tagging, is case-sensitive in a UNIX server, so just assume that it is all case-sensitive. For example, if you place a file name that is *lowercase* in the body of your text, and then place the file (that is to be loaded) into a server where it is *uppercase*, the link will not work. This is especially problematic for people who use PCs. Most people recommend that if you are using a PC, put all file names (e.g., CH1.HTM) in uppercase.

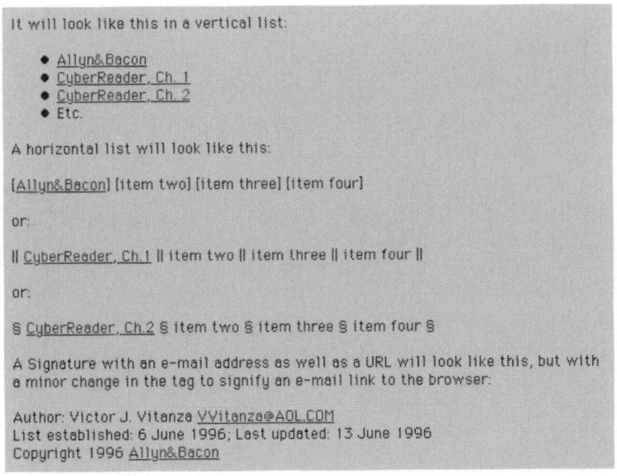

It will look like this in a vertical list:

- Allyn&Bacon
- CyberReader, Ch. 1
- CyberReader, Ch. 2
- Etc.

A horizontal list will look like this:

[Allyn&Bacon] [item two] [item three] [item four]

or:

|| CyberReader, Ch.1 || item two || item three || item four ||

or:

§ CyberReader, Ch.2 § item two § item three § item four §

A Signature with an e-mail address as well as a URL will look like this, but with a minor change in the tag to signify an e-mail link to the browser:

Author: Victor J. Vitanza VVitanza@AOL.COM
List established: 6 June 1996; Last updated: 13 June 1996
Copyright 1996 Allyn&Bacon

FIGURE 8

One additional aspect of linking that you should understand and practice is the difference between *absolute* and *relative* links. These differences can be confusing but must be understood; if not, files will not be found or will not work, that is, they will not load on a monitor. An absolute link is best described as the full URL. A relative link is an abbreviated one that will work under certain circumstances. This form of linking can cause you problems if not done with great care.

How does a relative link work? Let's first understand the conventional structure of a URL. It is composed of `<http://>` which establishes that the link is to follow the "hypertext transfer protocol." Thereafter, the address, by domain name, will direct the search to a particular machine, or server, somewhere on the Web; for example, `<http://www.abacon.com/>`. The domain name here is abacon for Allyn&Bacon. Once the link has been made, you will see the home page, on which will be a number of links to other pages/files. What is added to the URL for this home page in terms of the links on and from it are directory, subdirectory, and page/file names. For example, if at the Allyn&Bacon site you click on the image link for *CyberReader*, you will go to a page that has this URL: http://www.abacon.com/cyber/public_html/Cyber.html, which is the welcome page. Once you are on the welcome page, you will, yes, find more links, one of which is to http://www. abacon.com/cyber/public_html/Ch01.html. In both examples, you will find:

- The directory cyber,
- The subdirectory public_html
- The file, or page, Cyber.html and Ch01.html, which is in the subdirectory

You can always tell the difference between a directory, no matter at what level, and a file; the latter always has .html or .htm at the end of it. (For a Mac file the designation is html; for a PC, it is htm. PCs are deficient in this way, among others!) However, notice here that a directory can have html as part of its name, with an underscore (_), never a dot (.). What we are talking about here are hierarchies. There would be no problem whatsoever if Web people for a particular server put all their files in the same directory, that is, if they had one directory. And yet that would cause tremendous problems, which I will not go into here. Let it suffice to say that we like to place our information into categories so that we can generally know where it is so that we can retrieve it.

Perhaps the best way to see the hierarchical arrangement of directories and files is in terms of how it actually looks in the server's directory on a Web tree (hierarchical branchings). When I, or anyone else sends a file (FTPs, File Transfer Protocols) to a server, we can visually see the directories and files with the help of the program WS_FTP (for PCs) or Fetch (for Macs). I will explain this at greater length in a later chapter, but this is how it basically looks in Fetch, which I have superimposed over the various Chapter links at the CyberReader welcome page, with its links to the Chapters:

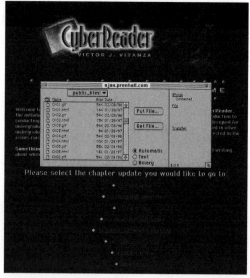

FIGURE 9

Note that Fetch is in the public_html directory, in which the various Chapter files (.html) and the GIFs (.gif) are visible. If I were to sustain a click on the arrow to the right of *public_html* directory, I would be able to see in a menu all the directories in both hierarchical directions and slide from one to the next.

You should now have a general understanding of how a URL works and what it is constructed of in terms of an address with a domain name and directories and files. Therefore, let's return to the question: *What is a relative link?* If you have a page/file within a directory and links to files within the same directory, you can use an abbreviated form of the URL. For instance, let us say that every file in the same directory (cyber_html) has a file to each other. If so, all that is necessary for the URL, if in a list, is:

```
<UL>
<LI> <A HREF="/cyber_html/Ch01.html">Chapter 1</a>
<LI> <A HREF="/cyber_html/Ch02.html">Chapter 2</a>
<LI> <A HREF="/cyber_html/Ch03.html">Chapter 3</a>
Etc.
</UL>
```

In other words, whereas in the *absolute* form, you would have to type <A HREF="http:// www.abacon.com/cyber/cyber_html/Ch01.html">, in the *relative* form you do the above abbreviated version. (Absolute and relative forms/paths are discussed at much greater length in later chapters, especially Chapter 7.)

Destination Markers and Jump Links

What we have been looking at is how generally to link file to file, or page to page. Let's look at how to link a specific section of one page to a specific section *on the same page* or to a specific section *of another page in the same directory.* If a file/page is long with several headings or items in a list, you will often find that the author uses internal links (destination markers or jumps) to precise sections of (lines on) the page. Often the author uses links to return the reader to the headings. The purpose of the links (jumps) is to keep the readers from having to scroll their way down or back.

To jump down (or return) to a specific section on the same page, use <#marker_name>. For example, if in a series of headings or a table of contents, you have one heading that reads "Links (marker and jump)," you would code it as:

```
<H2><A HREF="#links">Links (marker and jump)</A></H2>
```

Then at the specific location, or line, that you would have your reader jump to, you would write:

```
<H2><A NAME="links">Links (marker and jump)</A></H2>
```

To jump to a specific section of another page/file in the *same* directory, use <filename.html#marker_name>. The addition here is the name of the file placed before the marker name. For example, to jump to a section that might be at midpoint on a page/file with the name "works.html," you would write:

```
For counterarguments, see my summary of <A
HREF="notes.html#JonesTarget">Jill Jones's position</A>
```

At the specific location in the file "notes.html" that you would have your reader jump to, you would write:

```
<A NAME="JonesTarget">Jim Jones's argument</A>
```

There are other codes for jumping to files located in subdirectories and other locations, but to simplify matters I will leave the possible jumps to these two and move on to the questions: *What else can be a link?* Text and graphics/pictures. And *What can these be a link to?* More text and graphics but also to audio files and video files. Let's take a look at graphics now.

Pictures/Graphics (JPEGs and GIFs), Tagging and Linking, Aligning Text Blocks/Graphics, and Resizing

One thing you will eventually come to understand is how to design and develop graphics; we will see how to do this in later chapters. The purpose now is to show how to:

- Tag a graphic so that it will upload on a page
- Situate text in relation to it
- Make it into a link and resize a graphic if necessary

Graphic files generally come in what are called JPEGs or GIFs. When coding, you use the tags: IMG SRC (image source). Or you write `<IMG SRC="name.jpg">` or `<IMG SRC="name.gif">`. (Usually, JPEG is shortened to JPG.) The first thing to understand is that while the text on a page with a tag to a graphic will be in one file, the graphic will always be in a separate file, and usually in the same server and directory. In other words, they are two separate files, with one file calling the other on to its page by way of a URL; they are nested. The coding on one text file with a link to a graphic that is to load up on the text file will look like this:

```
<IMG SRC="greeneye.gif" ALT="[image]">
```

Comment

The tag `<ALT=>` does something that is very important here. First of all you do not necessarily need the ALT tag to get the image to become visible on Netscape; you should include it, however, because those using browsers such as Lynx will not be able to see the image and therefore might like to have some indication that an image is present. The necessity for adding this tag for Lynx, however, will become exceptionally important when the graphic is a link itself. Why? Again, because the link will not at all be visible to the user of Lynx; and if you have a page with graphics as links and no ALT tags, then nothing appears! Let me repeat: In the first case it is a courtesy to add the ALT tag; in the second, it is a necessity.

If you want to add text to the icon and make the text a link follow this model:

```
<IMG SRC="greeneye.gif" ALT="[image]"> <A HREF="http://domain
name/file name">The song "Green Eyes"</A>
```

If you want to add text to the icon and make both the graphic and the text a link follow this model:

```
<A HREF="http://domain name/file name"><IMG SRC="greeneye.jpg"
ALT="[image]"> The song "Green Eyes"</A>
```

The insertion of the text to the right of the JPEG places it automatically to the right; if you would like it to the left, then place it there:

```
<A HREF="http://domain name/file name">The song "Green
Eyes"<IMG SRC="greeneye.gif" ALT="[image]"></A>
```

The text can be at both the left and right with the image in the middle.

```
Here is my favorite song <A HREF="http://domain name/file
name"><IMG SRC="greeneye.gif" ALT="[image]"></A> "Green
Eyes"
```

It is merely a matter of manipulating the placement of the URL, which makes the link, and the URL for the graphic, which calls up and loads the picture on the monitor, and the text. (See Figure 10.)

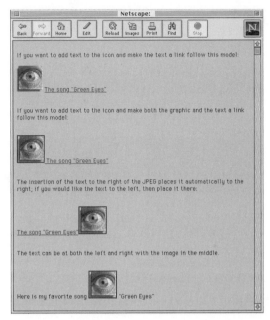

FIGURE 10

Notice how the second through the fourth images have a black box around them and the first one does not. The first one is not an image that is linked.

Let's examine some niceties of graphics in terms of their *alignment* to each other and to text and their *resizing*. In aligning them next to each other, you can create a horizontal/vertical list or menu. For example, a horizontal list would be tagged as:

```
<A HREF="http://domain name/file name"><IMG
    SRC="greeneye.gif" ALT="[image]"></A>
<A HREF="http://domain name/file name"><IMG
    SRC="greeneye.gif" ALT="[image]"></A>
<A HREF="http://domain name/file name"><IMG
    SRC="greeneye.gif" ALT="[image]"></A>
<A HREF="http://domain name/file name"><IMG
    SRC="greeneye.gif" ALT="[image]"></A>
```

Now take a look at Figure 11.

A vertical list would be tagged as:

```
<UL>
<LI> <A HREF="http://domain name/file name"><IMG
    SRC="greeneye.gif" ALT="[image]"></A>
<LI> <A HREF="http://domain name/file name"><IMG
    SRC="greeneye.gif" ALT="[image]"></A>
```

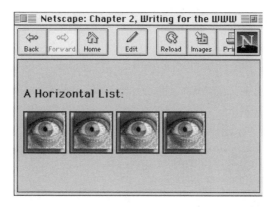

FIGURE 11

```
<LI> <A HREF="http://domain name/file name"><IMG
    SRC="greeneye.gif" ALT="[image]"></A>
<LI> <A HREF="http://domain name/file name"><IMG
    SRC="greeneye.gif" ALT="[image]"></A> </UL>
```

Please look at Figure 12. You can, of course, use text (words) along with these images. The codings would be similar to those done for graphics with text and links. Again, once you learn the basics you can manipulate the pictures, text, and links in a variety of ways.

FIGURE 12

Let's think now in greater terms of manipulating graphics and text. We have been learning about spacing in terms of the paragraph tag `<P>` and the break tag `<BR>`, and we have learned that text usually defaults to the bottom of an image that it is placed next to. Now what needs to be learned is how to align graphics and text in other ways. If you want to align text to the middle of a picture, tag the relationship as:

```
<IMG SRC="panthereye.jpg" align=middle>
```

You can also substitute "align=top" for "middle."

Other options are vertical and horizontal tags. These are handy because if you have more than just a small amount of text and that text line gets bumped down because of the size of the browser frame, the text line will be broken to below the graphic. This can be prevented by using V/H tags. For example, as with rules or bars, you can manipulate space and sizing by adding a number value equal to pixels. The number below for horizontal space (*hspace*) designates to the browser the distance between the image and text:

```
<IMG SRC="panthereye.jpg" align=left hspace=30> "Tiger, Tiger,
Burning Bright, <BR>In the Forest of the Night"<BR CLEAR=ALL>
```

Notice that when the break `<BR>` is added to drop the line, you should terminate it with `<BR CLEAR=ALL>`. (When we take a look at Tables later, there will be similar ways of manipulating pixels on your monitor.) If you want to designate vertical values, then, you would use the vertical space (*vspace*) tag:

```
<IMG SRC="panthereye.jpg" align=left hspace=30 vspace=60>
"Tiger, Tiger, Burning Bright, <BR>In the Forest of the
Night" ... <br> What's the rest of the poem?<BR>I can never
remember the rest of the poem!<BR> Let's see: "Tiger,
Tiger, Burning Bright,<BR> In the Forest of the
Night" ... <BR>Dahhhh!<BR CLEAR=ALL>
```

All these alignments of graphics and text are in Figure 13.

Larger chunks of text can be placed in juxtaposition with graphics in the same ways as demonstrated above. Here are two examples with some basic tags and chunks of text (the ellipses in both examples signify text not included here since the purpose is to demonstrate tags; text is included in its entirety in Figure 14):

```
<IMG SRC="winking.jpg" ALIGN=LEFT> Clifford Geertz, in his
discussions about the interpretations of cultures, tells
us....
```

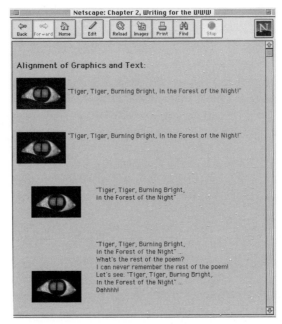

Alignment of Graphics and Text:

"Tiger, Tiger, Burning Bright, In the Forest of the Night!"

"Tiger, Tiger, Burning Bright, In the Forest of the Night!"

"Tiger, Tiger, Burning Bright,
In the Forest of the Night"

"Tiger, Tiger, Burning Bright,
In the Forest of the Night"
What's the rest of the poem?
I can never remember the rest of the poem!
Let's see: "Tiger, Tiger, Buring Bright,
In the Forest of the Night" ...
Dahhhh!

FIGURE 13

and

```
<IMG SRC="winking.jpg" ALIGN=RIGHT> Clifford Geertz, in his
discussions about the interpretations of cultures, tells
us....
```

and

```
<P><IMG SRC="winking.jpg" ALIGN=LEFT HSPACE=40
VSPACE=20>Likewise with the wink. Geertz reminds us that it
is even in our own culture a complex sign:<UL><LI> It can
mean that we are kidding (joking),<LI> it can mean that we
are not kidding (serious),<LI> it can mean that we are
flirting,<LI> it can mean that we are practicing winking,<LI>
it can mean that we have something in our eye,<LI> it can
mean that we have a tic, etc.</UL>Outside of our culture, a
wink can be just as complex.<BR CLEAR=ALL><BR>
```

The first example has the simple tag of `<IMG SRC="winking.jpg" ALIGN= LEFT>`. The second, however, uses the Horizontal and Vertical space commands so as to adjust the text in relation to the image. Also take note of the simple list tags embedded in the tags. In the next two chapters and at this book's Web site, I will give additional examples of this kind.

Resizing an image is fairly easy to do, though I hesitate to give the tags. You need to be aware that sizing goes best in one direction, namely, from large to

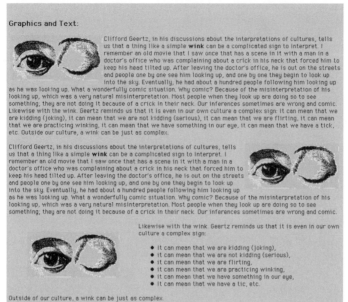

Graphics and Text:

Clifford Geertz, in his discussions about the interpretations of cultures, tells us that a thing like a simple **wink** can be a complicated sign to interpret. I remember an old movie that I saw once that has a scene in it with a man in a doctor's office who was complaining about a crick in his neck that forced him to keep his head tilted up. After leaving the doctor's office, he is out on the streets and people one by one see him looking up, and one by one they begin to look up into the sky. Eventually, he had about a hundred people following him looking up as he was looking up. What a wonderfully comic situation. Why comic? Because of the misinterpretation of his looking up, which was a very natural misinterpretation. Most people when they look up are doing so to see something; they are not doing it because of a crick in their neck. Our inferences sometimes are wrong and comic. Likewise with the wink. Geertz reminds us that it is even in our own culture a complex sign: it can mean that we are kidding (joking), it can mean that we are not kidding (serious), it can mean that we are flirting, it can mean that we are practicing winking, it can mean that we have something in our eye, it can mean that we have a tick, etc. Outside our culture, a wink can be just as complex.

Clifford Geertz, in his discussions about the interpretations of cultures, tells us that a thing like a simple **wink** can be a complicated sign to interpret. I remember an old movie that I saw once that has a scene in it with a man in a doctor's office who was complaining about a crick in his neck that forced him to keep his head tilted up. After leaving the doctor's office, he is out on the streets and people one by one see him looking up, and one by one they begin to look up into the sky. Eventually, he had about a hundred people following him looking up as he was looking up. What a wonderfully comic situation. Why comic? Because of the misinterpretation of his looking up, which was a very natural misinterpretation. Most people when they look up are doing so to see something; they are not doing it because of a crick in their neck. Our inferences sometimes are wrong and comic.

Likewise with the wink. Geertz reminds us that it is even in our own culture a complex sign:

- it can mean that we are kidding (joking),
- it can mean that we are not kidding (serious),
- it can mean that we are flirting,
- it can mean that we are practicing winking,
- it can mean that we have something in our eye,
- it can mean that we have a tic, etc.

Outside of our culture, a wink can be just as complex.

FIGURE 14

small, and not the other direction. If you take a small graphic (JPEG or GIF) and enlarge it, you are actually thinning it, adding spaces among the pixels, and this results in a poor quality graphic for most situations. Moreover, you should really do all of your resizing on PhotoShop or in a comparable program. Just because you might be making the image smaller, don't think that you are actually making the graphic file smaller. Understand that browsers will still have to upload larger than necessary graphics. The longer it takes for your page to upload on a visitor's monitor, the greater the probability that visitors will lose patience and click elsewhere. Perhaps the best reason for knowing and using the tags for resizing is that you can experiment with size during the drafting of pages. Once you know what size you want for the image, you can copy it down and then use those measurements later in Photoshop.

To resize the image, you add width and height values, but you must be careful that the proportions are maintained, unless you want purposefully to distort the image for special effect:

```
<IMG SRC="panthereye.jpg" align=left height=40 width=70>
```

Rules, Bars, Balls, Buttons, Backgrounds/Tiling, Color Codes

Rules are easy. The code is `<HR>` and it will create a line from the far left to the far right of your page. Rules usually form a shadow effect on the page, but you can tag the basic code in this manner `<HR NOSHADE>` and the results will be a solid line.

How do you vary a Rule? You can do it in terms of placement, width, and size (height and thickness). Placement by default is to the left. Width by default is across the complete page. Size by default is 2 pixels. Some examples:

```
<HR ALIGN=LEFT WIDTH=50%>
```

or

```
<HR ALIGN=CENTER WIDTH=30% SIZE=8>
```

or

```
<HR NOSHADE ALIGN=CENTER WIDTH=3% SIZE=10>
```

Here's how they look on a Netscape page:

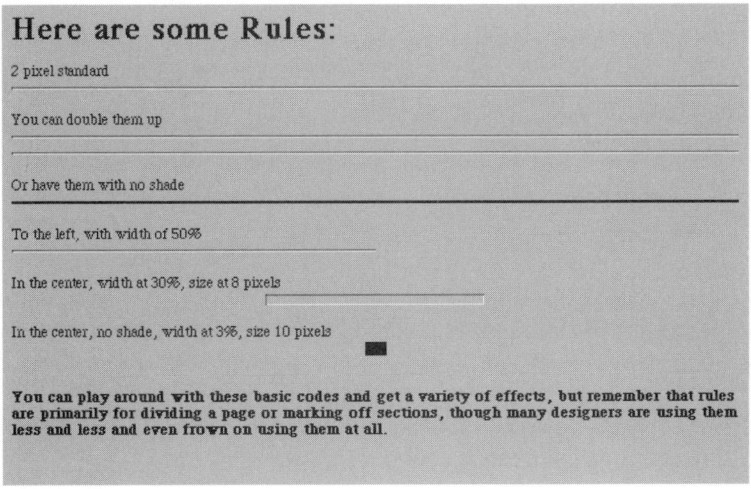

Here are some Rules:

2 pixel standard

You can double them up

Or have them with no shade

To the left, with width of 50%

In the center, width at 30%, size at 8 pixels

In the center, no shade, width at 3%, size 10 pixels

You can play around with these basic codes and get a variety of effects, but remember that rules are primarily for dividing a page or marking off sections, though many designers are using them less and less and even frown on using them at all.

FIGURE 15

Bars are easy. You already know how to tag a graphic, which is exactly what a Bar is; in fact, it's what Bars, Balls, Buttons, Backgrounds are. Unlike Rules, you will either design a Bar, Ball, etc., or find one on the Web to download as a JPEG or GIF. Yes, there are places, many places, you can browse to on the Web and legally download all kinds of what is called eye-candy. (See the URLs at the end of Chapter 3 for locations of where you will find what you need; also be sure to check out the Web site for this book.)

Like Rules, Bars are used for dividing a page, and since they are a graphic file, they are coded in the same way that all such files are tagged: `<IMG SRC="bar1.gif">`. Place them the same way that you situated a Rule: `<P><IMG SRC="bar1.gif"><P>`. You can adjust the placement and size of the Rule with code. For example:

```
<P><IMG SRC="bar1.gif" align=center width=250><P>
```

This is about the right midsize, or you can vary it.

As with Bars, the tag for *Balls* and *Buttons* is just as easy and can follow the same pattern as for an unordered list with bullets, which is what they are usually used for. You can also adjust the size to a preferred 10 pixels:

```
<UL>
<IMG SRC="15.gif" width=10> First item
<IMG SRC="15.gif" width=10> Second item
<IMG SRC="15.gif" width=10> Third item
</UL>
```

Backgrounds (virtual wallpaper) and *Color codes* (background and links) are somewhat different. To use backgrounds, you will enter the code at the top of the page in the Body:

```
<Body Background="crumpledpap.jpg">
```

What this particular placement and tag will do is tile the image across and down the page so that it will be a consistently distributed image over which all other text and graphics will be visible.

Along with the background, the color codes also go into the Body. Instead of using a graphic to be tiled, it is possible with the right tag and color (hexadecimal) code to change the default color gray to any other color. I usually use black and then a series of colors for links. For example:

```
<BODY BGCOLOR="#000000" TEXT="#FF0000"
LINK="#FDD90D" VLINK="#FDD90D">
```

There is a lot of information here. First of all, however, understand that there are three formats known as RGB, which get spread out 2 × 3 as #RRGGBB. RGB refers to the amounts of Red, Green, and Blue. The two digits of Red, etc., are hexadecimal numbers and letters that run from 0, 1, 2, 3, 4, 5, 6, 7, 8, 9, A, B, C, D, E, F. The range, then, is from black to white on the hexadecimal spectrum. The *background color,* in the above example, is black, for which the hexadecimal code is all zeros. (Hexadecimal codes always come in a unit of

6 and can be all numbers or letters or a combination.) For white, it is all "#FFFFFF". Hexadecimal codes, which differ for every color and shade, etc., can be found out at various Web sites, so I am not going to spend any more time on what they are in this chapter but in a later one. (See the URLs at the end of this chapter.) The color codes that work for backgrounds also work for establishing the nondefault colors for the *text* and for the *links*. Besides these, there are ways of putting in colors for *VLINKs*, which stands for *visited links*, and *ALINKS*, for *active links*, that is, the color a link takes while you are clicking on it. I tend not to use them.

Caveat

Be very careful not to use backgrounds and color combinations that are garish, for they tend to make it difficult to read what is on the page. People new to setting up Web pages tend to overuse them, just like a kid who gets his hands on a lot of candy. When confronted with such pages, people will just click themselves to another Web site.

Tables

The codes for Tables are not all that easy upon first glance, and yet, once you understand the logic in the pattern, they become easy. Tables are visible or invisible cells in which you can locate text and graphics. If you recall the horizontal list of graphics, which had the code of IMG SRC and then another one and another one, we can construct the same list in a Table and gain more control over it in terms of its stability and spacing. (While a list of images can lose their horizontal relationship if the frame of Netscape is narrowed down, a Table will hold that relationship.)

Here are the basic tags (mumbo jumbo) that you will be using:

```
<TABLE>Everything that is a Table fits in between these two
    codes</TABLE>
<BORDER=number> Will determine whether or not you want a
    Border and what size.
<CAPTION>The Caption for the Table</CAPTION>
<TR>Everything in a Table Row goes between these codes</TR>
<TH>Table Headers can be horizontal (row) or vertical (column)
    headers and are emphasized text</TH>
<COLSPAN=number> stretches a cell horizontally into the space
    of a designated number of cells
<ROWSPAN=number> stretches a cell vertically ...
```

```
<TD>Table Data, everything in the cell</TD>
<VALIGN=top/center/bottom ALIGN=left/center/right> control
    the alignment of information in <TR> and <TD> tags and
    within cells
<CELLPADDING=number> determines the amount of space around
    the contents in a cell
<WIDTH=number or %> determines the width of the table
```

Let's take a look at the most *basic* code for a simple Table. One thing to re-member is that Tables divvy things up into vertical columns and horizontal rows. (You really need to think of the space in Netscape in terms of vertical and horizontal space and how you want to represent the information that you want to tag.) Tables are good for a variety of things from calendars/ schedules to spreadsheets to situating chunks of text and graphics. Here's an example of tags for a very basic Table that can organize your life: *two rows, three columns.*

```
<TABLE WIDTH=400>
<CAPTION ALIGN=CENTER><B>This is a basic Table</B>,<br>set
at a width of 400 pixels, with two rows, each with three
columns<br>and no border</CAPTION>
<TR>
<TD ALIGN=CENTER>Item One, row one</TD>
<TD ALIGN=CENTER>Item Two, row one</TD>
<TD ALIGN=CENTER>Item Three, row one</TD>
</TR>
<TR>
<TD ALIGN=CENTER>Item One, row two</TD>
<TD ALIGN=CENTER>Item Two, row two</TD>
<TD ALIGN=CENTER>Item Three, row two</TD>
</TR></TABLE>
```

The caption should explain it all. Here's another: *two rows, three columns, with variations.*

```
<TABLE BORDER=2 WIDTH=500 CELLPADDING=3>
<CAPTION ALIGN=CENTER><B>This is a basic Table</B>,<br> set
at a width of 500, with different widths and alignments,
and a cellpadding of 3</CAPTION>
<TR>
<TD ALIGN=LEFT WIDTH=250>Item One, row one</TD>
<TD ALIGN=RIGHT>Item Two, row one</TD>
<TD ALIGN=RIGHT>Item Three, row one</TD>
</TR>
```

```
<TR>
<TD ALIGN=LEFT WIDTH=250>Item One, row two</TD>
<TD ALIGN=RIGHT>Item Two, row two</TD>
<TD ALIGN=RIGHT>Item Three, row two</TD>
</TR></TABLE>
```

Read the caption; it tells the story. Here's another Table: *three rows and three columns.*

```
<TABLE BORDER=1 WIDTH=100% CELLPADDING=10>
<CAPTION ALIGN=CENTER><B>This is a basic Table</B>,<br>set
at a width of 100%, with three rows, three columns, and
different alignments with a cellpadding of 10</CAPTION>
<TR>
<TD ALIGN=LEFT>Item One, row one</TD>
<TD ALIGN=LEFT>Item Two, row one</TD>
<TD ALIGN=LEFT>Item Three, row one</TD>
</TR>
<TR>
<TD ALIGN=CENTER>Item One, row two</TD>
<TD ALIGN=CENTER>Item Two, row two</TD>
<TD ALIGN=CENTER>Item Three, row two</TD>
</TR>
<TR>
<TD ALIGN=RIGHT>Item One, row three</TD>
<TD ALIGN=RIGHT>Item Two, row three</TD>
<TD ALIGN=RIGHT>Item Three, row three</TD>
</TR></TABLE>
```

Now look at Figure 16.

We can make Tables into more complicated schemes and even have fun with them. They are exceptionally useful, again, because they allow us *to control chunks of information.* Here's a Table with headers for both rows and columns:

```
<TABLE BORDER=2 CELLPADDING=5 WIDTH=100%>
<CAPTION ALIGN=CENTER><B>This is a Table with headers for
rows and columns</B>,<BR>with a border of 2 pixels, width
of 100%, cellpadding of 5 pixels</CAPTION>
<TR>
<TH></TH>
<TH>Header One</TH>
<TH>Header Two</TH>
```

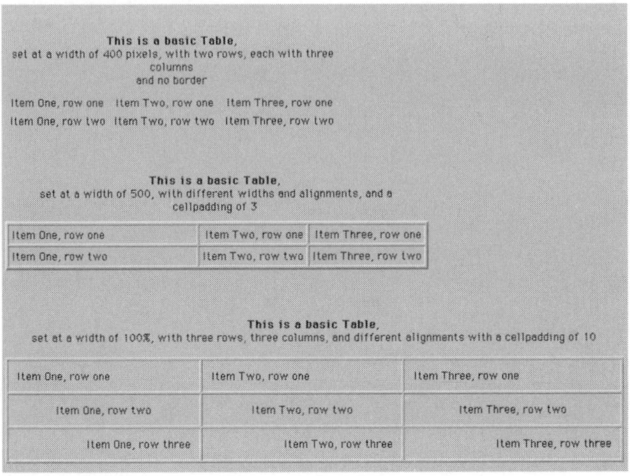

FIGURE 16

```
<TH>Header Three</TH>
</TR>
<TR>
<TH>Header A</TH>
<TD ALIGN=CENTER>Item One, row one</TD>
<TD ALIGN=CENTER>Item Two, row one</TD>
<TD ALIGN=CENTER>Item Three, row one</TD> </TR>
<TR>
<TH>Header B</TH>
<TD ALIGN=CENTER>Item One, row two</TD>
<TD ALIGN=CENTER>Item Two, row two</TD>
<TD ALIGN=CENTER>Item Three, row two</TD>
</TR></TABLE>
```

Here is a table with chunks of text and graphics that tell a story:

```
<TABLE WIDTH=100% CELLPADDING=10>
<CAPTION ALIGN=TOP><B>This is a Table with Text and Graph-
ics, </B><BR> with no border, mixed rows, <BR>width of
100%, cellpadding of 10 pixels</CAPTION>
<TR>
<TD ALIGN=LEFT>"Tiger, Tiger, Burning Bright, In the Forest
of the Night. What Fearful Tables...." ????<P><CENTER><B>1.
</CENTER></B></TD>
<TD ALIGN=CENTER><IMG SRC="panthereye.jpg"><P><B>2.</B></TD>
```

```
<TD ALIGN=LEFT>Let's See: "Tiger, Tiger, Burning Bright, In
the Forest of the Night. What Fearful Symmetry Tabled...."
????<P><CENTER>3.</B></CENTER></TD>
</TR>
<TR>
<TD ALIGN=CENTER><IMG SRC="panthereye.jpg" HEIGHT=60
WIDTH=80><P><B>4.</B></TD>
<TD ALIGN=LEFT>Again, "Tiger, Tiger, Burning Bright, In the
Forest of the Night. Who Tabled thy Fearful
Symmetry?"<P><CENTER><B>5.</B></CENTER></TD>
<TD ALIGN=CENTER><IMG SRC="winking.jpg"><P><B>6.</B></TD>
</TR></TABLE>
```

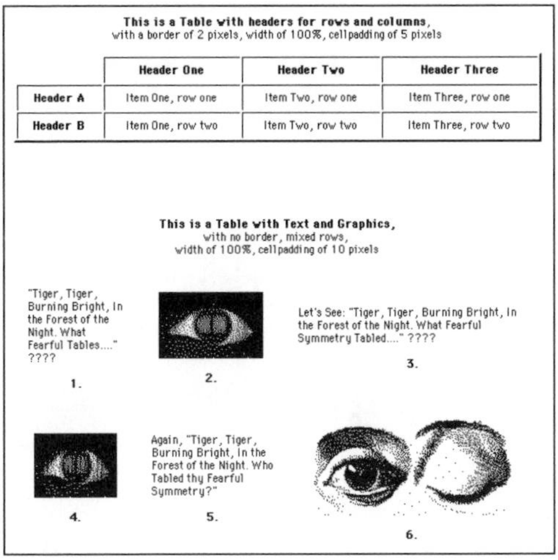

FIGURE 17

If you study the above examples, you will have some paradigms to think with about what makes for a Table. A good way to study them, however, is while developing a Web site, so we will return to them and discuss them in greater length. Another way of studying them is finding them on the Web and pulling down the source document to see how they are constructed. The Web is a textbook itself, the world's largest!

Special Characters

There are some tags for special characters that even your word processing program must use. For example, if you want to accurately spell the name

Hélène Cixous, with the acute (é) and grave (è) accents over the e, you need to know the tag/code. For the acute accent, the tag is "é" or "é". For the grave accent, it's "è" or "&#egrave;". Therefore, the name would be rendered in a sentence of a paragraph as: H"é"l"è"ne Cixous. When the browser reads it, it appears as "Hélène Cixous." This kind of tagging is a rather simple substitution. Be aware that these codes do *not* go into right- and left-angled brackets, "< >".

Tip

So many graphic designers have not yet discovered the code for indenting a paragraph. Instead, what they do is to create a graphic (a GIF) with the same color as the background and place it at the beginning of a paragraph. An alternative is to use the tag " ". You will have to repeat this tag perhaps five or six times in a row to get a full indentation. (Note that this code is not placed in right-angled brackets.)

All of the above are some of the basic tags. What we will take a look at in the next chapter are some of the trappings (developing conventions) that define pages on the Web.

COMMENTS AND SUGGESTIONS

Templates

The best way to see and accumulate these codes is for you to type them (precisely as I have given them to you here or any variation thereof) on a *text only* formatted page. Begin, as you might expect, with the simpler codes and progress to the more complicated ones. Save each file onto your hard disk and use all of them as templates. Be sure to have one for Tables or, even better, have several for a variety of formatted Tables. When you need to construct Tables, then, all you have to do is launch the appropriate template. As you build more and more files, you will be building your repertoire of HTML formats and designs, which you can use over and over again by simply cutting and pasting.

Differences Among Browsers

There is little consistency from one browser to another. Remember that many people are still probably using Lynx, which is a text browser and, hence, does not read graphics of any kind. Even among the browsers that do read graphic files, there are numerous differences in how HTML can get interpreted and rendered on a monitor. For example, *Font size control,* found on Netscape V.2.01. is not available on America On Line V.2.6 Mac or V.2.5 PC. *Vertical and horizontal spacing commands,* available on Netscape, are not represented on many other browsers. *Tables and Frames,* available on Netscape, are not representable on several browsers. (Netscape 2.01+ can read both Tables and Frames.) (We will learn a few things about Frames in Chapter 8.) Therefore, if you use Netscape remember that what you design and see on your monitor, others will not necessarily see. It is worth noting that more and more browsers are being reprogrammed in their version updates to include many features such as Tables and Frames.

Making Web Sites Accessible for Sight- and Hearing-impaired

Since Lynx does not read graphic files, the solution, as I have pointed out, is to include the <ALT=> tag and a description of the image. But access to Web sites can be greatly enhanced not only for users of Lynx but also for the sight- and hearing-impaired. Since the interest in making Web media more accessible is growing along with major developments in the technology, I suggest that you intermittently visit the Web site for the National Center for Accessible Media (NCAM): http://www.boston.com/wgbh/pages/ncam/ncamhome.html. The NCAM has numerous links to "Blindness Resources," "Deafness/Hard of Hearing Resources," and "General Disability Resources." A rather new suggestion, to accompany the <ALT=> tag, is the placement of a *"D"* link with every graphic and audio file, which gives a fully developed description of the graphic or a transcription of an audio file.

Netscape: Obtaining a Copy

You can always purchase a copy of Netscape, but since you are a student, Netscape Navigator is free for your use. It is a very large program, so you must be sure to have the memory and correct operating system to run it. If you are online, that is, have a connection from your own computer to the Net, you can simply go by way of the text-only browser Lynx, or you can go by way of FTP software to Netscape and download a copy. (You can obtain a copy of *WS_FTP* for DOS or Windows or a copy of *Fetch* for Mac from a friend since it will fit on a floppy disk.) If you use Lynx, the URL is *http://home.netscape.com/*; if FTP, the URL is *ftp20.netscape.com.* (Your user ID will be "anonymous" and your password will be either "guest" or your e-mail address. The directory will be */pub.* Once in, double click on the directory *Navigator* and download whatever version you will need, which will most likely be 2.0 if still available; the suffixes are Mac-hqx; Windows 3.1-N16; and Windows95 or NT versions-N32. You may wish to download 3.0 or higher, but I would be very careful in terms of specifications, that is, whether or not you will be able to use either version 2.0 or 3.0. Much depends on the amount of RAM, memory, that you have installed.)

If you are not online, then you are confronted with a problem that can be solved in one of three ways:

1. Get a copy from a friend: The program is too large to be placed on a simple 1.4MB floppy disk. You will have to find someone who has a ZIP Drive or some other removable storage drive that allows for disks that hold more megabytes than a simple floppy in order to transfer the file to your hard disk. If you do it in this fashion, be sure to transfer Netscape in the Installer format so that the browser with all of its additional files will be installed correctly in your hard drive.

2. Sign up for America Online, or some comparable provider, for the free hours and then download all the software you can. But be careful, once you exceed the free time you are going to start paying, paying, paying.

3. Get a CD with freeware or shareware. Often magazines such as *.NET* come with such CDs.

WEB SITE RESOURCES

HTML Web sites

Following are some URLs to Web sites that will be helpful in further exploring the basics of HTML. Also be sure to visit the Web site for this book, where you will find these URLs and many additional ones:

A Beginner's Guide to HTML
`http://www.ncsa.uiuc.edu/General/Internet/WWW/HTMLPrimer.html`

HTML Tutorial
`http://www.mcli.dist.maricopa.edu/tut/Writing`

HTML Quick Reference
`http://kuhttp.cc.ukans.edu/lynx_help/HTML_quick.html`

Guides to Writing HTML Documents
`http://union.ncsa.uiuc.edu/HyperNews/get/www/html/guides.html`

How To Write HTML Files
`http://kcgl1.eng.ohio-state.edu/www/doc/htmldoc.html`

HTML: Adding More
`http://kcgl1.eng.ohio-state.edu/www/doc/htmlmore.html`

3.0 Announcements
`http://www.hp.co.uk/people/dsr/html3/CoverPage.htmlHTML`

Composing Good HTML
`http://www.cs.cmu.edu/~tilt/cgh/`

Style Guide for Online Hypertext
`http://www.w3.org/hypertext/WWW/Provider/Style/Overview.html`

Netscape extensions to HTML
`http://home.mcom.com/home/services_docs/html-extensions.html`

Web Developer's Virtual Library: HTML
`http://WWW.Stars.com/Vlib/Providers/HTML.html`

TableMaker
`http://www.missouri.edu/~c588349/tablemaker.html`

Color, RGB, Hexadecimal Codes

You will find loads of information concerning color codes at these sites.

Color Information
`http://www.yahoo.com/Computers_and_Internet/Internet/World_Wide_Web/`
`Page_Design_and_Layout/Color_Information/YAHOO`

Hexadecimal Color Code where you get the colors of the rainbow+ for your
backgrounds and various links.
`http://www.webmotion.com/Websurfshop/Colorcode/index.html`

Background Color Hex Converter
`http://www.echonyc.com/~xixax/Mediarama/hex.html`

RGB Made Easy
`http://www.ukshops.co.uk:8000/tc/rgb.html`

Update on Changes in Browsers (Netscape Navigator, Netscape Explorer, etc.)

Browser Watch
`http://www.ski.mskcc.org/browserwatch/browsers.html`

Yahoo
`http://www.yahoo.com/Computers_and_Internet/Internet`

▶ 3

The Elements of Hyperstyle: Page Conventions

Words and Images (Content and Style, Substance and Glitz)

Length and Width: The Problem of Scrolling

Connections/Linkages (No Dead Pages!)

Logo (Identity)

Statement of Purpose (Why? and Who?)

Table of Contents, Headings, and Subheadings

Graphics and Photographs (Worth a Thousand Words)

Disposition of Chunks of Prose and Images

Disposition of Pages/Files

Signature with Credits

References (Books and Articles)

Web site Resources
    General Guides to Writing and Designing on the WWW
    Copyright
    Icons and Graphics
    Special Services

Having discussed the basic tags for HTML, I now want to spell out what the basic *visible elements* or conventions are for generic Web pages. This will continue throughout the next few chapters and more so in context. By *conventions*, I do not mean to suggest that Web designers or teachers of Web writing agree that all these elements are necessary. It may very well be that your teacher/facilitator suggests that some elements are not to his or her liking. There is plenty of room for disagreement or differences in taste or choice when it comes to writing for print and writing and designing Web sites. You must be flexible in relation to these differences, knowing when to use some and not others.

As you look over the list of elements in this chapter's outline, note that many elements are similar to those used in writing for print and, in a few cases, specifically advertising. Therefore, I am going to take up the first element, which deals with the ever-present, hotly debated issue of substance *and* (or *versus*) glitz.

WORDS AND IMAGES (CONTENT AND STYLE, SUBSTANCE AND GLITZ)

When asked to write papers for class, you are expected to produce a well-developed group of paragraphs that all contribute to the realization of your purpose for the writing, whether it be for informing the audience (exposition) or for changing the opinion of your audience (argumentation). This is all achieved by way of words carefully selected and strategically given. Usually there are no images except for occasional analogies or other forms of figurative language; seldom, if ever, are there images as in graphics.

One thing most authors of textbooks on writing will tell you—and for good reason—is to avoid the overuse of figurative, flowery language, especially if it is filled with clichés. In fact, never use figurative language unless it helps illustrate a difficult, abstract point, or makes it memorable. Such advice works fairly well in the medium of writing for print, but does not always work in electronic writing and designing. Though the Web and writing for it are fairly new, those of us who have studied it, specifically how people write for it, have come to understand that "words, words, words" do not alone or in quantity make for good, successful Web pages. In fact, too many words can be a major turn off, and will cause your audience to click off to some other site.

Does this mean, then, that a successful Web page must have lots of graphics? No. While you have had to learn and perhaps still are learning to use words effectively and in relation to a particular economy, you will now need to learn to use words and graphics in a completely different economy.

By "economy" I mean the amount or number of words and graphics that you are going to place on a page, their interrelationships, and their purpose; in other words, the amount of what is often referred to as content and style, substance and possible glitz, and how you are going to expend them. Writing and designing for electronic media are just as filled with possible hazards, if not more so, than writing for print. Therefore, writers and designers, beware! Unfortunately, there is no algorithm, or rule-governed procedure, that I can offer. At best, be very careful of the difference between telling and showing. The *Web*, for many people, is more about showing than telling. The former can be quick and 'insiteful' [sic]; the latter, in the medium of a Web site can be laborious and annoying.

Showing over telling does not mean, however, that you must abandon all of the critical, argumentative strategies you have learned in writing for print. Is it not the case, for example, that when you turn to the editorial page in a newspaper, you will find editorial cartoons, which by way of *showing* are just as effective, if not more so, in critiquing someone's thinking or a governmental policy? Often the editor will run a written editorial (telling) along with an editorial cartoon (showing)—an extremely effective combination. You must learn *why* and *how* it is effective and how to use it on the Web.

Showing over telling does not mean that you must abandon lengthy pieces of prose either. In this and the next two chapters we will take up the issue of how to deal with lengthy prose. What has become clear, I think, is that the medium of the Web does not invite lengthy articles or books, but there are ways of designing for them.

After building several Web sites and studying the WWW with someone who can tell you what to look for, you will begin to gain an ethical, political, aesthetic—and very practical—sense of what does and does not work. Complicating the whole matter of learning, however, is the incredible speed at which the technology of electronic media is changing. As soon as you learn a technique, there are new developments that have an impact on the usage of all that you have learned, which then causes you to relearn what you thought you understood and could do well.

With this said about substance and style, let us now turn to some specifics concerning conventions. Keep in mind, however, that the word "conventions" is used loosely in all cases.

LENGTH AND WIDTH: THE PROBLEM OF SCROLLING

Perhaps one of the most argued about issues right now among teachers and designers of Web pages is *their overall size*. Some argue that everything on the first, or hub/core page should fit on a standard 14-inch monitor, while others see nothing wrong with having their readers scroll down a long page. Some argue that the width of a page should be no wider than 600 pixels, while others will establish multiple rows and columns that push the width out of the so-called normal viewing area. (I recently read an article in an electronic magazine whose width was set at 2800 pixels but whose length or height was set at 300 pixels. All of my scrolling, therefore, was horizontal.)

I am going to assume the real point is not simply length and width in themselves and some rule-governed notion about staying within limits, but how well the writer and designer can interest and seduce their readers into scrolling. Content and style (when blended together successfully) should dictate everything, including length and width. Having made this point, however, I feel that I need to warn you that if you do not know what you are doing, you can get yourself into a heap of trouble with some rather ridiculous, to coin a word, "scrolly" problems. Be careful. And at first simplify, simplify, simplify.

Let's take a look at some different styles: The first example (Figure 18) is a simple and straightforward student home page, which fits comfortably within a 14 inch monitor (http://www.uta.edu/english/daver/).

The second example (Figure 19) is an electronic newspaper that is exceptionally well organized in a consistent style, which promises the viewer that everything he or she wants is just a click away. For many people, however,

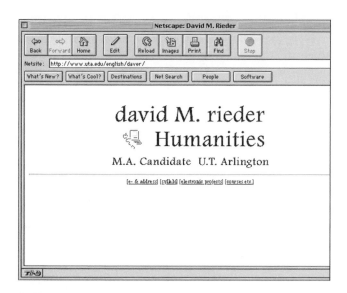

FIGURE 18

FIGURE 19

this site might appear to be "cluttered"; I find it aesthetically pleasing and well-ordered. (http://www.cnet.com/).

The third example (Figure 20) is another student home page, which has a few animated GIFs and lines connecting object to object, thereby inviting the reader to scroll horizontally so as to follow the thread. (http://www. uta.edu/english/cgb/home/index.html).

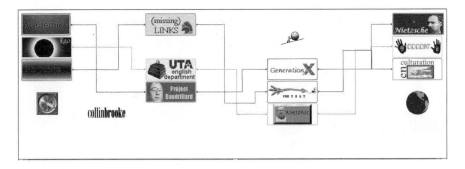

FIGURE 20

CONNECTIONS/LINKAGES (NO DEAD PAGES!)

When linking pages from the primary or hub/core page, you should always include on every page a link back to the previous page. It *is* the case that if readers jump from one page to the next on Lynx or on Netscape, all that they have to do to return is strike the left arrow key for Lynx or the Back button at the top of Netscape. But if potential readers find one of your files/pages on the Web by way of a search engine and enter in the middle of several contiguous files, they cannot simply return to where they have not already been! They should be able to get to what we call the "top" of your page.

The importance of linking pages also suggests the importance of using *markers* and *jumps* within a long page so that the readers will not have to scroll to (re)locate a section. (See HTML tags, Chapter 2.)

Hence, include some form of interpage (across pages/files) and intrapage (within a single page) navigational system. You will learn to do this in a variety of ways in subsequent chapters.

Here are some examples of different kinds of navigational devices (Figure 21):

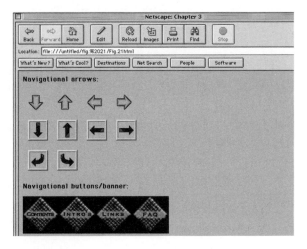

FIGURE 21

LOGO (IDENTITY)

The very idea of having a logo, which is often associated with corporations, may appear immediately out of place here in relation to the kind of writing you will be asked to do. And yes, it certainly is. In most cases, I suspect, your instructor may want you to skip this section, but I include it here because there is every reason for me to believe that you will eventually be creating Web sites that can use and will benefit from using a logo. As you will note later, I will be giving you sample templates that use logos effectively.

When I started thinking of this book, specifically a title for it, I started thinking in terms of a logo. I typed (as if doodling) these combinations:

```
<WWWW>, <W4>, ==W4==, VV4
```

The purpose of a logo is for instantaneous recognition.

For my own personal home page (http://www.uta.edu/english/Victor_.html), I developed not a single logo, but a variety of optical images, or more simply put, variations on the image of an eye or eyes. This image has been around for a long time and especially in relation to television (the CBS logo) and all things concerning the WWW. (Pick up any magazine about the Web or electronic environments and you will find the image of the eye going through all kinds of metamorphoses.) Instead of designing one eye and laying claim for its specificity, I played with a variety of images: some would be single eyes (human or animal), some animated GIFs, etc. I also decided to make academic (e.g., psychoanalytic and rhetorical) allusions with them, and then appropriate links from them. (Hence, I decided that I would imitate what was taking place on the whole Web itself and in many magazines.) Moreover by not being specific with a logo, I figured that I could phase it out easily, if I decided to do so, and then slowly phase in yet another.

So give some thoughts to developing a logo for some of your pages. Remember, it's about your identity, whether stable, ever-changing, or . . . .

STATEMENT OF PURPOSE (WHY? AND WHO?)

One of the most important conventions for communication by way of any medium—whether through speech, print, or electronic discourse—is a statement of purpose, or an answer to the questions *Why?* and *Who?*, or an answer to a question from your WWW audience, such as *Now that we are here, what are you going to show and tell us?* Communicating instantaneous answers to these questions is not always easy to accomplish, but you must spend whatever amount of time it takes to discover in the simplest terms the premise for your site. (You have probably heard that busy CEOs usually give people only a few minutes to put forth a premise or concept. Most likely, people who visit your Web site will give you much less time!

One of the tried and tested ways to discover why and who is to jot down some ideas, graphically connect them, and then attempt to summarize them in a couple of sentences. Another way is to construct a storyboard (a narrative) and then summarize it. Another is to browse the Web in search of what you might want to do and then learn from the examples you find. In any case, it is necessary for you to have arrived at a purpose and then communicate it succinctly.

Here is an example of a brief statement of purpose:

Welcome to the Bandwidth Conservation Society

Last June, a loosely knit group of web developers put up a couple of pages about making gif files smaller in bytesize (hence, faster web delivery). The mail was phenomenal, we were even able to answer some of it (but, having day-jobs, spouses, spawn, etc., the BCS was pretty static.) Here is v2 of the Bandwidth Conservation Society.

The goal is that this site becomes a resource for web developers with an interest in optimizing performance, but still maintaining an appropriate graphic standard. The conviction (or perhaps hallucination) that there is a balance between a pleasing page and an economical, low-bandwidth delivery of that page [sic].

We invite you to contribute, criticize, compliment, or just cruise.

—JOHN-MICHAEL KEYES APRIL 1996

In this example from the Bandwidth Conservation Society Web page (http://www.infohiway.com/faster/index.html), the statement of purpose begins with a historical explanation of how a group of people got started and then evolved into the present Web site with its growing concerns. (By the way, this is a site well worth visiting for information on how to establish pages with graphics that are low in number of kilobytes and, consequently, will load fast and conserve bandwidth, through which all Web data must pass.)

Here is one (http://www.eff.org/) that is even more succinct:

The Electronic Frontier Foundation is a non-profit civil liberties organization working in the public interest to protect privacy, free expression, and access to public resources and information online, as well as to promote responsibility in new media.

Often, a statement of purpose is implied or communicated by way of the overall appearance (including logo, title, and list of items). Figure 22 (http://www.uta.edu/english/mal/sein/seinfeld.html) illustrates this point.

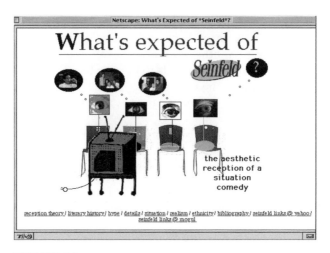

FIGURE 22

TABLE OF CONTENTS, HEADINGS, AND SUBHEADINGS

A table of contents (TOC) can be especially helpful to readers of Web documents that are exceptionally long, running the length of a standard book in print. While the importance of the TOC should be rather obvious, the importance of headings may be less appreciated. Nothing is more difficult to read than a continuous flow of words on a monitor; therefore, it is best to place the prose (if you have a lot of it, for example, in an article or even in a Web book) into brief paragraphs that are occasionally introduced by headings, subheadings, etc. In this way, your readers will have sign posts all along the way, both guiding and enticing them to continue reading. The wording of the headings needs to be informative.

It is exceptionally important to make your headings decrease in size (<H1> to <H6>) as you enter the various levels of subheadings, and to avoid going beyond this sequence of hierarchies: headings, subheadings, or subsub headings. Or in terms of a book: title, table of contents, topics, subtopics. (If you get too detailed in your dividing and subdividing, your reader will only get lost.) Remember: The point is to make information easier to process, not more difficult.

Figure 23, taken from Beth Baldwin's book *Conversations* (http://www.missouri.edu/~rhetnet/baldwin/), illustrates how a table of contents can be used effectively. This same site also shows how large and long pages/files of words can be effectively formatted by moving from regular to boldface print:

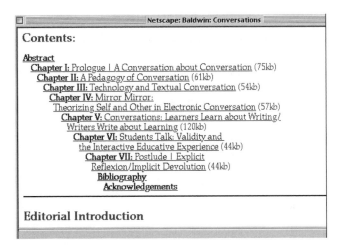

FIGURE 23

Comment

This form of dividing up the flow of a single page into Headings is important enough for me to bring it up again in the next chapter, and I will do so in terms of breaking up long pieces of prose into many separate files that are linked and, therefore, read without having to scroll down but by having only to point and click from section to section. The tags used are Destination Markers and Jumps. The designer of the above examples uses these tags.

GRAPHICS AND PHOTOGRAPHS (WORTH A THOUSAND WORDS)

Again, the Web is about multimedia, not just words, words, words. Therefore, instead of being good only as a wordsmith, you must learn how to be good at developing and selecting graphics and photographs and at preparing them for your Web sites. There are some general rules (conventions) that you should follow:

- Learn the differences between JPEGs (Joint Photographic Experts Group) and GIFs (Graphics Interchange Format) and when to use one or the other (as you might expect, there are more arguments than agreements among designers about which graphic format is better than the other and for which purpose)

- Understand that you should keep the size (i.e., the number of bytes) to a minimum so as to avoid long uploading times, which will try the patience of your audience
- Learn to prepare photographs carefully, cropping them so as to remove unnecessary image space
- Respect copyright laws when using graphics and photographs

DISPOSITION OF CHUNKS OF PROSE AND IMAGES

Try to maintain some balance, as a general rule, between words and images. Perhaps the best way to prepare yourself for combining words and images is to study magazines, a wide variety of them, to get a sense of layout. And also, of course, study the WWW. When studying print layout, you will note that every attempt is made by designers to break up long flows of words by constructing:

- Columns and, at times, rows
- Boxes with additional information and graphs for illustrations
- Pictures and images
- Pull-quotes invisibly boxed (i.e., no borders) between columns

Each of these techniques can be simulated on the Web. The HTML tags for Tables will be most helpful in controlling the disposition and flow of information (pixels that constitute both words and pictures) on the page.

Comment

I have not forgotten the importance of *audio* and *video* in electronic media. Since this book is an introductory one, concerned with the most basic principles, I leave these other forms of information to later or other books. As you progress, into this book, however, you will notice that audio and video files are intermittently taken into consideration, laying the groundwork for later developments.

DISPOSITION OF PAGES/FILES

As with the disposition of paragraphs in an essay or theme and that of chapters in a book and, as I have suggested, the disposition of units of information (words and images) on a Web page, the *arrangement and se-quencing (linkings) of pages/files on a Web site need to be thought out carefully and strategically.* In thinking about the disposition of files, you most certainly need to use flowcharts and read as much material on this subject as possible.

There is so much to say about this aspect of writing and designing for the WWW that it is a book in itself. The best I can recommend, at present, is Siegel's *Building Killer Websites,* in which the author examines what he calls first- through third-generation Web sites. The latter distinguish themselves from the former by establishing, in part, differences between *entrances* and *exits.* (The influence of electronic games may be at work here.) For example, it is typical in first- and second-generation Web sites to have a standard introductory first page with a *statement of purpose* and a *quasi-TOC* or *list of links* and finally a *Signature.* In third-generation sites, however, there is an entrance tunnel through which the audience passes to get to this information. Often the first page(s) are exceptionally simple and automatically transport the audience (by way of a *push* tags) to the next page(s) until, after being escorted to the main page, the audience finally regains control and gets to select for itself what it wants to visit. What the audience sees, however, are not the traditional conventions of statement of purpose, etc., all on one page; for these conventions, too, may be displaced from their expected positions, yet nonetheless easy to find. Like the entrance, the exit is composed of a series of tunnels.

SIGNATURE WITH CREDITS

Along with a logo, which usually appears at the very top or bottom of a page, you will need to incorporate a Signature with credits. In the previous chapter on HTML, I suggest a way of tagging Signatures. In addition, you need to know where and what kind of information to include. Your Signature should appear at the bottom on what you consider to be your primary page, from which all primary links branch out. In the Signature, you might include:

- Your name
- Copyright statement (though this is *not* really necessary for most pages)
- Your e-mail address as a link (a `<mailto:>` tag),
- The date you first established your Web site and the date last modified
- Any credits, that is, names of people you should acknowledge for giving assistance

FIGURE 24

Figure 24 shows how I have arranged, in a very bland style, the Signature on my home page.

In Chapters 4 through 6, we will take a more detailed look at a variety of ways to develop first (primary, a.k.a. *hub* or *core*) pages and then additional pages branching from them. We will also examine some basic ways to revise and further develop Web sites and finally how "to publish" them, that is, place them into a *server*, which is the computer (machine) that makes them available to everyone.

REFERENCES (BOOKS AND ARTICLES)

Baldwin, Beth. *Conversations: Computer-Mediated Dialogue, Multilogue & Learning.* (http://www.missouri.edu/~rhetnet/baldwin/)

Merholz, Peter. "Tricks for Laying Out Your Web Page: Case Study: The Voyager Site." *.Net* (June 1996): 52–53.

Siegel, David. *Creating Killer Websites Online: The Art of Third-Generation Site Design.* Indianapolis, IN: Hayden Books, 1996. This is an advanced book that distinguishes among first-, second-, and third-generation Web sites. (See Siegel's Web site: http://www.killersites.com/.)

Waters, Crystal. *Web Concept and Design: A Comprehensive Guide for Creating Effective Web Sites.* Indianapolis, IN: New Riders, 1996. A basic book for developing mostly commercial sites. (See Waters's Web site: http://www.typo.com.)

Weinman, Lynda. *<deconstructing web graphics> Web Design Case Studies and Tutorials.* Indianapolis, IN: New Riders, 1996. As the title suggests, this book is a study of the development of select commercial Web sites such as HotWired and Discovery Channel Online (See Weinman's accompanying Web site: http://www.lynda. com/decon.)

———. *<designing web graphics>: How to Prepare Images and Media for the Web*. Indianapolis, IN: New Riders, 1996. This book is a more basic book than *<deconstructing. . . .>*. (See Weinman's Web site: http://www.earthlink.net/~lyndaw *Or* http://www.lynda.com/.)

———. *"Word:* Portrait of an Online Magazine." *.Net* (May 1996): 54–56. This is an excellent study of the revisions made at the *Word* site [http://www.word.com/] and is not included in Weinman's book *<deconstructing>*.

WEB SITE RESOURCES

General Guides to Writing and Designing on the WWW

Creating Net Sites (Netscape)
`http://home.netscape.com/assist/net_sites/`

NCDesign HP (This is an exceptionally good site for HTML Design Guide, VRML, Web Material, and Design Research.)
`http://ncdesign.kyushu-id.ac.jp/`

Lynda's (Weinman) *Homegurrlpage* (great information here)
`http://www.lynda.com/`

Web Design Tips
`http://home.earthlink.net/~lyndaw/tips.html`

Sun Microsystems, Guide to WebStyle
`http://www.sun.com/styleguide/`

BOBAWORLD: Bob Allison's HP: The Web Master
`http://gagme.wwa.com/~boba/masters1.html`

A general styleguide
`http://www.book.uci.edu/Staff/StyleGuide.html`

How to make your Web site "reader-friendly"
`http://www.anet-dfw.com/~tsull/webtips/35252.html`

Web development by John December
`http://www.december.com/web/develop.html`

Zen and the art of developing Web sites
`http://www.tlc-systems.com/webtips.html`

Writing a Web space
`http://www.wiu.edu/users/mflll/writing.html`

Copyright

Copyright is an extremely important issue. Every time someone downloads a graphic from a Web site into his or her hard disk, that person potentially violates copyright law. One of the most misunderstood concepts is that of "fair use." You should spend some time visiting the sites listed below and reading about copyright. For this book, I did two things: I made my own graphics by taking pictures or constructing designs on PhotoShop; or I downloaded graphics from public domain sites such as the first two listed below under "Icons/Graphics" and wrote the Web meisters of these sites a note of inquiry and intention.

World Wide Web Issues (general statement)
`http://www.benedict.com/webiss.htm`

Copyright FAQ (Frequently Asked Questions)
`http://www.cis.ohio-state.edu/hypertext/faq/usenet/Copyright-FAQ/`
`top.html`

10 Big Myths about copyright explained, by Brad Templeton
`http://www.clarinet.com/brad/copymyths.html`

The Copyright Website (This site is especially helpful in terms of graphics and multimedia. Be sure to read the sections on the fair-use doctrine.)
`http://www.benedict.com/`

Copyright, Intellectual Property, and Publishing on the WWW, by Jeff Galin
`http://www.pitt.edu/~hypertch/copyright.html`

Icons and Graphics

(Be sure whether or not the contents of these sites, as well as others like them, are in the public domain.)

The Icon Browser, search engine (Many of the graphics in this book come from this site.)
`http://www.cli.di.unipi.it/iconbrowser/icons.html`

Barry's Clip Art (Many of the graphics in this book come from this site.)
`http://www.barrysclipart.com`

WebSurfshop
`http://www.webmotion.com/Websurfshop/index.html`

Randy's Icon and ImageBazaar
`http://www.infi.net/~rdralph/icons/`

Yahoo, Icons (many links)
`http://www.yahoo.com/Computers/World_Wide_Web/Programming/Icons/`

Ventana's Clip Art Archive (Spend some time here looking around and be sure to visit Ventana's links to other sites, where you will find some animated Gifs in the public domain.)
`http://www.vmedia.com/archives/clipart/index.html`

Desktop Publishing Com: The Ultimate Desktop Publishing (some free material).
`http://www.desktopPublishing.com/open.html`

Clip Art
`http://www.n-vision.com/panda/c/`

Dingbats for your pages
`http://sparc2.lib.cuhk.edu.hk/~ernest/gifs/dingbats.html`

Special Services

(Web-Counters and Bots)

Web-Counter Usage Page
`http://www.digits.com/web_counter/usage.html`

Free Services Page, from E-Mail Robots to Various Kinds of Synthesizers
`http://www.netmind.com/NetMind`

▶ 4

Constructing Web Pages: Personal Home Page

PAGE-TO-PAGE (FILE TO FILE) CONSTRUCTION

In the future, everybody will have a Web page. I mean everybody on Earth.

—DOUGLAS COUPLAND

This section will give you specific examples, along with step-by-step instructions and suggestions, for how to construct various kinds of Web sites. We will be specifically concerned with only the *first page* of the page-to-page (file-to-file) construction of the various kinds of Web pages that you will most likely be asked as a student to construct. What you learn in doing these first pages, however, is what you will be able to use when constructing any kind of Web page that you might have to do later for an employer or for your own professional or personal identity and, let's not forget, your pleasure. As we proceed, I will make suggestions for particular projects that you yourself might do alone and as collaborative projects, that is, those that you can do with classmates and friends. In Chapters 5 and 7, we will look at how to connect additional pages to first pages.

THE PERSONAL HOME PAGE: A BEGINNING

On the Web, the idiom for constructing a "home" identity is to assemble a "home page" of virtual objects that correspond to one's interests. One constructs a home page by composing or "pasting" on it words, images, and sounds, and by making connections between it and other sites on the Internet or the Web. . . . People link their home page to pages about such things as music, paintings, television shows, cities, books, photographs, comic strips, and fashion models.

—SHERRY TURKLE

Deciding on Categories of Content

What would you *expect* to find on a personal home page? When you want to know something about someone or communicate basic facts about your own life, what do you ask for and what do you give? This is a tricky question because there are certain things that should and should not be told, right? What would it be to be conventional, that is, to be in tune with what someone might expect for you to tell them and what they might feel comfortable knowing about you? When you are asked in a regular, conventional writing class to draft an *expressive,* or self-expressive, essay, what do you say about yourself and your relations with others? Certainly, you do not tell everything, I hope. And I am sure your teachers hope as well.

But the question is still more complicated. If the Web space is being provided by your university, let's not forget that your page of expressive discourse and graphics is not something written on several sheets of paper and turned in *only* to your teacher but is at least one electronic file that is theoretically and potentially available to everyone in the world. Consequently, there is a tremendous shift in context. Again, if the Web space is being provided by your university, let's not forget that your page is in the much larger context of the university and most likely in the context of your particular academic department. In other words, there are all those other files in the server and department server that are around yours. This should be taken into consideration. What you say about yourself has an impact on the larger contexts in which others will view your Web site. If, however, you have Web space elsewhere in a commercial server that you are purchasing, then you would not have to be concerned with an institutional context, but with the basic conventions of what would be acceptable to communicate to others. Commercial Web space providers have their rules as well. Another way of saying all this is that *you need to be concerned with your audience.* Though the whole wide world is your potential audience, the context in which you place yourself helps frame you for a more specific audience that has specific expectations. Anyone can tell by simply looking at the URL for your site that your page is in a server at an educational institution (edu) or a commercial one (com).

I am not telling you flat out that you *must* be overly conventional. Far be it from me, given my Web sites, to expect you to be totally conventional. What I am suggesting, however, is that you be sensitive to basic conventions and, when breaking them, know that you are going against the grain. With that said, let's return to the question of *What might you expect on a personal page?*

The best initial suggestion that I can make is for you to surf the Web and look at Web sites that are personal pages. Look at those established at your own university and for your academic department. Look at both faculty members and students, if available. Look at other university sites to get a feel of what is expected of you.

I have spent a lot of time looking at academic and nonacademic personal home pages and they do have a few things in common. Academics tend to give for the most part professional information and a minimum of personal information; they give their degrees (where earned), publications, classes taught, etc., namely, the kind of information you would expect to find on their resumes. And students? If they are graduate students who are teaching for an academic department, they will have a mixture of personal (their hobbies, favorite links) and professional (past and present courses), degrees already earned or working on, etc. Undergraduates will have information of a similar kind, but for the most part tend to stick to personal things such as hobbies, favorite links, photos of themselves with friends, and in some cases collaborative work.

Okay, let's say you are an undergraduate—probably midway through your degree—and that you have the opportunity to develop a personal home page. What should you include? Again, surf the Web. Learn from others. What you will most likely find are some of these elements:

- A Title for your first page
- Some basic information about
  - your life: date of birth, home town, etc. (obviously, you should be careful about the information you give)
  - your family and friends (you might include some pictures)

- your school, perhaps your secondary school and your university
- your aspirations and plans for the future
- your interests and hobbies
- your friends/classmates/favorite courses and links (URLs) to their pages
- your frequently visited Web sites (which would be as much for your own advantage as for providing information to others)
- A Signature (including the date you established the site, the date it was last updated, and a link to your e-mail address so that you can be contacted)

These, then, would be things to begin with. (There's nothing surprising here, is there? There shouldn't be! Remember the importance of convention.) It's important to set up housekeeping, or let's say, home page-keeping, on the Web; once you get your home page established, you can start adding other things that might distinguish your Web site from others. And perhaps, even push against convention. My middle son, David, who completed the requirements of secondary school not too long ago, has put up his own home page and has many of these elements. I will not embarrass him here any further by including his page as an example.

> *The best way to get started when you want to create a home page is to "borrow" other people's code. Find a page you like, and look at how its creator organized cool ideas and nifty links, and provided easy-to-use navigational choices. . . . Feel free to steal what I have done, since it's well known that thievery is the first rule of becoming a Web master.*
>
> —CRYSTAL WATERS

Preparing to Tag a Page

So let's start tagging a page that you might set up for yourself and include a few of the possible categories I mentioned. Essentially, what we are going to do is to establish a *template* that you can use and modify to satisfy your own interests and purposes. Though the categories of autobiographical statement, your interests and hobbies, etc., are conventional, the method of presenting and formatting them do not necessarily have to be. As Crystal Waters and I suggest, surf the Web and find personal Web sites that interest you and download the source codes as Text Only (ascii) files to keep them as templates that you might eventually study carefully and learn from. You might also print out the page from Netscape so that you will have a copy of what it looks like on the Web. (Often, if you return to a Web site, it will have been revised and be totally different, so it is good to print out a copy.)

First, we will do a vanilla page, and then we will take Waters's advice and use the formatting for her own home page to turn vanilla into another flavor. (Please do not misunderstand: vanilla does not mean bad or simple-minded; sometimes vanilla is precisely what is called for.) We will wait to accomplish this shift from one flavor to another after constructing a whole series of different kinds of first pages, personal and otherwise; we will use Waters's page at the beginning of Chapter 5 when we attempt to pull together a number of the examples we develop here. The title of Waters's article from which I quoted is "Steal My Web Page!" We will do just that but *not* for the purpose of copying it precisely *as is* but for getting ideas about formatting.

Caveat

It is not considered plagiarism when you download the source document in Netscape any more than it is considered stealing when you follow conventions or even follow unconventional conventions. But you *definitely do not* want to simply take someone's code from a highly stylized page, strip away the text, and then put in your own. Waters, however, has given us permission in her article to borrow from her page and thereby has placed her page in the *public domain*. Unless given such permission, forget the wholesale use of another's page; otherwise you will be violating copyright laws. And yet, what could Waters mean when she says, "thievery is the first rule of becoming a Web master"? I take it that she is being comically ironic; I can take it, given the law, no other way. See the note at the close of this chapter on copyright law and multimedia.

You need to open a Word or Note Pad document/file (Word or Windows, PC) or a Simple Text document/file (Mac) and start putting in notes such as whatever your categories might be. It is recommended that you work in these mini-word-processing programs instead of an elaborate one, which has features that will slow you down and perhaps only get in your way. You can, of course, use the elaborate program and just save your document as Text or Text Only (ascii), but as I suggested in the previous chapter, you can get in trouble later.

The first thing you will want to do after you have opened your Text only file is to type in the basic HTML page sections. I would suggest that you keep a template of this in a Text only (ascii) file in your hard drive so that you can subsequently just use it when you start a new page/file. As you develop more and more different kinds of pages, you should keep each of them clearly marked as templates and in a folder on your desktop. This is the most basic template:

```
<HTML>
        <HEAD
                <TITLE> </TITLE>
        </HEAD>
        <BODY>
        MOST OF YOUR TEXT WILL GO IN THIS SECTION
        </BODY>
</HTML>
```

Let's assume for the sake of brevity here that after jotting down ideas over a period of time, you decide on what you want to include in the first appearance of your page, which includes a photo, some basic information, and a Signature.

With the HTML template typed on the page, you can type in the Title as it will appear on the heading of the Netscape frame or whatever graphical browser you might be using. Next, you can put in the Heading with your name, using the `<H>Heading</H>` tags; you can perhaps include a photograph of yourself, using the `<IMG SRC=" ">` tags. (See Appendix B for scanning a photo and preparing a JPEG or GIF file of it.) Then, continue tagging the sections as you might want them to appear in the Body of the page. Perhaps you will use a format for a List of some kind: If an Unnumbered List, then you will use the tag `<UL>` and then for the first item `<LI>`, etc. And finally you will type in the Signature section just prior to the end of the Body.

Correcting and Revising as You Build Your Page

While you are tagging this Text Only file, you should begin intermittently looking at it on Netscape. (See the references at the end of this chapter for how to obtain a copy of Netscape.) In Chapter 2, I explained how you could and should use Netscape as a means of checking on your work as you develop it. Let me explain again but in greater detail just how this use of the browser works.

First of all you need to understand that you can use Netscape without an online connection. All that you will need is Netscape, preferably at least version 2+. If you use Netscape without an online connection, you will notice, however, that Netscape, or Mosaic, will look for a connection or a socket. When you get a dialogue box saying that Netscape can't find a connection, just click on *okay* or any comparable word; most likely, you will have to click on a second or at times even a third box.) However, if you are working at home with an online connection or in a computer lab and your computer is directly wired to the mainframe/server, don't worry; for you will have no problems with having to deal with these dialogue box messages.

Once you have launched Netscape and it is stable, go to File (top far left) in the menu and pull it down to Open Files, which will then open a dialogue box showing either your hard disk contents, desktop contents, or the various drives (A, B, C), where you will find the Text Only file you are developing. (If it does not show or is faint and not accessible to a click, then you most likely have not converted your word processing document into a Text Only file. If you have not, then do so.) Just double click on that file in the Open Files dialogue box and Netscape will allow you to view your file as if it were in the mainframe or server. Or—and this is so much easier—if you are using Netscape Navigator or comparable for Mac and if you are using operating system 7.5+, all you have to do to see your coded files is to drag and drop the file onto Netscape, after it's been launched, and you will see the page you are working on. Or if you have a lot of Text Only files in a folder, just drag and drop them onto Netscape and you will get an index file, which allows you to click on the various files and see your work. Obviously this is easier than having to work through the menu commands. (By the time this book appears, Netscape and DOS or Windows will most likely have the drag-and-drop capability.)

What you see on the Netscape browser is what you will see precisely when your document/file is placed from your hard disk into a server and you call it up with a URL. (Later, in Chapter 7, I will explain how to place your files in a server.) Once you have seen the file in Netscape, it will be easy for you to work on the file and then to see again whether you are coding correctly. You will find that this shuttling back and forth from the Text Only file to Netscape is how you write and revise step by step along the way (and correct your errors). It has become much simpler to revise in the past few months as the technology has improved; and by the time this book appears it will be even easier.

Example of a Generic Home Page

More specifically, now, I am going to take you through the process of filling in the HTML template. I will build a generic home page for a student and, as I do so, will comment on each section. Remember that this is to be a generic, or the vanilla-generic, template for a home page. (See Figure 25.)

```
<HTML>
<HEAD>
<TITLE>John or Joan Student HP</TITLE>
</HEAD>


<!--author: John or Joan Student--------------------------->
<!--date created: 9 June 96; last modified: 20 June 96----->
<!--document name: Generic Personal Page------------------->
<!--purpose: To establish a beginning example------------->
```

As previously discussed, you might want to use these invisible format tags and identify the project.

```
<BODY>
<P><P><BR><BR>
<IMG BORDER=1 SRC="picture.jpg" ALIGN=RIGHT WIDTH=150
HEIGHT=150 HSPACE=10 ALT="PHOTO OF MYSELF">
<H1><B>John or Joan Student</B></H1><P>


[<A HREF="http://domain/file.html">UT, My university</A>]


<P><P><BR><BR>
```

Within the Body section (above), a space is immediately created for a photo/JPEG. It is aligned so as to be on the right side and sized in both width and height to be 150 pixels. To create blank space around it, I used the horizontal space command and put in a value of 10 pixels. Also, for people who are not using graphical browsers such as Netscape but something like Lynx, which is a browser that renders text only, I put in the ALT tag, which will tell someone there is a photo. Special software for the sight impaired will also be able to read the statement "photo of myself" along with the rest of the text. Please take the time to insert ALT tags.

I composed the rest of the Body (below) as an Unnumbered list that has a bullet <LI>, "•," in front of each item. The categories are in bold, <B>Personal:</B>. I used a paragraph <P> tag between each category. And I included a few links with the <A HREF> tags. This kind of page/file is all rather simple and will eventually be second nature for you as you do more and more of them.

```
<!-------BEGINNING OF UNNUMBERED LIST---->
<UL>

<LI> <B>Personal:</B> I was born July 14, 1977, in San
Francisco, CA.<P>

<LI> <B>Family:</B> My parents now live in San Diego and I
have a brother and sister in school in California and
Missouri.<P>

<LI> <B>Schooling:</B> I graduated from Smith High School
and am now a student at the University of Texas, where I am
an English Major and Communications Minor. I am presently a
Sophomore, though I am taking advanced classes.<P>
```

```
<LI> <B><Plans for the Future:</B> I intend to pursue a
Masters degree in Graduate School. I am thinking about
becoming a university professor. I would also like to be a
Web Graphics Designer.<P>

<LI> <B><Interests and Hobbies:</B> I am a member of the
Young Democrats, Sigma Tau Delta (English), and Foreign
Films Committee. I play the piano and I enjoy going to
movies and concerts.<P>

<LI> <B><Friends and Classmates:</B><BR>
<A HREF="http://domain name/file.html">Fred Smith</A>
(friend from high school), who has his own home page.<BR>
Janice Jones (classmate), who does not have a HP, but I am
going to help her establish one.<P>

<LI> <B>Favorite Courses I am Taking:</B><BR>
ENG2375: American Literature: Poetry<BR>
HIST3365: Western Civilization<BR>
<A HREF="http://www.uta.edu/english/V/E3371.html">ENG3371:
Writing for the WWW</A> (This is the best! It has every-
thing online such as the syllabus, resources, and student
papers. I learned in this course the basics of how to
construct my HP.)<P>

<LI> <B>My Most Used Links:</B><BR>
Yahoo (Directory)<BR>
AltaVista (Search Engine)<P>
</UL>
<!------END OF LIST------------>
```

Finally, we reach the end of the page with the Signature. Notice the invisible
tags throughout, which are there to distinguish each block of tags and text.
Signatures are usually in smaller fonts. Note the change in size to a -1 and
the use of <CODE> for fixed-width font.

```
<HR>
<!-------SIGNATURE------------>
<P><FONT SIZE=-1>
<CODE>Established: February 23, 1996; Last Updated: February
28, 1996.<BR>
<A HREF="MAILTO:UserID@System">E-Mail me:
JSMITH</A></CODE></FONT>
```

```
<P><BR>
</BODY>
</HTML>
```

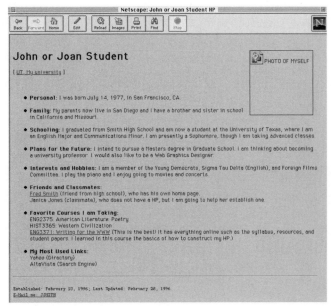

FIGURE 25

As you can see in Figure 25, this is not only fairly easy—which is the way to start—but also a very plain, minimalist home page. Is there a way, however, to spif up this home page? Yes. Let me suggest to you one of the clever, yet still somewhat generic ideas that I got from browsing not the Web, but magazines. (It's interesting to watch how magazines are attempting to simulate Web designs and, of course, vice versa.) The revision that I am going to suggest is only a slight enhancement, for as we progress we will develop more elaborate and innovative Web sites.

An Attempt at Revision

Looking through magazines, I found a question and answer format—the kind you yourself can find—on the last page of the magazine *Vanity Fair*. This format is very common; it is found in other magazines and even in many newspapers. I decided to mimic, more or less, this last page of *Vanity Fair*, which the editor calls the "Proust Questionnaire," as the format for a home page. (If you are a student of literature, there is a good chance that you have heard of the French novelist Marcel Proust.)

I have decided to imitate one of these pages and yet stick with the conventions of a home page, which means that I will end up with a *hybrid*. I will take the principles of print culture and apply them to electronic media and then reverse the approach by sticking to the conventions of a home page. Instead of calling the questionnaire format after Proust, I will call it the "Ada Questionnaire," after Ada Lovelace, the first programmer. (Recall my discussion about mixed media in the Preface.) According to the design conventions of the *Vanity Fair* page, I must include a photo and some brief questions with even briefer answers.

Let's assume that I already know what questions I want to ask and what my answers will be. I said that I was not going to embarrass my middle son, David, but I need a real, not a generic person—and certainly not myself—so David is now the generic student. Let's say that David picks a photograph he thinks appropriate, scans it and turns it into a JPEG. (See Appendix B.) He has a choice of two ways to tag/code the page: one that is very simple; the other is more complicated because it is tagged with tables.

As in the previous example (Fig. 25), I have included here blocks of tags and of text with my comments interspersed, explaining what David is doing when necessary. (See Figure 26, David's Web Study):

```
<HTML>
<HEAD>
<TITLE>DAVID'S WEB STUDY</TITLE>
</HEAD>
<BODY BKGROUND COLOR="#FFFFFF" TEXT="#000000">
<P><P><BR><BR>
<CENTER>
[<A HREF="http://www.texnet.net/">TEXNET, Work</A>]
[<A HREF="http://www.tstc.edu/~1dmv6922/">TSTI, School</A>]
[<A HREF="http://www.texnet.net/david/">HP</A>]
</CENTER>
<P><P><BR><BR>
```

David decides not to use the default colors for background and links, but instead a simple white (FFFFFF) background and black (000000) text. Immediately introducing one of the conventions of a Web page, is the horizontal list of links for work, school, and the home page. (This list functions here as a top Signature; sometimes Web designers will include a Signature at the top and the bottom.) There is a redundancy in the horizontal list (the link to his home page), because we are seeing this link from the home page itself; but David places it there most likely for future purposes, which will become evident as we progress. This page is under construction, but David does not put out an icon announcing this. All pages on the Web are under constant reconstruction; some more than others.

Tips

As mentioned in Chapter 2, it is *not* necessary to use all capital letters in the tagging. Browsers are not sensitive to this aspect of the tags. I, and others, tend to use all caps because it is easier for me to tell the difference at a glance between tags and content. Remember, however, that URLs are case-sensitive.

Let's continue with the layout of this page:

```
<IMG BORDER=2 SRC="dmv.jpg" ALIGN=LEFT HEIGHT=200 WIDTH=200
VSPACE=20
HSPACE=35 ALT="photo of myself"><br>
<H1>"My Web Study"</H1><P><P>
<Font Size=+20>D A V I D<BR> V I T A N Z A</font><P>
<FONT SIZE=+2>This Month ... David publishes his homepage,
proving that even he can construct a clever page, as he
demonstrates in the Web's<BR> <I>Ada Questionnaire</I>
</FONT>
```

In the first line of the tag is a JPEG file <dmv.jpg>, which is a scanned picture of David. Notice the border of 2 pixels around it. Such decisions are a matter of taste and of basic principles of design. David has resized the JPEG with the Height and Width tags and at 200 pixels, and then inserted pixel values also for vertical and horizontal space, which allow him to maneuver the relationship between the picture and the text that is to be aligned to the left.

David puts the title in headers that are size 1 (<H1> </H1>) and two paragraph tags, <P><P>. To simulate the look of the single page in *VF*, he uses the font size tag and places spaces between the letters of his name, D a v i d.

Tips

Common coding mistakes are to leave out the close tag, for example, </FONT> and, consequently, all the rest is +20 or +2 or whatever value that was initially assigned. Therefore, it is good to check, as you would with quotations, the beginning and end of the tag.

```
<P><BR><HR NOSHADE>
```

There is no rule in the *VF* page, but it is included here for design reasons. Remember that another person might not like a horizontal rule used in this way at all. (Many authors of Web design books and articles advise their readers to avoid the horizontal rule.) It really depends on which design principles and special effects builders of home pages want. This page has a rule with no shade `<HR NOSHADE>`.

```
<B>Where were you born?</B>.....Urbana, IL.
<BR><B>Where do you live?</B>.....Texas! and the WWW!
<BR><B>What do you do?</B>.....I'm a student and a systems
administrator.
<BR><B>What do your teachers say about you behind your
back?</B>.....He's the best!
<BR><B>And your boss?</B>.....He's the best!!
<BR><B>Whom would you invite to Your Fantasy
Dinner?</B>.....Ada Lovelace, Phiber Optik, John Perry Bar-
low, Bruce Sterling, and Eric Bloodaxe.
<BR><B>What are you most proud of?</B>.....Being Sicilian!
<BR><B>What is your mode of transportation?</B>.....I surf
the Net!
<BR><B>Your best Asset?</B>.....People skills.
<BR><B>Your favorite movie?</B>.....<I>Hackers</I>.
<BR><B>What languages do you know?</B>.....German, HTML,
CGI, and JAVA among others.
<BR><B>Where do you like to Vacation?</B>.....IRL: Germany.
I go there often.
<BR><B>Best advice you could give a 40 something and
above?</B>.....Start over by surfing and writing code.
<BR><B>What are your favorite links?</B>.....<A
HREF="http://www.texnet.net/david/social_distortion/">Social
Distortion</A>
& <A HREF="http://www.uta.edu/english/V/english/
Victor_.html">Victor Vitanza's---My Dad's---Page</A>
```

Here we have a simple list with boldface tags `<B>` for the question and plain font for the brief answers. Note that some of the categories are drawn from my earlier example and that a theme holds his questions together. This section ends with a couple of links.

Tip

There is a lot of code thrown in here and hence the opportunity to make mistakes. Again, a common mistake is to leave out the tag that closes the *bold* font `</B>` and then to have everything that follows all in bold.

In general, this simple, single-spaced list is difficult to read, especially on the Web. David will remedy this flaw in the design when he revises this page in the next example, using tags for a definition list.

```
<P><P>
<HR NOSHADE>
<P><P>
<code><FONT SIZE=-1>
David M. Vitanza <a
href="mailto:dvitanza@textnet.net">DMV</A><BR>
Established: 10 June 1995; Last Updated: 18 June 1996.<BR>
Copyright &#169; 1995, 1996 David M. Vitanza
</FONT></code>
<P><P><BR><BR>
</BODY>
</HTML>
```

Here we conclude with a Signature, which somewhat repeats the horizontal list at the top and includes a copyright notice, although, given copyright laws, really is not necessary. But, as David would say, it has a certain "special effect."

Much of what you see here is (again) layout for print culture but with touches of electronic discourse included (Fig. 26). This is a transitional piece,

FIGURE 26

with very few links. When this is revised and has more tags and docu-
ments/files to click to, the whole thing will take on a different look.

A Second Attempt at a Revised, More Complicated Revision

When David places the same page content in tags for Tables and uses the tags
for a definition list and double spaces the content, he gains more control over
the pixels on the monitor, this allows him to change the graphic design and
come up with, I think, a more interesting looking design. The completed
tagged page, with invisible comment tags included, can be found at the end
of this chapter on pages 81–84. "Fully Tagged Pages" is the completely coded
page with invisible comment tags included. Study these tags carefully, for
once you get a sense of how they work, you will be able to do a lot with them.
You should find ample explanations of the changes in the invisible tags. (See
Figure 27.)

Okay, now you need to stop for a while, if you have not already, and type
in each of these three versions of home pages into a Text Only file/document
and fill them in with your own content, photo, etc. You will probably make
some typing mistakes and find as you test a file in Netscape that you are not
getting what is represented in Figures 20–22. If this happens, go back over
what you have typed and find the errors. *Making, finding, and correcting such*

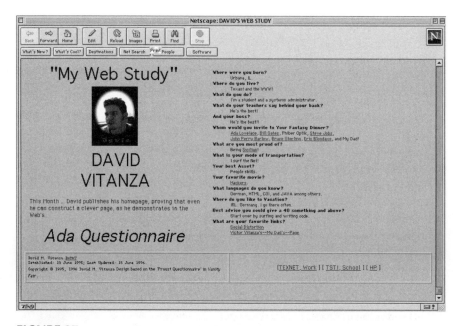

FIGURE 27

errors are how you learn! Making mistakes is part of the process. It may be frustrating, but you will eventually overcome it all.

We will return to the personal home page, but we need to move on to another equally important genre—the essay. In our discussion, we will limit ourselves to several possible first pages and return to the home page in passing. Keep in mind then that we have only begun to work on the home page as a genre and the different ways of revising it; in fact, we will continue to revise David's page up through Chapter 6 as we begin to build files branching out of, linking from, first pages.

SUGGESTIONS

As suggested at the end of Chapter 2 and intermittently throughout this chapter, you might again type much of the code included as examples printed in this book, or visit the Web site for this book and download by way of the menu on Netscape (View/Source) the code for whatever sites might be available from time to time. And again, you will find it valuable to create a folder with templates for each of the genres (personal home page, informational page, collaborative page, etc.). As you surf the WWW, you will find many sites that you will want to download the code for and eventually study and perhaps use, with some modification, as a template.

When you build your own personal home page, you might begin with the various suggested formats here and in the chapters to follow. (Don't forget the fully tagged page below.) Or you might be on the lookout for how other students or professionals have constructed their home pages. Or as you begin to develop confidence in the use of the codes and how to maneuver them, you might try to construct—from your own vision—a home page that is unique yet conventional.

FULLY TAGGED PAGES
(REFERRED TO IN CHAPTER)

HTML tags for Figure 27

```
<HTML>
<HEAD>
<TITLE>DAVID'S WEB STUDY</TITLE>
</HEAD>
<!--author: DAVID VITANZA--------------------->
<!--date created: 9 June 96; last modified: 20 June 96---->
<!--document name: David's Web Study------------->
<!--purpose: to establish Table version----------->
```

```
<BODY BKGROUND COLOR="#FFFFFF" TEXT="000000">
<P><P>
<!----------FIRST CELL----------------------->
<!----the width is set to span the full page----->
<!----cellpadding creates space between cells----->

<TABLE WIDTH=100% CELLPADDING=15>
<TR>
<!---the width of the first cell, lesser percentage of 100-->
<TD ALIGN=CENTER WIDTH=45%>
<Font Size =+8> "My Web Study" </font>
<BR>
<IMG BORDER=2 SRC="dmv.jpg" HEIGHT=125 WIDTH=100 VSPACE=5
HSPACE=5 ALT="photo of myself">
<BR>
<Font Size=+15>DAVID<BR>VITANZA</font>
</CENTER>
<BR>
This Month ... David publishes his home page, proving that
even he can construct a clever page, as he demonstrates in
the Web's<P>
<CENTER><FONT SIZE=+4><I>Ada Questionnaire</I></FONT></CENTER>
</FONT>
</TD>


<!----------SECOND CELL-------->
<TD ALIGN=LEFT WIDTH=55%>
<!-----the width of the second cell, greater percentage--->
<!-----David is learning to add links to his page---------->
<DL>
<DT><B>Where were you born?</B>
<DD>Urbana, IL. <P>
<DT><B>Where do you live?</B>
<DD> Texas! and the WWW! <P>
<DT><B>What do you do?</B>
<DD> I'm a student and a systems administrator. <P>
<DT><B>What do your teachers say behind your back?</B>
<DD> He's the best! <P>
<DT><B>And your boss?</B>
<DD> He's the best!! <P>
<DT><B>Whom would you invite to Your Fantasy Dinner?</B>
<DD> <A HREF="http://www.cs.yale.edu/homes/tap/Files/ada-
bio.html">Ada Lovelace</a>, <A
```

```
HREF="http://www.microsoft.com/corpinfo/bill-g.htm">Bill
Gates</A>, Phiber Optik, <A
HREF="http://www.sun.com/sunergy/Bios/jobs_bio.html">Steve
Jobs</A>, <BR><A
HREF="http://www.eff.org/~barlow/barlow.html">John Perry
Barlow</a>, <A
HREF="http://www.dscga.com/~dragoncon/people/sterlib.html">B
ruce Sterling</A>, <A
HREF="http://freeside.com/phrack.html">Eric Bloodaxe</a>,
and My Dad! <P>
<DT><B>What are you most proud of?</B>
<DD> Being <A
HREF="http://www.sicily.cres.it/">Sicilian</A>! <P>
<DT><B>What is your mode of transportation?</B>
<DD> I surf the Net! <P>
<DT><B>Your best Asset?</B>
<DD> People skills. <P>
<DT><B>Your favorite movie?</B>
<DD> <A HREF="http://www.mgmua.com/hackers/">Hackers</A>.
<P>
<DT><B>What languages do you know?</B>
<DD> German, HTML, CGI, and JAVA among others. <P>
<DT><B>Where do you like to Vacation?</B>
<DD> IRL: Germany. I go there often. <P>
<DT><B>Best advice you could give a 40 something and
above?</B>
<DD> Start over by surfing and writing code. <P>
<DT><B>What are your favorite links?</B>
<DD> <a href="http://www.texnet.net/david/social_distor-
tion/">Social Distortion</a>
<DD> <a
href="http://www.uta.edu/english/V/Victor_.html">Victor Vi-
tanza's My Dad's Page</a>
</DL>
</TD>
</TR>
</TABLE>
<!----------Table is closed------------->
<!---New Table opened for signature and list----->
<!---with 2 cells, border, cell, and alignments-->
<!---different font sizes and acknowledgment given to VF-->
<TABLE BORDER WIDTH=100% CELLPADDING=10>
<TR>
```

```
<TD WIDTH=50% ALIGN=LEFT VALIGN=CENTER>
<code><FONT SIZE=-1>
David M. Vitanza <a
href="mailto:dvitanza@textnet.net">D=M=V</A><BR>
Established: 10 June 1995; Last Updated: 18 June 1996.<BR>
Copyright &#169; 1995, 1996 David M. Vitanza</FONT></code>
<FONT SIZE=-2>Design based on the 'Proust Questionnaire' in
<I>Vanity Fair</I></FONT>.
</TD>
<TD WIDTH=50% ALIGN=CENTER VALIGN=CENTER>
[<a href="http://www.texnet.net/">TEXNET, Work</a>] [<a
href="http://www.tstc.edu/~1dmv6922/">TSTI, School</a>] [<a
href="http://www.texnet.net/david/">HP</a>]
</TR>
</TABLE>
<!--------------New Table closed---------->
<P><BR>
</BODY>
</HTML>
```

REFERENCES (BOOKS AND ARTICLES)

Coupland, Douglas. "An Interview with. . . ." *USA Weekend* June 28–30 (1996): 10–11.
Merholz, Peter. "Approaching the Perfect Interface." *The Net. 2.3 (August 1996):* 42–43.
Turkle, Sherry. *Life on the Screen.* NY: Simon & Schuster, 1995.
Waters, Crystal. "Steal My Web Page!: A Home Page Template for the Web-o-Rama-Challenged." *The Net.* (April 1996): 36–39.

WEB SITE RESOURCES (HOME PAGES)

Home pages often are called "Vanity" pages. Take a look at some of these VPs at the Web Site Reviews OnLine Blue Pages, from the magazine *The Net.* (While at this site, you might also check out other genres of Web pages.)

```
http://www.thenet-usa.com/blue_pages/bluepage.html
```

Home Page Generator v.2.0 (Yes, this page allows you to quickly put up your own page, but in a very limited fashion.)
```
http://www.cs.uoregon.edu/~jolson/generator/
```

And one other thing: Go to various university home pages and then to the English department and check out the graduate student pages.

▶ 5

Constructing Web Pages: The Electronic Essay

PAGE-TO-PAGE (FILE TO FILE) CONSTRUCTION (CONTINUED)

In this chapter, we will continue to work with first pages, but now we are going to turn primarily to the genres of *essays,* both traditional and experimental. About midway, when dealing with the traditional and the experimental essay, we will go beyond single pages/files ("traditional" texts) and begin introducing ways of connecting multiple pages ("hyper"-texts).

This distinction between "traditional" and "hyper"-texts can be confusing, so I want you to begin to get a sense of what the distinction might mean and how it will be used in this chapter. As we proceed into each of the sections in the chapter, we will do the following three things.

First, we will take the "traditional" text (the academic essay) and write it into a single file/document to be placed on the Web. We will examine how a book can be placed in a single file and then on the Web. We will also examine a few other incidental forms of traditional writing as well.

Second, we will take the "traditional" text (again, the academic essay) and, instead of writing it into a single file, we will take the essay in its entirety and partition it into brief sections (two to three pages at the most) and place each of the sections into separate files while maintaining the original sequence of paragraphs. In other words, there will be one "first" page, which we will call the title or beginning page, *and* there will be a series of additional pages. Therefore, with a fifteen-page essay, we might end up with:

- one "first" page, and
- five to six additional pages/files, with each sequentially linked

When we move from placing the complete essay into one file to placing the essay into multiply connected files, we are reconfiguring the essay into the format of a "hyper"-text. These links may be made at the end of a page/file to the beginning of the next sequentially logical file; or these links may be made anywhere on a page/file to another file that is logically connected. For example, if in a paragraph on a single page/file the author uses the word *literacy,* he/she has two choices:

- defining the term in the body of the paragraph on that page/file
- making the word a logical link to another file that has perhaps a set of paragraphs with the full definition

The advantage of the latter choice is that if someone already knows what the word means, he/she may not want to waste time reading through the explanation, but just go on. However, if someone does want the definition and perhaps further explanation, then, it's just a matter of clicking on the word *literacy* and getting the author's definition. Once having read the definition, the reader must have a link back to the previous page/file. Though this link is imperative, it should not preclude the possibility of additional links in the definition page/file to yet another file, say, to one with sources (bibliographical references) for the various definitions.

This is where some of us might get confused, for what is usually referred to as a "hypertext" has another, very different meaning, which we will reserve for the third thing that we will do in this chapter. The prefix "hyper" means *extended* (text). Let me stipulate that when I use the spelling "hyper"-text, I mean a text (essay, book, etc.) that is extended from being placed in one file to being placed in many files. The connections or links, however, are always logical, discursive, linear links. When I use the word "hypertext," I am referring to the third thing that we will be doing.

Third, we will examine *what* "hypertext" can variously be and *how* it differs from multimedia. Put briefly, because we will expound on it later, "hypertext" is basically a nonlogical, nonlinear movement of text (words, discourse) that is structured by way of psycho-logic or associational logic or poetic and dream logic. Whereas "hyper"-text is more expository or argumentative, "hypertext" is more poetic.

One other point: both "hyper"-text and "hypertext" can be in the multimedia format. However, whereas both are limited to words or discourse alone, multimedia includes not only words but also video and audio.

Here are the stipulated terms we will be using in this chapter:

- "traditional"-text
- "hyper"-text
- "hypertext"
- multimedia

Now, what are the differences among them?

THE FIRST PAGE: THE ELECTRONIC ESSAY AND THE PRINT ESSAY

Traditional Disposition of Essay

In this section we will consider and examine how to prepare and place the "essay" in an electronic environment with the purpose of publishing it on the Web. As with the personal home page, we will consider the essay in terms of both print and electronic environments and their various respective standard and evolving conventions. Initially we will look at *discursive writing*, the kind of writing normally expected at the university in English courses and on exams. Discursive writing is linear and propositional; it is also hierarchical, i.e., it is composed of sentences in paragraphs in sections in chapters. The author of discursive writing begins with a promise *to inform* the readers about some particular subject (anything from defining allegory to describing Zen Buddhism) or *to convince* the readers to take some particular action (anything from protecting *a*rable land to sending financial support to Zaire). After making this promise clear, the author continues very systematically by giving explanations (a variety of definitions, a discussion of part/whole or part/part relationships, comparison/contrast, cause/effect, etc.) or reasons (logical arguments in support of a position). When done well and successfully, discursive writing should not veer from its stated purpose to inform or convince; in this sense, it can be seen, in yet another sense, as a "traditional" or "flat"-text. (At least, for some people, there is the illusion that it is unidirectional and flat.) To begin with, we will place discursive ("traditional") writing in single files only, which will contribute to its being contained. When we get to "hyper"-text, we will place a "traditional"-text into multiple files, and when we get to "hypertext," we will take a few initial steps toward understanding *how* an essay can be reconfigured in nonlinear ways.

Essay Arranged Discursively as "Traditional" text

We are going to introduce and examine briefly a variety of *first pages of an electronic essay.* Initially, we will look at a first page that is simply

    a "traditional" essay posted in a server

so that it can be accessed via the Web; then, a first page that is

    a "traditional" table of Contents (TOC) with the contents

as it would appear in print culture; next,

    a page with icons and pictures interspersed to form
    "traditional" exposition

that is often found in print culture as a compromise with earlier forms of writing such as pictograms and also can be found, more so, in electronic discourse. Next, we will take another look at the

    TOC (of this book, W4) formatted in "hyper"-text

to be published on the Web. We will then return briefly to

    David's home page to revise it by adding multimedia
    "hyper"-text links to other sites

and finally I will return to, so as only to suggest, what the

TOC (W4)**,** formatted with **M**ultimedia "hyper"-text links to the same site**,**

might look like. (The first multimedia page—though a "hyper"-text format, as I have defined it—will remain basically a "traditional" page but with links to video and audio sites on the WWW. The second multimedia page will be a "hyper"-text page, with links to pages/files as part of the same project in the same server.) As we progress, therefore, from one kind of page/file to the next, we will be moving from print culture to electronic culture.

I can only simulate these difference in this book, for all these differences could be so much better illustrated on the Web itself, which is precisely what I will do on the Web site for this book. I also promised in the Introduction that I would re-present that print genre of the "Introduction" itself as an electronic essay on the Web site for this book. Yes, you will actually find yourself—if you pursue this book as I suggest—holding the book in one hand while looking at the monitor and holding the mouse and clicking the links in the other.

As you might have noticed, the above paragraph has been formatted in a rather odd way. In other words, I did not list and format—in a conventional way—the kinds of examples that we will be covering:

- an essay for print but on the Web ("traditional")
- a table of contents to a book for print but on the Web (TOC, "traditional")
- a page with icons and pictures interspersed (pictography, "traditional")
- a table of contents to a book for the Web (TOC, "hyper"-text)
- a home page revised with multimedia links to other sites ("hyper"-text)
- a table of contents to a book for the Web with multimedia links to same site ("hyper"-text)

(I've had to change some of the wording when taking the unconventional list out of context.)

In what follows, be aware that I am going to *abbreviate* each of the examples in terms of tags and length to make my various points as quickly as possible. The coding/tagging of these pages is really very simple compared to what we have already done in designing personal home pages, so you will be able to supply the missing sections easily.

Comment

Let's see if the copy editor—who usually must follow the rules of print culture—will let me violate the rules, as I did above, so I might illustrate differences between the two cultures in using print conventions on the Web and electronic conventions on paper. It's this way when **we are learning** to be *amphibians* as I suggested in the Preface and the Introduction. (By now, you should realize that I am not a strict separatist when it comes to the various kinds of discourse. And I hope that you realize that you cannot be if you want to be successful)

An Essay for Print But on the Web ("Traditional"):   Turn to any page in an old magazine or a scholarly journal and what do you find? Words, words, words, and occasionally a picture or a graphic. Turn to any contemporary magazine and what do you find? Words and pictures and graphics and pull-quotes and different fonts, font sizes, and colors. It is remarkable how magazines such as *Time* and *Newsweek*—which were fairly conservative in layout over a decade ago—have been influenced by electronic discourse (and by the programs that allow for special layouts and graphics). And what about the newspaper *USA Today?* My wife and I subscribe to about two dozen magazines, one of which is *Allure.* Though it is my wife's magazine, I grab it first to look at the layout. It is—and there are others like it—a remarkable example of experimentation in layout, graphics, color, etc. And besides, it's a magazine that even spoofs itself. And then there are all kinds of underground magazines and comics that are influencing Web designers.

Earlier we were thinking in terms of a vanilla-generic site. How is such a site tagged? What does it require to be able to be truly vanilla? Well, if you know one code—namely, for paragraphing (<P>)—you will in a sense be a success. And if you know how to tag for bold (<B> </B>), then, you are moving along. As an example of minimalist approach to tagging (see Figure 28),

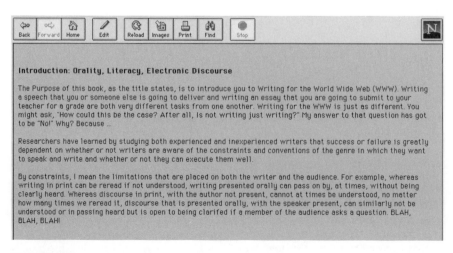

FIGURE 28

let's take the opening pages of my Introduction. Assuming the basic HTML framework, we would tag it thus:

```
<B>Introduction: Orality, Literacy, Electronic Discourse </B>
<P><P>
The Purpose of this book, as the title states, is to intro-
duce you to Writing for the World Wide Web (WWW). Writing a
speech that you or someone else is going to deliver and
writing an essay that you are going to submit to your
teacher for a grade are both very different tasks from one
another. Writing for the WWW is just as different. You
might ask, "How could this be the case? After all, Is not
writing just writing?" My answer to that question has got
to be "No!" Why? Because ...

<P>Researchers have learned by studying both experienced and
inexperienced writers that success or failure is greatly de-
pendent on whether or not writers are aware of the con-
straints and conventions of the genre in which they want to
speak and write and whether or not they can execute them
well.

<P>By constraints, I mean the limitations that are placed
on both the writer and the audience. For example, whereas
writing in print can be reread if not understood, writing
presented orally can pass on by, at times, BLAH, BLAH, and
BLAH! <P><P>
```

Comment

Anyone who is Web-savvy will tell you that this is far too many words for the WWW. Moreover, the sentences are too complex in their structure for readers to read on a monitor. Therefore, remember that what I have tagged here is what I originally wrote for print. This raises the question: How should I rewrite these sentences so that people can easily read them on a monitor? One possible answer is that I or any writer should make the **sentences** (throughout the Introduction) simple sentences with few subordinate clauses and more monosyllabic words; or double space the lines; or put them in a larger font size (`<FONT SIZE=+1>`). Another possible and different answer, which I prefer, is that this many words in this environment simply do not work well if the author actually intends for them to be read on a monitor.

People who grew up with books and are used to reading words in print might try to read all these words on the screen or might print out the full page/file and then read all these words. However, people who have grown up with electronic media (television, music videos, games, etc.) might just click themselves away to another Web site. Therefore, I want you to understand that it is never simply a matter of writing sentences that are easy to process in an electronic environment. It is more so a matter of mixing words with images and of chunking this mixture in ways that are both easy and a pleasure to read. Does the medium of writing for the Web present us all with having to think about new ways of writing? You bet!

As we progress into this chapter, I will have more to say about writing for the WWW, and will attempt to answer these questions:

- Why, then, should someone insist on putting so many words on the Web?
- Is there not a middle ground between placing all these words at once on a page and mixing them with graphics?

A Table of Contents to a Book for Print But on the Web (TOC, "Traditional").   Here is the TOC for *W4*, followed by the entire text (Fig. 29), on the Web:

```
<CENTER><H1>Writing for the World Wide Web (W4)</H1></CENTER>
<P><P><BR>
<CENTER><H3>Table of Contents</H3></CENTER>
<P><P><BR>
Preface to Students (and Facilitators)
<P>Introduction: Orality, Literacy, Electronic Discourse
<P>1. First Questions and Concerns
<P>2. The Elements of HyperStyle: A General Guide to Hypertext
Markup Language (HTML)
<P>3. The Elements of HyperStyle: Page Conventions
<P>4. Constructing Webpages: The Personal Home Page
<P>5. Constructing Webpages: The Electronic Essay
<P>6. Constructing Webpages: Collaborative Genres
<P>7. Beyond the Single Page/File: Disposition of Pages
(Directories/Files)
<P>8. Publishing Your First Webpage (Elementary and Advanced
Considerations of Placing Files in Directories)
<P>9. Tips and Suggestions for Web Writing and for Assessing
and Revising Drafts of Webpages: A Checklist, with some opinions
<P>10. The Future is Now: From HTML (Hypertext) to Multimedia
(Audio and Video)
```

```
<P>Appendices
<P><P>
<HR NOSHADE>
<HR NOSHADE>
<P><P>
<CENTER><H2>Preface to Students (and
Facilitators)</H2></CENTER>
<P><P>
```

The Purpose of this book, as the title states, is to introduce you to Writing for the World Wide Web (WWW). Writing a
speech that you or someone else is going to deliver and
writing an essay that you are going to submit to your
teacher for a grade are both very different tasks from one
another. Writing for the WWW is just as different. You
might ask, "How could this be the case? After all, Is not
writing just writing?" My answer to that question has got
to be "No!" Why? Because ...

```
<P>
```

AND HERE, BELIEVE IT OR NOT CONTINUES THE REST OF THE
BOOK...! section by section, Kbites by Kbites....

```
<P><P>
```

And so it goes!

The previous two examples are all "traditional" (or "flat") texts; that is, they are not "hyper"-texts. Although they are formatted in HTML (hypertext markup language), there are no links from these first-and-only files, each of

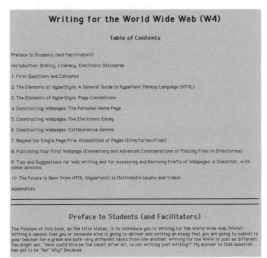

FIGURE 29

which could be broken down into separate sequential files. There are no "extended" (i.e., "hyper-") texts here. We will demonstrate in another example how a large text/file can be "hyper"-texted into several files, yet still be very linear. For now, however, we will look at another treatment of a "traditional" and "flat" text, one without any links, but varied by graphical and iconographic design. In a way, the introduction of icons and pictures does extend a text.

A Page with Icons and Pictures Interspersed (Pictographic, "Traditional"): You have already seen the kind of writing you will see here. It originates as the pictogram. What we have done is to mix pictograms and alphabetic writing.

With this example (Fig. 30), we return to David's work, whose home page we drafted previously in various ways. Earlier today, I spoke with David informing him that he was writing about me on the Web. He wanted to know what he was saying! Let's see:

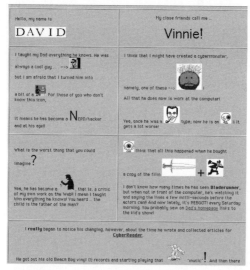

FIGURE 30

(The complete HTML tags are to be found at the end of this chapter.)

Comment

David has retained the Border (as part of the Table) to guide the reader from section to section. There is in our cul-ture the convention of moving from left to right in rows and columns; perhaps readers of this Web site might not, therefore, have problems following the thread if presented without Borders. What do you think? (In Chapter 2, Figure 17, I numbered the blocks of text and icons to assure myself that the readers would read in the direction I wanted them to.) This example could have been written and redesigned without Borders, and yet with the same results, by chunking the information of words and images in a staggered pattern, with that to the left a bit higher than that to the right. There are many other ways that the disposition of the information could be established so as to invite the reader to read it. What might these other ways be?

Caveat

Many Web designers recommend turning off the Borders of Tables, in other words, to use the code `<BORDER=0>`. Therefore, you might think of limiting your use of Borders.

Reminder

Open up your basic HTML template, which is in Simple Text or NotePad, and type in the above tags, or those at the end of this chapter, from beginning to end. Then see what they look like on Netscape. Change the content and add your own graphic files to suit your own purposes. Play around with ways of chunking the words and graphics so as to make them more "reader friendly." Search for methods of disposition on the WWW and in magazines. When done, keep the versions you generate as other templates. Soon you will have a repertoire of templates from which to choose and reuse.

A Table of Contents to a Book for the Web (TOC, "Hyper"-Text):   Now we are going to begin putting in more and more hypertext links, and thereby move from a "traditional" text that is "flat" to one that disperses the information by chunking it into many different, yet logical files (Figure 31). With this new approach, the text will begin to explode, and yet in an orderly manner, with a first-page file and subfiles and sub-subfiles. Later we will discuss just how this is to be done in a flowchart. For now, however, you can see how such a first page might be coded and look on the Web.

Notice right away the difference between this TOC and the previous one (Figure 29). And compare the tagging and the tags for links (`<A HREF=>`). You will see that I have returned to a more complicated coding, using a set of Table tags with no Borders so that I could line up precisely the chapter numbers and the titles. Without a Table tag, there would be no proper alignment. Also, notice that Borders is turned off (`<BORDER=0>`):

```
<CENTER>
<I><FONT SIZE=+20>Writing</FONT><BR>
...   <FONT SIZE=+15>for the World Wide Web</FONT></I><BR>
<FONT SIZE=+2>==W4==</FONT>
```

```
</CENTER>
<P><P><BR><BR>

<CENTER><H3>Table of Contents</H3></CENTER>
<P><P><BR>

<TABLE CELLPADDING=5>
<TR>
<TD></TD>
<TD ALIGN=LEFT>
<A
HREF="http://www.abacon.com/Directory/Filename.html">Preface
to Students (and Facilitators)</A>
</TD></TR>

<TR>
<TD></TD>
<TD ALIGN=LEFT>
<A HREF="http://www.abacon.com/Directory/Filename.html">
Introduction: Orality, Literacy, Electronic Discourse</A>
</TD></TR>
Etc.........
```

(The tags remain very much the same all the way down to the Signature. See the complete HTML tags for this page, Figure 31, at the end of this chapter.)

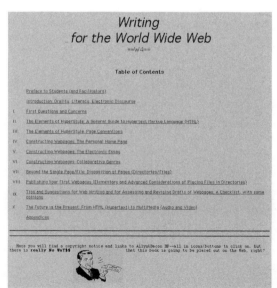

FIGURE 31

The information here is consistently tagged in a recognizable pattern. At this point you might stop reading and look back at Figures 25–31 to refresh your memory of the differences. I have insisted on this progressive sequence of presentation, instead of putting Figures 28 and 30 and Figures 29 and 31 following each other. Again the development is more and more toward a fuller expression of the basic potentials of electronic discourse. We don't get a real taste of this potential until we get to the Web itself and to multimedia presentations.

A Home Page Revised with Multimedia Links to Other Sites ("Hyper"-Text):   All I can do at this point in our discussion is to suggest what multimedia is all about in terms of a *first page*. A fuller explanation will be offered in Chapter 10 after we have discussed the potential capabilities of hypertext, which is strictly limited to text and occasionally supplemented with icons and pictures, whereas multimedia includes not only text but also audio and video. (My distinction is not as fixed in the community of Web designers as I make it sound here, but it allows me to establish some semblance of a difference.)

Though we are exemplifying in this section the electronic essay (and print essay), let's return to one of David's personal home pages (Figure 27, in Tables) and see how we can transform it into a basic beginner's multimedia page. (We will return to the genre of the essay following this example.) We are going to add audio and video to David's home page (see Figure 32). To simplify matters at this point, however, we will make links to Web sites with sound and film files that are not in the same server but elsewhere. Remember that the examples here are primarily of first pages. One thing that happens with personal home pages is that people just keep adding on to them, like adding on to a home, one room at a time, which is what David is doing by adding onto his home page his new interest in RealAudio and QuickTime Movies. Instead of giving the entire page of codes from the top, I include only what is new:

```
<P><HR NOSHADE><P>
<CENTER>
Since I first ventured out onto the Web with my Ada
Questionnaire, I have become interested in RealAudio and
QuickTime movies: Check out these sites:
</CENTER><P>
<!-------ADD ON---NEW TABLE FOR MEDIA------->
<!---------WITH 2-CELLED TABLE-------------->
<TABLE BORDER=1 WIDTH=100% CELLPADDING=20>
<TR>
<TD WIDTH=50% ALIGN=LEFT VALIGN=TOP>
Visit the <a href="http://www.cnet.com/Content/Radio/">C|Net
```

```
Radio</A> Web site, which has a link to the <a href="http://
www.realaudio.com">RealAudio</A> page, where you can down-
load a copy of the RA Player for MAC or Windows. Be sure to
read what the minimum requirements are! After you have your
RA player set up and worked into your copy of Netscape
2.0+, then download some of the C|Net files and listen to
radio. Also, check out the archives! <P>Here are two of my
favorite sites:
<UL>
<LI> <a href="http://www.npr.org/">National Public Radio</A>
<LI> <a href="http://ww2.AudioNet.com/pub/koyn/koyn.htm">KOYN,
Paris, Texas!</A>
</UL><P>
</TD>
```

This first cell gives information about obtaining a RealAudio player and locations for copies of broadcasts, and then gives a couple of radio stations.

```
<TD WIDTH=50% ALIGN=LEFT VALIGN=TOP>
But what's sound without moving pics? Visit <a
href="http://quicktime.apple.com/">QuickTime Home</A>, where
you can download a MAC or Windows copy of the player. You
will find additional plug-ins at the site. <P>Here are a
couple of sites where you can download QT movies:
<!------>UNNUMBERED LIST---------->
<UL>
<LI> <A HREF="http://black.missouri.edu/~c588349/movies.html">
John Lennon</A>, Dad's favorite!
<LI> <A HREF="http://www.inwap.com/reboot/QuickTime.html">
ReBoot</A>.
</UL>
<!--------->LIST CLOSED------------>
You can find a lot more by going to <A HREF="http://www.
yahoo.com/">Yahoo</A> and searching for QuickTime Movies.<P>
</TD>
</TR>
</TABLE>
<P>
<CENTER>More later! I'm about to make some QT Movies of my
own. Bookmark my site and return later for David's Produc-
tions!</CENTER><P><P>
```

And here we have the same kind of introduction but to QuickTime Videos.

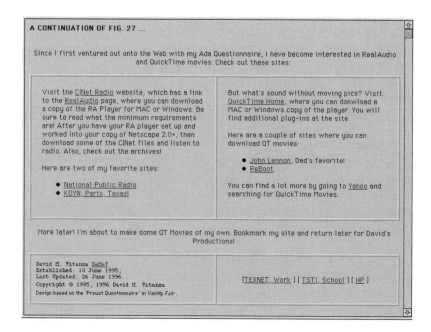

FIGURE 32

The site concludes with the promise of more to come.

A Table of Contents to a Book for the Web with Multimedia Links to Same Site ("Hyper"-Text):   Setting David's page aside, let's return to the TOC example (Figure 31) to develop it into a basic first page with multimedia files (i.e., with links to files with audio and video).

From the initial example of first pages in this chapter, I have limited myself (except for Figure 33) to only one file. It has been my goal to look at a variety of "traditional" first pages. Occasionally, when I have included links from these pages, the links have been to other individual or commercial sites. Now I am going to have to construct internal links/pages/files (not only text links as previously done but also audio and video links)—extending the first page considerably—so as to introduce in passing how such files work and to illustrate again what a basic "hyper"-text first page with multimedia files looks like and specifically how it is tagged. In returning to the TOC page for this very book, I will specifically demonstrate what it *might* look like on a Web site but as a Web book. In other words, I am putting together a *mockup* of how the entire book might be placed on a Web site, with links from each chapter of the TOC going to a separate file. Though this book will not be published on a Web site, there *are* books published by individuals on the Web.

Since I have made some changes in the TOC (Fig. 33), I am going to give the first section of the page, skip the middle, which has no changes, and then include for special discussion the new multimedia material. Here is the new format with tags for the opening of the page:

```
<HEAD>
<TITLE> Chapter 3, Writing for the WWW
</TITLE>
</HEAD>
<BODY BGCOLOR="#FFFFFF" TEXT="#000000">
<P><P><BR><BR>
<!-----OPENING TABLE-------------->
<TABLE WIDTH=100% CELLPADDING=4>
<TR>
<TD ALIGN=MIDDLE VALIGN=MIDDLE>
<I><FONT SIZE=+15>Writing</FONT> ...<BR>
for the <FONT SIZE=+15>World Wide Web</FONT></I><BR>
<FONT SIZE=+1><B>The WebBook</B></FONT>
</TD>
<TD ALIGN=MIDDLE VALIGN=BOTTOM>
<FONT SIZE=+12>==W4==</FONT><BR>
<I>by<I><P><FONT SIZE=+2><B>Victor J. Vitanza</B></FONT>
</TD></TR>
</TABLE>
<!------CLOSE OF TABLE------------------>
<HR NOSHADE><HR NOSHADE>
<P><P><P><P><BR><BR>
<!------OPEN OF TABLE-----TOC------------>
<TABLE CELLPADDING=5>
<TR>
<TD></TD>
<TD ALIGN=LEFT>
<B>T A B L E of C O N T E N T S</B>
</TD></TR>
<TR>
<TD></TD>
<TD ALIGN=LEFT>
<A HREF="http://www.abacon.com/Directory/Filename.html">
Preface to Students (and Facilitators)</A><BR>
</TD></TR>
```

(Hereafter to the closing of the TOC, the tags remain the same as in Figure 31.)

What has been added to the opening section is background and text colors (white and black) and a Table with two cells giving the title of the Web

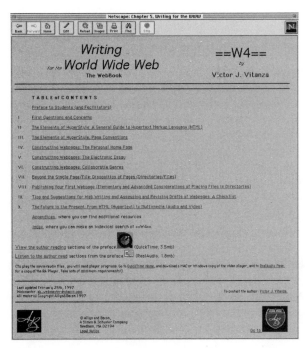

FIGURE 33

book and the author's name. After establishing the Table, I inserted a double unshaded Horizontal Rule (`<HR NOSHADE>`), which is followed by a new Table for the TOC. Notice how spaces are inserted between the spelled out letters of T A B L E of C O N T E N T S. Notice that most of this page is done in Tables with the Borders turned off. Also, notice in particular that two empty cells (`<TR><TD></TD>`) are created for the TOC and the Preface headings since they are not numbered as the chapters are. If I had turned on the border tags, tracing each cell, you would see the two empty cells. (If you need to refresh your memory about Tables, return to Chapter 2.)

Tip

When constructing Tables, especially of the kind in Figures 31 and 33, it might be helpful to turn on the Borders (`<BORDER=1>`) so that you can see precisely where the various chunks of information are. When finished, it's best to turn off the Border (`<BORDER=0>`).

Recall, in this context, that Borders are automatically, by default, turned on. I suggest, however, that you include the full tag so that you can later simply substitute a zero value (=0) for the assigned value (=1).

What follows toward the end of the page is the introduction of multimedia information and files. I am including here a *new* item in the TOC because when a book is published on the Web, a reader should be able to make a database search of its contents:

```
<TR>
<TD ALIGN=LEFT>
<TD ALIGN=LEFT><P><A
HREF="http://www.abacon.com/Directory/Filename.html">Index</A>,
where you can make an indexical search of ==W4==.
</TD></TR></TABLE><P>
```

The next set of tags establishes the multimedia aspect of the first page, with audio and video files of the author reading the Preface. (One has to laugh, but this can be and is done.) Along with the links is given the size of the files so that the person downloading can anticipate the amount of space and time it will take. Also, at this point, it is courteous not only to give this kind of information but also to give links to where a person might find the programs necessary to play these files. Hence, I have provided links to the appropriate sites:

```
<A HREF="www.abacon.com/Directory/File"><FONT SIZE=+1>V
</FONT>iew the author reading</A> sections of the preface.
<IMG SRC="quicktime.gif"> (QuickTime, 3.5mb)<BR>
<A HREF="www.abacon.com/Directory/File"><FONT SIZE=+1>L
</FONT>isten to the author read</A> sections from the preface.
<IMG SRC="iconsound.gif"> (RealAudio, 1.8mb)<P>
<FONT SIZE=-1>(To play the movie/audio files, you will need
player programs. Go to <a href="http://quicktime.apple.com/">
QuickTime Home</A>, and download a MAC or Windows copy of
the video player, and to <a href="http://www.realaudio.com">
RealAudio Page</A>, for a copy of the RA Player. Take note
of minimum requirements!)</FONT>
<P><P>
<HR NOSHADE><HR NOSHADE>
<P><P>
```

From here on to the end of the page, there are Signatures, logos, and <MailTo> links to the Web meister and the author:

```
<!-------NEW TABLE, WITH SIGNATURE AND MailTo TAGS------->
<TABLE WIDTH=100%>
<TR><TD ALIGN=LEFT VALIGN=BOTTOM>
```

```
<FONT SIZE=-1>
Last updated February 25th, 1997
<BR> Webmaster: <!-- MailTo TAG -->
<A HREF="MAILTO:ab_webmaster@abacon.com">
ab_webmaster@abacon.com</A><BR>
All material Copyright Allyn&Bacon 1997
</FONT>
</TD>
<TD ALIGN=RIGHT VALIGN=BOTTOM><FONT SIZE=-1>To contact the
author:
<!-- MailTo TAG -->
<A HREF="MAILTO:vvitanza@AOL.com">Victor J. Vitanza.</A>
</FONT><BR><BR>
</TD></TABLE>
<!-------END OF TABLE------->
<HR NOSHADE>
<!-----NEW TABLE, WITH SIGNATURE AND LOGOS/RETURN LINK----->
<TABLE WIDTH=100%><TR>
<TD VALIGN=BOTTOM>
<IMG SRC="A&BLogo.gif">
</TD>
<TD VALIGN=BOTTOM>
<FONT SIZE=-1>&#169; Allyn and Bacon,<BR>
A Simon & Schuster Company<BR>
Needham, MA 02194<BR>
<A HREF="http://www.abacon.com/cyber/public_html/
ABNotice.html">Legal Notice</A>.</FONT>
</TD>
<TD ALIGN=RIGHT VALIGN=BOTTOM>
<A HREF="http://www.abacon.com/">Go to<IMG SRC="abhome2.gif">
</TD></A>
</TR></TABLE>
<!-----END OF TABLE/PAGE----->
<BR><P><P>
</BODY>
</HTML>
```

It is highly unlikely that you as a student will be publishing a book on the
Web, but one never knows. Many of the first pages, however, that I have
given you examples of so far—the personal home page and essay—you *will*
most likely use. Such genres are for students who would write for and publish on the Web.

Comment

Why publish essays and books (words, words, words) on the Web? I raised this question earlier in the light of the question, How to write for the Web? The answer to Why publish essays? is simple. So as to make them available to anyone who might want the information you have. Just because essays in the form of "traditional"-texts are not in some ways appropriate for the electronic medium does not mean they should not be published in the medium. If you think that you have something of value to other people and you want to publish it and you have the means, then, publish, publish, publish. Anyone who wants your information can download it from the so-to-speak WWW Library and read it. The reason for publishing books is the same for publishing essays.

Besides the genres we have studied in this section, there are others, specifically, Promotional/Information pages and, if not books, other kinds of electronic publications such as Zines and collaborative projects that you can work on with your classmates. These two are taken up in great detail in the next two chapters. For now, however, we will turn to the electronic essay strictly in terms of multiple pages. Whereas up to this point I have only suggested how first pages with links might be coded, I will now concentrate on how you should construct those files according to their varying conventions and how you should tag them.

FROM FIRST PAGE TO MULTIPLE PAGES: THE ELECTRONIC ESSAY AND THE EXPLODING TEXT

What we are going to consider in this section is how to make the text *explode*, that is, how to *divide* it. In other words, instead of having just one page/file, we will now divide and distribute the contents of that page into a first page/file with multiconnected files.

However, when I use the phrase the "exploding text," I am referring to two additional, more general, yet crucial concepts:

- *Experimental texts* (i.e., writing done with the purpose of extending the print genres of the essay and the book and perhaps to discover new genres)
- *Electronic texts* (i.e., writing specifically discovered/invented and developed for electronic environments and more specifically for the Web)

What all three of these notions and concepts have in common is the attempt to discover how to write in an appropriate manner for the Web.

Experimental Disposition of Essay

Writing for print is old. Writing for the Web is new. Some people argue that writing for the Web should not be done—though it can be done and is done—as if for print. Other people argue that it should be done and not as if for print. What this alternative method of writing would be, however, has not yet been satisfactorily determined. Writing for the Web will continue to be experimental in one form or another; since it is new, it has to be invented. (As Steven Brand says, we are "inventing the Future.") In general, however, there is a tendency among experimenters to explode and fragment the text, which is the easiest way of avoiding the conventions or literacy (though not completely), for newspaper and magazine editors use this technique with the help of jump tags. There are other more experimental ways of dealing with the problem, but they are exceptionally difficult.

The easy way: Making the text explode with a measure of success is easier to do if limited to discursive rather than nondiscursive forms. In other words, if a "traditional" text is to become a "hyper"-text and is exploded or fragmented into sections and its linear development is maintained by way of logical, sequential links, then all a writer has to do is follow the basic conventions of linking pages. As suggested in Chapter 3, hardware, along with software, can determine the evolving conventions of writing for the Web. For example, I am thinking of the width of the average monitor measured diagonally, which is 15 inches. There are some writers and designers, therefore, who would have us limit the length of a page/file to what can be seen on this average monitor, that is, without having to scroll. What the writer would do in this case is to measure the length of the essay to determine how many files would have to be created. The rest of the task would be limited to placing the equally and logically exploded text into the files and, as suggested, linking them all. There are a few academic, scholarly journals that have this approach as their format.

The difficult way: If a traditional essay were to be exploded and fragmented into sections and its linear development were not maintained but rearranged in terms of nonlogical, appositional links, then a writer and Web designer would have to discover precisely how those experimental links are to be made. This is important to understand. It is possible to take a "traditional" essay and cut it up randomly and mix the parts randomly and then link them randomly, but the outcome most probably will not be very effective. When changing from "traditional" to "hypertext" writing, it is necessary to rely less on randomness and more on art-fulness. What stands for logical connections is partially replaced, therefore, by aesthetic or metaphorical connections that are art-fully linked together. Having said this, however, I am not ruling out the possibility of art-fully produced random cuts. *They do happen.*

Comment

William S. Burroughs writes about the cut-up method, which he calls the "fold-in method." Burroughs gets his idea of cutting the text from Brion Gysin. (You might be interested in reading Burroughs's novels *Nova Express* and *The Ticket That Exploded*.) Whatever method you yourself might use, you will have to invent it. That is why I refer to the second way that I will discuss here, but only in passing, as *the difficult way.*

We will take a long look at the first, easy way; and a brief look at the second way, reserving a fuller exemplification of the latter at the Web site for this book.

Arranged Discursively as "Hyper"-text

In the previous section I demonstrated how to place the Introduction to this book (W4) into a file and how to tag it. Now we will take that "traditional" mode of writing and place it into the format of "hyper"-text, which means that we will have to create *a first or title page and several accompanying pages/files.* The process is easy, but there are some definite conventions that you should follow. The overall collection of pages should have the following:

- Links from one file/page to the next
- The final page linked back to the title/first page
- The title/first page linked to your home page (if possible)
- A Signature (i.e., your name, linked e-mail address, etc.) on the title/first page.

Along with these basic conventions, you should make sure that the basic layout of the title, your name, and the various paragraphs and endnotes, content notes, and works cited should be easy to read and are cross-linked.

The Introduction to W4 in "Hyper"-text:
I "exploded" the Introduction into eight different files and entitled the files/documents "intro1.html" through "intro8.html." (See Figures 34–41.) The first file is tagged in the following manner:

```
<HTML>
<TITLE>
Introduction, "Orality, Literacy, and Electronic Discourse"
</TITLE>
```

```
<BODY BGCOLOR="#FFFFFF" TEXT="#000000" LINK="#FF0000">
<P><P><BR>
<CENTER><H2>Introduction: Orality, Literacy, and Electronic
Discourse</H2><P>
by Victor J. Vitanza</CENTER>
<P><BR>
```

The headers are in <H2>. I think that <H1> is far too large for use in this case. (It's a matter of taste.) Notice that I centered both the title and my name. Often beginners feel that they have to center and then close the centering (<CENTER></CENTER>) for each line, which is a waste of energy. I have kept my name in the default font size of 10 points.

```
     <B>For the Students:</B> The
Purpose of this book, as the title states, is to introduce
you to Writing for the World Wide Web (WWW). Writing a
speech that you or someone else is going to deliver and
writing an essay that you are going to submit to your
teacher for a grade are both very different tasks from one
another. Writing for the WWW is just as different. You
might ask, "How could this be the case? After all, Is not
writing just writing?" My answer to that question has got
to be "No!" Why? Because . . . <P>
```

This is the first paragraph of the Introduction. I tagged the first sentence five times with the code   so as to create space for a paragraph indention. (Remember: Do not place the code   into right and left angles < >.) I then put the section title in boldface (<B>) and turned off the boldface (</B>). What follows in subsequent paragraphs is routine; each has been shortened for the sake of brevity.

```
     Researchers have learned by
studying both experienced and inexperienced writers that
success or failure is greatly dependent on whether or not
writers are aware of the <I>constraints</I> and <I>conven-
tions<\I> of the genre in which they want to speak and
write and whether or not they can execute them well.<P>
         By constraints, I mean the
limitations that are placed on both the writer and the au-
dience. For example, whereas writing for print can be
reread if not understood, writing presented orally can pass
on by, at times, without being clearly heard. Whereas dis-
course in print, with the author not present, cannot at
```

```
times be understood, no matter how many times we reread it,
discourse that is presented orally, with the speaker pre-
sent, can similarly not be understood or in passing heard
but is open to being clarified if a member of the audience
asks a question. . . . [Note: Shortened for sake of
brevity]<P>
          By conventions, I mean the
commonly accepted genres of communicating (or kinds of dis-
course) for different purposes and media. Listeners and
Readers have certain expectations, given their understanding
of the purpose of the communication, that they desire to be
fulfilled. For example, if you want to appeal a grade you
received in a class, there is a time-honored way of formu-
lating your request to be heard and a way of linking to-
gether good reasons for the request to be granted. . . .
[Note: Shortened for sake of brevity]<P>
```

Once I reached the limit of the screen on the monitor as an area to fill with text, I marked this first page as one of eight, then typed in links back to the home page for the site that this essay is linked from, then I put in a link to page two of eight (2 of 8). Since this is the first page, I included a Signature.

```
     (page 1 of 8) <B><-----<A
HREF="index.html">h o m e</A> || <A
HREF="intro2.html">c o n t i n u e</A>-----> . . . </B>
<P><BR>

<SIGNATURE FONT=-1><A HREF="MAILTO:VVITANZA@AOL.COM">
VVITANZA@AOL.COM</A><BR>
Established 8 Oct. 1996; last modified 9 Oct. 1996<BR>
Introduction to <I>Writing for the World Wide Web</I>.
Allyn&Bacon, 1997.</SIGNATURE><BR>
<P></BODY></HTML>
```

Here is the second page/file:

```
<HTML>
<TITLE>
Vitanza, Introduction, "Orality, Literacy, and Electronic
Discourse"
</TITLE>
<BODY BGCOLOR="#FFFFFF" TEXT="#000000" LINK="#FF0000">
<P><P><BR>
```

This second page/file (2 of 8)—like all subsequent files making up the Introduction, since they are separate files to be placed into the server—must have the complete basic tags repeated at the top, that is, the <HTML>, <TITLE>, <BODY>, etc. And these must be closed at the bottom.

```
     What you will read about in
this book are some of the evolving conventions of writing
for the WWW. Yes, though the WWW is a fairly new medium, it
is possible at this point in time to begin thinking about
conventions. This does not mean, however, that they will be
set and will not change. What the Web is all about <I>is</I>
change. And yet, there are some basic principles of commu-
nication, even in electronic discourse, that are not going
to change that rapidly, if change at all. . . . [Note:
Shortened for sake of brevity]<P>
         Let's recoup and slightly
reformulate and elaborate. What I have suggested thus far
in passing is that there are constraints on and conventions
for<P>
    <UL><LI>speech (oral discourse on sound waves), for
    <LI>writing (printed discourse on paper), and for
    <LI>electronic discourse/WWW (magnetized pixels on black
and white or colored monitors).</UL><P>
```

This second paragraph has a simple tag for a list with bullets, <UL><LI>, etc., </UL>:

```
We know from experience and study that if someone writes a
speech that has very complicated sentences that are not
necessarily broken up into parallel repetitive structures,
but that are labyrinthine in structure, twisting and turning
while exploring different avenues of thought, the audience
will most likely be at a loss to follow what is being
said. . .  . [Note: Shortened for sake of brevity]<P><BR>

(page 2 of 8)
<PRE>
<B><------<A HREF="intro1.html">r e t u r n</A> || <A HREF=
"intro3.html">c o n t i n u e</A> ------>  . . . </B>
</PRE><BR><P><BODY></HTML>
```

This page/file ends like the first, with the page two of eight in parentheses, but this file has both a *return*-to-the-previous file link and a *continue*-to-the-next file link in preformatted tags. Note that I did not include a Signature on this page. All subsequent files, except for the last, should be structured in making links like this second one.

In the sixth page (6 of 8), I made a link to the Works Cited file, which is the eighth file (8 of 8). The sentence, which is in the last of the second paragraph, is:

```
As <A HREF="intro8.html">Michael Joyce</A> says, we must be
"Of Two Minds." I would interpret to mean that we must
firmly place one writing hand on paper and boldly move one
typing hand in(to) the future.
```

Here, as you can see, I linked the author's name, Michael Joyce, to the Works Cited page, which is file eight, and which has the following as its contents:

```
<HTML>
<TITLE>
Vitanza, Introduction, "Orality, Literacy, and Electronic
Discourse"
</TITLE>
<BODY BGCOLOR="#FFFFFF" TEXT="#000000" LINK="#FF0000">
<P><P><BR>
Works Cited:<P><P>
<HR NOSHADE><P>
Joyce, Michael. <I><Of Two Minds</I>. Ann Arbor: University
of Michigan Press, 1995. (return to <A HREF="intro6.html">
page 6</A>)<P>
```

Because I introduced a link on page six to the Works Cited page, I need to establish a link back to that file/page. Hence, I include the return link here.

```
McLuhan, Marshall, and Quentin Fiore. <I>The Medium is the
Massage: An Inventory of Effects</I>. NY: Bantam, 1967.
(return to<A HREF="intro5.html">page 5</A> or <A HREF=
"intro7.html">page 7</A>)<P>
```

Since I had other links to this WC page, I have links back to those respective pages.

```
<HR NOSHADE>
<P>
<B>P.S.:</B> There's something new on the Web that you might
enjoy. It's called "The Main Quad: A Global Community for
College Students." Visit <A HREF="http://www.mainquad.com/
```

```
">http://www.mainquad.com/</A>. You might want to enroll.
<P><BR>
<HR NOSHADE>
<P>
(page 8 of 8)
<PRE>
<B><-----<A HREF="intro1.html">r e t u r n</A></B>
</PRE><P></BODY></HTML>
```

Here is my link back to the first/title page of the essay.

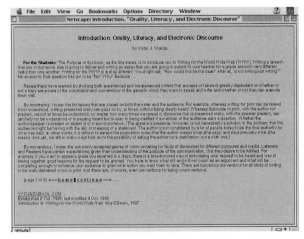

FIGURE 34

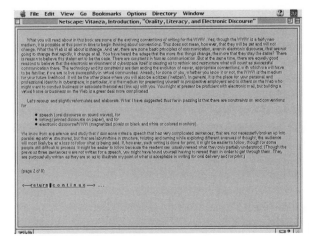

FIGURE 35

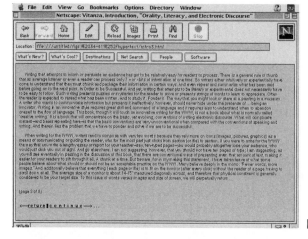

FIGURE 36

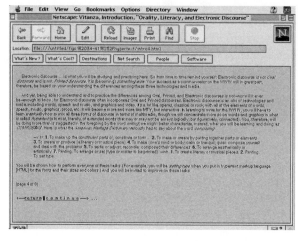

FIGURE 37

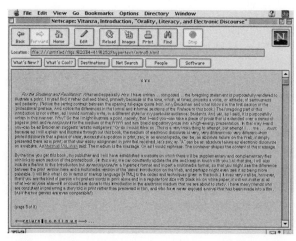

FIGURE 38

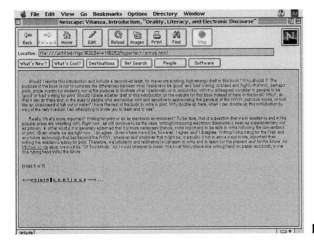

FIGURE 39

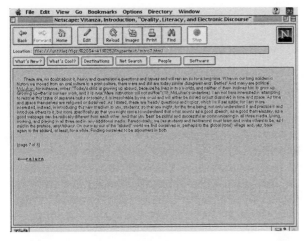

FIGURE 40

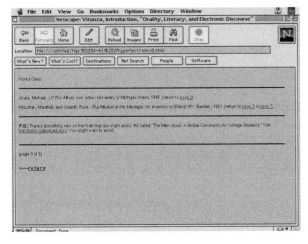

FIGURE 41

Some Options with Destination Markers and Jumps

When I tagged the references in the Introduction to authors and their works (M. Joyce and M. McLuhan), I used simple links to the files. It is possible, however, to use a destination marker and jump links, which will position readers on the precise line I want them to jump to and return them to the precise line originally jumped from. Instead of giving all or most of the contents of each file again, I will abbreviate and give only the necessary changes. On page five (5 of 8), the tag `<A HREF="intro8.html">` should be changed to `<A HREF="intro8.html#mcluhan">`. On page eight (8 of 8), "McLuhan, Marshall," should be changed to `<A NAME="mcluhan">McLuhan, Marshall</A>`. What these two changes accomplish is to give a destination marker `<#mcluhan>` to where I want the readers precisely to jump to, which is the author's tagged name `<mcluhan>`.

But now I will want the readers to return to the precise line or end of sentence from which they departed (5 of 8). To accomplish this return, we need to put in reverse tags. Here is the sentence as I originally wrote it so as to jump to the page 8 of 8:

```
<A HREF="intro8.html">Marshall McLuhan</A> said: The medium
is the massage. Or as I would rephrase: The container
shapes the content of the message.
```

The necessary additional change in this sentence is the inclusion of the `<A Name=>` tag, which I would place in this way:

```
<A Name="medium">The medium is the massage</A>. Or as I would
rephrase: The container shapes the content of the message.
```

Remember that this name "medium" is the round-trip destination. In order to arrive here, I need to return the readers. Therefore, I will need a destination marker on page eight (8 of 8):

```
return to <A HREF="intro5.html#medium">page 5</A>
```

In sum, then, the section on page five (5 of 8) will now be tagged:

```
<A HREF="intro8.html#mcluhan">Marshall McLuhan</A> said: <A
NAME="medium">The medium is the massage</A>. Or as I would
rephrase: The container shapes the content of the message.
```

And the section on page eight (8 of 8) will now be tagged:

```
<A NAME="mcluhan">Marshall McLuhan</A>, and Quentin Fiore. <I>The
Medium is the Massage: An Inventory of Effects</I>. NY: Bantam,
1967. (return to <A HREF="intro5.html#medium">page 5</A>.)
```

The other pages/files (6 of 8, 7 of 8) will need similar destination markers and names. (For a fuller explanation of marker destination and jumps, see Chapter 2.)

Note

Be sure to *read* and *experience* at the Web site for *W4* each way that I have reworked the Introduction. First, as a "traditional" essay (as done in the previous section); then, as a "hyper"-text (as done in this section); and finally, as a "hyper"-text greatly enhanced with layout and graphics. Remember that you have it presented and rendered in this very book. And also remember that you can download the *source documents* for each of the pages/files by going to the menu of Netscape and pulling down *view*.

Pages Arranged Appositionally as "Hypertext" and Multimedia

In what follows I can only suggest how to write "hypertext" pages/files. I can only suggest such writing because it is very much in the realm of what goes for poetry (or so-called "creative writing"), or it is in the realm of being able to see and to construct juxtapositions that make meaning in an analogical or paralogical way, that is, not in strictly logical ways. Such writing is really beyond the purpose of this book, which is geared to more traditional, academic forms of writing for the Web. However, I do not want you to think that HTML, or hypertext in general, is used solely for linear, discursive purposes. And so let's at least take a look at a couple of examples, leaving for a later time and book an advanced exploration.

Signatures

If you recall, intermittently we have examined Signatures and their placement on a Web page. (In general, they go at the bottom of the first page/file.) If you know anything about the art of letter writing, you know that there are the conventions of *salutation* (Dear X) and *complimentary close* (Sincerely, Yours truly, Best wishes). Other somewhat similar forms of electronic communication have conventions for saying hello and naming who you are. It's making simple contact: Hello, welcome to my home page; I am so-and-so, and this is how you can contact me.

What Signatures (and a logo such as "W4") are all about is *identity*, which in many forms of experimental prose is not necessarily presented in a stable manner as in a traditional home page or a letter, but being perpetually discovered, lost, and researched. Invented! Identities change; they, in other words, metamorphosize (or morph) into something else and yet again something else. As you well know this shape-shifting of identity is common in literature, film, and multimedia. It can be active or passive and can be done by a force from within or from without.

Rethinking and Reinventing Signatures

As an example of an appositionally structured Web page with subpages linked off of it (a "hypertext"), we can begin to rethink and reinvent Signatures (the question of identity). Jacques Derrida and Gregory Ulmer have done just this kind of writing and designing: Derrida in writing for print, and Ulmer in writing for electronic discourse. Both writers go by multiple names: Derrida refers to himself, for example, as "Reb Derrisa"; Ulmer often refers to himself as "glue." In a textbook entitled *Text Book,* Ulmer writes:

> According to the French philosopher, Jacques Derrida, there are at least three ways in which an author signs a work. The first dimension or register of signing is the signature "proper"—the proper name placed on the title page identifying the source of the writing. The second register refers to what is commonly called "style"—"the inimitable idiom of an artist's work"—such that even without the availability of the proper name an experienced reader might recognize the author of a work. . . . [The] third register of the signature is the most complex, involving *the heraldic placement of the name in the depths of the text.* At this level the writer's name is seen as the seed out of which the text has grown, by a process of metaphorical and intertextual development. Retracing this process, an interpreter can find the author's name, hidden in the depths—or, to use Derrida's word, the 'abyss'—of the text. (256; emphasis added)

In an attempt to illustrate how this *third signature* works (plays), I am presently building a Web site based on my name (Victor Vitanza) and developed "by a process of metaphorical and intertextual development." It is surprising what I have been able to discover in many mixed terms of my name. For example, I can tell you now that my last name is composed of two separate Italian words (Vita anzi[a]). Turning to an Italian dictionary, I discover the following lexigraphical meanings:

vita signifies *Life*

anzi signifies *contrary to, against,* etc.

Therefore,

Life + against = (or signifies) Death?!

This is a rather disconcerting discovery, no? However, my first name,

Victor, signifies *Conqueror*

So when put all together, my full name can signify:

Conqueror of Death

Not bad, huh? This is only a beginning step in reinventing other connections between my name and other words and other texts, which I promise to illustrate on the Web page for this book. It must be done in an electronic medium, for any number of reasons, which I am sure you can figure out by now.

Rethinking and Reinventing Signatures into a Fetish Page

The Web site will not be an attempt at what we have been calling a home page; it, instead, will be a *fetish page,* again, developed by Ulmer. (A fetish is generally understood as a substitute item for some other object that we want.) If we question identity, we question our sense of place and home, which we can begin to see as "unhomely" (strange) or as a substitute item for what we really don't have in the first place. And what that might be becomes the driving question. We are not at home, because there is something we don't have. Hence, the building of not-at-home pages, or fetish pages, so as to continue to invent who we are and to record our findings, ever so provisionally in virtual space on the Web. (I will not only attempt to illustrate such a page but will give you from the Web site numerous links to fetish pages so that you can learn from them.)

I hope that this is enough to whet your appetites, create suspense, and get you ready to build your own fetish pages. So light out for the virtual territory ahead and check out those pages, whence I continue this sentence and discussion. . . .

SUGGESTIONS

As suggested in this chapter and at the end of Chapter 4, you might again type much of the code included as examples printed in this book, or visit the book's Web site and download by way of the Menu on Netscape (View/Source) the code for whatever example sites might be available from time to time. And again, you will find it valuable to create a folder with templates for each of the genres ("traditional" text, "hyper"-text, "hypertext"). As you surf the WWW, you will find many sites whose codes you will want to download and eventually study and perhaps use, with some modification, as a template.

FULLY TAGGED PAGES
(REFERRED TO IN CHAPTER)

HTML tags for Figure 30

```
<HEAD>
<TITLE>
Chapter 3, Writing for the WWW
</TITLE>
</HEAD>
<BODY>
<P><P><BR><BR>
<!----------TABLE WITH THREE ROWS AND TWO COLUMNS---->
<TABLE BORDER WIDTH=100% CELLPADDING=15>
<TR><TD ALIGN=LEFT VALIGN=MIDDLE>
Hello, my name is<P><IMG SRC="AlphD.jpg" WIDTH=30
HEIGHT=30><IMG SRC="AlphA.jpg" WIDTH=30 HEIGHT=30><IMG
SRC="AlphV.jpg" WIDTH=30 HEIGHT=30><IMG SRC="AlphI.jpg"
WIDTH=30 HEIGHT=30><IMG SRC="AlphD.jpg" WIDTH=30 HEIGHT=30>.
</TD>
<TD ALIGN=MIDDLE VALIGN=MIDDLE>
My close friends call me ... <P><FONT SIZE=+8>Vinnie!</FONT>
</TD>
</TR>
<!-------END OF FIRST ROW----->
<TR>
<TD ALIGN=LEFT VALIGN=MIDDLE>
I taught my Dad everything he knows. He was always a cool
guy . . . <B>--</B> <IMG SRC="italmanshades.gif">,
<P>but I am afraid that I turned him into
<P>a bit of a <IMG SRC="whacker.gif">. For those of you who
don't know this icon,
<P>it means he has become a <FONT
SIZE=+4>N</FONT>ERD/hacker . . . and at his age!!
</TD>
<TD ALIGN=LEFT VALIGN=MIDDLE>
I think that I might have created a cybermonster,<P>namely,
one of these --> <IMG SRC="crazy.gif"> ! <P>All that he
does now is work at the computer!<P>Yea, once he was a <IMG
SRC="bob.gif"> type; now he is an <IMG SRC="eyeguy2.gif"> !!
It gets a lot worse!
</TD>
</TR>
<!-------END OF SECOND ROW----->
<TD ALIGN=LEFT VALIGN=MIDDLE>
```

```
What is the worst thing that you could imagine<FONT
SIZE=+5>?</FONT> <P>Yea, he has become a <IMG
SRC="critic.good.gif">, that is, a critic of my own work on
the Web!! I mean I taught him everything he knows! You
heard . . . the child is the father of the man?
</TD>
<TD ALIGN=LEFT VALIGN=MIDDLE>
<IMG SRC="eyeguy_front2.gif"> think that all this happened
when he bought
<P>a copy of the film <IMG SRC="sword.gif" HEIGHT=50
WIDTH=100>
<font size=+8>+</font>
<IMG SRC="runman.gif" HEIGHT=50 WIDTH=50>.
<P>I don't know how many times he has seen <B>Bladerun-
ner</B>, but when not in front of the computer, he's watch-
ing it and saying the lines a few milli-seconds before the
actors can!! And now lately, it's REBOOT! every Saturday
morning. You probably saw on <A HREF="http://www.uta.edu/
english/V/Victor_.html">Dad's homepage</A> links to the
kid's show!</TD>
</TR>
<!----------END OF THIRD ROW----->
<TR>
<TD ROWSPAN=2 COLSPAN=2 ALIGN=MIDDLE VALIGN=MIDDLE>
I <B>really</B> began to notice his changing, however,
about the time he wrote and collected articles for <B><A
HREF="http://www.abacon.com/">CyberReader</A></B>.<P>He
got out his old Beach Boy vinyl (!) records and starting
playing that <IMG SRC="surfer.gif"> "music"<FONT
SIZE=+18>!</FONT>. And then there was the first . . . or as
he would spell it . . . the phirst (!) . . . Book.
</TD>
</TR>
</TABLE>
<P><P><BR> <CENTER>
<FONT SIZE=+3>And now it's <B>W4</B>, as he calls
it!</FONT></CENTER>
<P><P><BR><BR>
</BODY></HTML>
```

HTML tags for Figure 31

```
<HEAD>
<TITLE>
Chapter 3, Writing for the WWW
```

```
</TITLE>
</HEAD>
<BODY>
<P><P><BR><BR>
<CENTER>
<I><FONT SIZE=+20>Writing</FONT><BR>
...   <FONT SIZE=+15>for the World Wide Web</FONT></I><BR>
<FONT SIZE=+2>==W4==</FONT>
</CENTER>
<P><P><BR><BR>
<CENTER><H3>Table of Contents</H3></CENTER>
<P><P><BR>
<TABLE CELLPADDING=5>
<TR>
<TD></TD>
<TD ALIGN=LEFT>
<A HREF="http://www.abacon.com/Directory/Filename.html">
Preface to Students (and Facilitators)</A>
</TD></TR>
<TR>
<TD></TD>
<TD ALIGN=LEFT>
<A HREF="http://www.abacon.com/Directory/Filename.html">
Introduction: Orality, Literacy, Electronic Discourse</A>
</TD></TR>
<TR>
<TD ALIGN=LEFT>
<P>I.</TD>
<TD ALIGN=LEFT><A HREF="http://www.abacon.com/Directory/
Filename.html">First Questions and Concerns</A>
</TD></TR>
<TR>
<TD ALIGN=LEFT>
<P>II.</TD>
<TD ALIGN=LEFT><A
HREF="http://www.abacon.com/Directory/Filename.html">The
Elements of HyperStyle: A General Guide to Hypertext Markup
Language (HTML)</A></TD></TR>
<TR>
<TD ALIGN=LEFT>
<P>III.</TD>
<TD ALIGN=LEFT><A HREF="http://www.abacon.com/Directory/
Filename.html">The Elements of HyperStyle: Page Conventions</A>
</TD></TR>
<TR>
```

```
<TD ALIGN=LEFT>
<P>IV.</TD>
<TD ALIGN=LEFT><A HREF="http://www.abacon.com/Directory/
Filename.html">Constructing Webpages: The Personal Home
Page</A>
</TD></TR>
<TR>
<TD ALIGN=LEFT>
<P>V.</TD>
<TD ALIGN=LEFT><A HREF="http://www.abacon.com/Directory/
Filename.html">Constructing Webpages: The Electronic Essay</A>
</TD></TR>
<TR>
<TD ALIGN=LEFT>
<P>VI.</TD>
<TD ALIGN=LEFT><A HREF="http://www.abacon.com/Directory/
Filename.html">Constructing Webpages: Collaborative Genres</A>
</TD></TR>
<TR>
<TD ALIGN=LEFT>
<P>VII.</TD>
<TD ALIGN=LEFT><A HREF="http://www.abacon.com/Directory/
Filename.html">Beyond the Single Page/File: Disposition of
Pages (Directories/Files).</A>
</TD></TR>
<TR>
<TD ALIGN=LEFT>
<P>VIII.</TD>
<TD ALIGN=LEFT><A HREF="http://www.abacon.com/Directory/
Filename.html">Publishing Your First Webpages (Elementary and
Advanced Considerations of Placing Files in Directories)</A>
</TD></TR>
<TR>
<TD ALIGN=LEFT>
<P>IX.</TD>
<TD ALIGN=LEFT><A HREF="http://www.abacon.com/Directory/
Filename.html">Tips and Suggestions for Web Writing and for
Assessing and Revising Drafts of Webpages: A Checklist, with
some opinions</A>
</TD></TR>
<TR>
<TD ALIGN=LEFT>
<P>X.</TD>
<TD ALIGN=LEFT><A
HREF="http://www.abacon.com/Directory/Filename.html">The
```

```
Future is the Present: From HTML (Hypertext) to MultiMedia
(Audio and Video).</A>
</TD></TR>
<TR>
<TD ALIGN=LEFT>
<TD ALIGN=LEFT><P> <A HREF="http://www.abacon.com/Directory/
Filename.html">Appendices</A>
</TD></TR>
</TABLE>
<P><P>
<HR NOSHADE><HR NOSHADE>
<P><P>
<CODE> . . . Here you will find a copyright notice and links
to Allyn&Bacon HP--all in icons/buttons to click on. But
there is <B>no way$$</B> <IMG SRC="bob.gif" ALIGN=TOP
ALT="Bob"> that this book is going to be placed out on the
Web, right?</CODE><BR><P><P>
</BODY></HTML>
```

REFERENCES (BOOKS AND ARTICLES)

Brand, Steven. *The Media Lab: Inventing the Future at MIT.* New York: Viking, 1987.

Burroughs, William S. *Nova Express.* New York: Grove, 1965.

Burroughs, William S. *The Ticket That Exploded.* New York: Grove, 1965.

Joyce, Michael. *Of Two Minds: Hypertext, Pedagogy, and Poetics.* Ann Arbor: University of Michigan Press, 1995.

Scholes, Robert, Nancy R. Comley, and Gregory L. Ulmer. *Text Book: An Introduction to Literary Language.* 2nd Edition. New York: St. Martin's Press, 1995.

WEB SITE RESOURCES

Writing "Hyper"-text and "Hypertext" Books

GNA: The Text Project Writing Hypertext Books, a Guide by Peter Muller
```
http://uu-gna.mit.edu:8001/uu-gna/text/
```

"Hyper"-text

Here you will find examples of "hyper"-texts, both articles and books.

Alt-X
```
http://www.altx.com
```

Electronic Book Review
```
http://www.alt.com/ebr
```

Gregory Ulmer, "A Project for a New Consultancy"
http://www.altx.com/ebr/ebr2.ulmer.html

Victor J. Vitanza, "Writing the Paradigm"
http://www.altx.com/ebr/ebr2.vitanza.html

Nancy Kaplin, "E-Literacies: Politexts, Hypertexts, and Other Cultural Formations in the Late Age of Print"
http://raven.ubalt.edu/Kaplan/lit/One_Beginning_417.html

"Hypertext"

Here are some sites where you will find excellent examples of "hypertext" files developed by noted authors of "hypertext."

Eastgate Systems (Home of 'StorySpace'/hypertext)
http://www.eastgate.com/

Hypertext
http://www.cudenver.edu/~mryder/itc_data/hypertext.html

Hypertext and Literary Things
http://www.aaln.org/~kmm/

The Search for Some Hypertext Fiction
http://is.rice.edu/~riddle/hyperfiction.html

George Landow's HP (Click on "World Wide Web Materials")
http://www.stg.brown.edu/projects/hypertext/landow/cv/landow_ov.html

Michael Joyce's HP
http://iberia.vassar.edu/~mijoyce/

Stuart Moulthrop's HP
http://raven.ubalt.edu/Moulthrop/sam_home.html

▶ 6

Constructing Web Pages: Additional, Collaborative Genres

THE FIRST PAGE

The Promotional/Informational Page

Since we have looked at more than an adequate number of examples—from discourse on the Web that mimics the conventions of print discourse, to the beginnings of a discourse, that looks for what the conventions of electronic discourse might eventually be—let's take a look now at two different types of Promotional/Informational pages that you will most likely find yourself having the opportunity to construct. Both are in the genre of exposition.

As a student, you most likely belong to some kind of club or organization, that will want to have a Web page. If it is a social fraternity/sorority, a service or honorary organization, or a committee responsible for a film series on campus or an organization for minorities or diverse students, etc., you will want your classmates to get necessary information about your group. Let's say that you don't have an office or a telephone or money to print announcements, etc., about your activities, but you do have access to Web space, which is a perfect place to put such information. But even if you do have an office, a phone, etc., you will still need a Web site so as to make your information available twenty-four hours a day. Correcting and revising information is easy and in general, hassle-free. Moreover a Web site is better than a telephone recording with information because all the information is present and consequently does not require the caller to recall your number so as to replay the tape.

If I go to my own university's home page (http://www.uta.edu), I find the following *Student Organizations with Web Sites* listed as having pages:

IEEE (Institute of Electrical and Electronics Engineers)
APICS (American Production and Inventory Control Society, Inc.)
Asian Christian Fellowship
Business Constituency Council
Conservative Students Association
Data Processing Management Association
Gorgias Society
Graduate Humanities Student Organization
International Student Organization
National Association of Business Economists
Olympus Mons, the Astronomy Society of UTA
Omicron Delta Epsilon, International Honor Society in Economics
Sigma Phi Epsilon
Society of Graduate Business Students
Society for Creative Anachronism—UTA, medieval re-creation
Student Congress
Tau Beta Pi
University Bands

(This list has grown rapidly and by the time this book appears will be somewhere between double and triple its size.)

In many ways, the promotional/informational page is like the personal home page, with the major exception that the focus shifts from expressive writing and designing (an individual's identity or interests) to exposition (a group's interests). (To be sure, this is not always the case. There can be a blurring of the different kinds, as you will note in the examples in Figures 42 and 43.) What is conventionally found on such a page? As you might expect, you may find:

- A list of the members of an organization (and hierarchically arranged by title or position and with links to files with specific information on each person)

- A list of scheduled events (with links)
- A list of associated organizations (with links to them), and so on

If it is not an organization but a special-interest page, then you might find links from that page to both files created by the owner of the list and links to other sites.

Let's first take a look at an organization's page, one linked off of a university's Web site, and then a special-interest, informational page, for example, one that might be linked off of a Music Department's page.

A Film Club Page

Often on campus there is a film club. Therefore, let's construct a Web site for such an organization. The site, according to the calendar of the academic year, can be established for a quarter or semester or for the entire year. We will construct one that is for a spring semester and that is devoted to "creature features." (This is not a serious film buff club, but a social club.) Here's what such a site (see Figure 42) might look like when tagged and with my interpolations:

```
<HTML><HEAD>
<TITLE> University of X: Film Club Page, "A Tacky Tomato!"
</TITLE></HEAD>
<BODY BGCOLOR="#000000" TEXT="#FFFFFF" VLINK="#FF0000"><P>
<CENTER>
```

Notice that I have used black for the background, red (blood) for visited links to match the theme of "horror" movies, and white for text.

```
<TABLE CELLPADDING=10 WIDTH=85%><TD ALIGN=MIDDLE VALIGN=MIDDLE>
<FONT SIZE=+3>Welcome to the U of X: <BR>A Tacky Tomato
Film Series!</FONT></TD>
<TD><IMG SRC="tomatoes.gif" WIDTH=125 HEIGHT=75><br>Innocent
Looking, right?</TD></TABLE>
<B><PRE>The S E R I E S</PRE></B>
<Font size=+1>W</FONT>e are pleased to announce the Spring
Semester's Film Series selection of ... <P>a John De Bello
<FONT SIZE=+2>Killer Tomato Retrospective</FONT>.
```

I opened with a two-celled Table (above) so as to have text to the left (with the title) and an image to the right (of tomatoes). The cellpadding is set at 10, and the width at 85 percent throughout. After closing the Table, I established the statement of purpose. Preformatting is used to set of the subheading "The Series." A couple of different font sizes are used.

```
<!----------TABLE ONE---------->
<TABLE WIDTH=85% CELLPADDING=5>
<TD ALIGN=LEFT VALIGN=TOP><A
HREF="www/directory/file.html">S c h e d u l e</PRE></A>
<LI> Attack of the Killer Tomatoes (1977, 1980)<BR>
<LI> Return of the Killer Tomatoes (1988)
<LI> Killer Tomatoes Strike Back (1990)
<LI> Killer Tomatoes Eat France! (1991)
<LI> Elvira Mistress of the Night ("Attack ... Tomatoes"
featured in, 1988: Director, James Signorelli)
</TD></TR></TABLE>
<!----------TABLE TWO---------->
<TABLE WIDTH=85% CELLPADDING=5>
<TD ALIGN=RIGHT VALIGN=TOP><PRE>T o m a t o   L i n k s:</PRE>
<A HREF="http://marconi.me.utexas.edu/~pholstie/rotel-3.
html">Rotel & the Hot Tomatoes</A> (Austin, TX, musical
group)<BR>
<A HREF="http://www.tomato.org/mart-pgs/factsm.htm">Facts
About Fresh California Tomatoes</a></FONT><BR>
<A HREF="http://www.cbs.com/lateshow/lists/940523.html">Good
Things About the Biologically Engineered Tomato: David Let-
terman, Top Ten</a><br>
<A HREF="http://probe.nalusda.gov:8000/otherdocs/tgc/vol8/
v8p4.html">The Tomato Breeders Group</a><br>
<A HREF="http://www.doubleclickd.com/iit.tomato.html">Insti-
tute for Integrated Therapies: Tomato Warning</a><p>
</TD></TR></TABLE>
```

There are two additional tables: the first lists the films, the *Attack of the Killer Tomatoes*, the original, and then the sequels. It also has a link that goes to a Web site that lists a great deal of information about the films. The second, playing on the comic theme, lists sites that play on the theme of tomatoes. The width stays the same, but the cellpadding changes from 10 to 5. Note that when I made the first list, I did not use the tag <UL>, but the <LI> for bullets. When I made the second list, I did not even use the bullets, since that cell is aligned to the right.

```
<!----SIGNATURE-------->
<TABLE BORDER=0 WIDTH=85%>
<TD ALIGN=LEFT VALIGN=MIDDLE><A HREF="http://www/directory/
file"><IMG SRC="tomat2.gif" WIDTH=40 HEIGHT=40>...return to
College of Fine Arts</A></TD><TD ALIGN=RIGHT VALIGN=BOTTOM>
<FONT SIZE=-1>WEBMEISTER: <A HREF="mailto:userid@film.edu">
```

```
AmericanBeauty</A><BR>
Established: 18 June 1995; last modified: 17 July
1996.</FONT></TD></TABLE>
<P><P><BR><BR>
</UL></BODY></HTML>
```

As might by now be expected, I ended the page with a Signature, again in a Table. I constructed a return button, aligned to the left, with the crossed-out image of a tomato as a link, and a Web meister e-mail address.

Comment

I use Tables throughout this site, as on many others, because they allow me to chunk information and place the chunks of words and images precisely where I want them. Tables are well worth learning how to use. They are still the best tags for thinking and placing information both vertically and horizontally on the page.

A Music (Jazz) Page

Now let's develop a site that would be linked off of a Music Department's home page and specifically concerned with jazz.

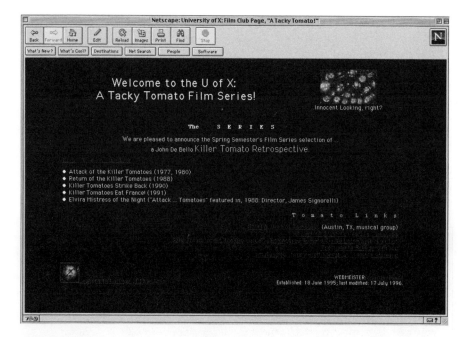

FIGURE 42

What I've done in establishing this page (see Figure 43) is generally to follow the basic schemes used before, with a couple of exceptions—using a Background Tile <BODY BACKGROUND="mus_not.gif"> and multiple Tables. I tend to avoid such Tiles because they make it difficult to read the page. The Tile that I have used is not intrusive in comparison to what you often see. You can find ready-made Background Tiles in the public domain or make your own. The one here is ready-made and is shareware (see notes at the end of this chapter). It is an empty musical staff repeated down the page.

Here's the tagged page in its entirety, with my interpolations:

```
<HTML>
<HEAD>
<TITLE>University of X: The Jazz Page<TITLE>
</HEAD>
<BODY BACKGROUND="mus_not.gif">
<P><P><BR><BR><P><P>
```

Because some Background Tiles are edged with a design on the left margin of the page, it is sometimes necessary to use a code that will move the text and images on the page about an inch to the right. I simply used the tag for Centering instead; but I could have used the Unnumbered List function for a similar purpose (<UL>). When we use a more pronounced left margin another time, I will demonstrate how the tag for lists can be used.

```
<CENTER>
<TABLE BORDER=1 CELLPADDING=15 WIDTH=80%><TD ALIGN=MIDDLE
VALIGN=MIDDLE>
<FONT SIZE=+8>Welcome to the University of X: <BR>The Jazz
Page</FONT></TD>
<TD><IMG SRC="musicstaff.gif"></TD></TABLE>
<P><P><BR><BR>
```

This page opens in the same way as the film page.

Comment

I found the <musicstaff.gif>, which is an AnimatedGif, on the Web by searching on AltaVista for animated GIFs. You must be careful that what you find is not copyrighted and be aware of the terms for your using a particular icon. In this case, the company placed this and other animated GIFs in the public domain. I discuss at length AnimatedGifs in Chapter 10.

```
<B>The  S  C  O  R  E</B>
<P>
<!---------TABLE ONE--------->
<TABLE WIDTH=80% CELLPADDING=5>
<TD ALIGN=LEFT VALIGN=TOP><FONT SIZE=+1>
<A HREF="http://web/directory/file/">Big Bands</A><BR>
<A HREF="http://web/directory/file/">Small Groups</A><BR>
<A HREF="http://web/directory/file/">Concert Schedules</A><BR>
<A HREF="http://web/directory/file/">Clinics</A></FONT><BR>
</TD>
</TR>
</TABLE>
```

As we get to the groupings of links, I've tried to illustrate what the author of such a special-interest page might want to represent. Here, the author is touting the local jazz bands, concerts and clinics to be held, and then moves on to the virtual publishing of a newsletter of additional information and a photo gallery, etc. It's possible to see a site like this as a hobby, and certainly as a form of publishing. (Whatever is put at this fictional site is underwritten, of course, by the music department at a particular university since space is being provided by the university.)

```
<!---------TABLE TWO--------->
<TABLE WIDTH=80% CELLPADDING=5>
<TD ALIGN=MIDDLE VALIGN=TOP><FONT SIZE=+1>
<A HREF="http://web/directory/file/">The NewsLetter</A><BR>
<A HREF="http://web/directory/file/">PhotoGallery</A>
(JPEG/Thumbnails)<BR>
<A HREF="http://web/directory/file/">Discographies</A><BR>
<A HREF="http://web/directory/file/">Manuscript
Archives</A></FONT><BR>
</TD>
</TR>
</TABLE>
<!---------TABLE THREE--------->
<TABLE WIDTH=80% CELLPADDING=5>
<TD ALIGN=RIGHT VALIGN=TOP><FONT SIZE=+1>
<A HREF="http://web/directory/file/">Links to Other Jazz
Pages</A><BR>
<A HREF="http://web/directory/file/">Links to RealAudio
Jazz</A><BR></FONT>
</TD>
</TR>
</TABLE>
<P><P><BR>
```

FIGURE 43

What follows is the Signature. Notice the link back to the music department. Remember things need to be connected on the Web, and that, in part, is what a Signature is all about.

```
<HR NOSHADE width=80%>
<P>
<TABLE BORDER=0 WIDTH=85%>
<TD ALIGN=LEFT VALIGN=MIDDLE><A
HREF="http://www/directory/file"><IMG SRC="return_icon.gif">...
return to Department of Music</A></TD><TD ALIGN=RIGHT
VALIGN=BOTTOM>
<FONT SIZE=-1>WEBMEISTER: <A HREF="mailto:userid@jazz.edu">Cozy
Cole</A><BR>
Established: 18 June 1995; last modified: 17 July
1996.</FONT></TD></TABLE>
<P><P><BR><BR></UL></BODY></HTML>
```

Electronic Publications

Campus Electronic Magazine (a.k.a. 'Zine)

Moving from information pages to major electronic publications such as electronic magazines and journals and other collaborative pages is a big leap. Though the first page of an electronic publication can be rather simple, it can be crammed with links that often have to fit into a minimum amount of visual space. In what follows I am going to construct one site, an E-'Zine (or electronic magazine) and construct it as a collaborative site for student work.

Have you thought about starting a magazine? Most likely some of you have, but immediately there is the realization of the enormous expense in terms of, let's say, paper and postage alone. Printing is not inexpensive either. With the advent of the Web, however, none of these expenses is there, although someone does have to pay for Web space.

Either your university will allot space to you or, if you can manage it, you can pay a personal provider for an account and, if necessary, for additional megabytes of Web space. The cost will be considerably less than you would pay for an actual printing of a magazine. However, there's no way that people are going to pay to subscribe to your magazine, so don't expect being able to charge for access. You can, but who is going to pay, at least right now? (No one, as far as I know, is at present charging for such magazines on line. There are, of course, items on the Web that people have to pay for to get access to, but we are not talking about such enterprises.) Most likely, making money for such work is far from your thoughts right now, and you are more interested in learning how to tag such pages and in communicating your interests. (In any case, let's begin.)

I am going to call the 'Zine . . . *Zine-Ith,* and exploit various spellings on the similarities of Zenith and the 'Zine of maga*zine.* The first page will have a tremendous amount of information put into a small amount of space. The previous sites I have constructed have been longer and required some scrolling, which allowed for the thinning of the density of links. There is a tendency for people involved in Web designs to want to keep a limited amount of information on each page, including the first page. But there is a countermovement to place more "clickable" information on the first page of an electronic magazine. Recently Peter Merholz made a study of the development of C|*NET* (http://www.cnet.com/), showing, when it first appeared, how it was originally simple in design and then progressively filled with about fifty links. I am going to attempt a similar approach, especially since my designs up to this point have been fairly simple. The idea is to ease you into the process of thinking about electronic space from simple to complex designs, though none of our designs will be truly complex in this book.

Comment

As I suggested earlier there is a mixing of techniques in paper magazines and 'Zines or E-Journals. If you have noticed, television advertisements are also taking on the kinds of designs that are common on the Web. Learn the differences and how they borrow from each other. When you watch television (advertisements and promotions) watch for the kinds of formats that you find on the Web. It's very easy to find the reverse.

These are the overall features of the first page: It will be in three columns (not rows) done in Tables. There will be Tables within Tables. (The layout could have been done in what are called Frames, which I have not yet given the coding for and will do in Chapter 10. I tend not to like Frames.) There will be a number of graphics (JPEGs and GIFs). And there will be mostly internal but a few external links.

There is an added feature mentioned previously, which is the file named `index.html`, so there will be two files for this example of a first page. It is necessary in this instance, when working with the genre of a publication that will appear periodically, to have a front door (the `index.html` file) and then multiple secondary front doors for each issue. What we are doing now is working ourselves not only from simple to more complex design but also from front page/file to additional files off of the front page. (This issue is the major concern of the next chapter.)

To begin with, therefore, let's take a look at the `index.html` page, which will serve as a terminus for getting us to our volume 1 issue number 1 of *'Zine-Ith.* (See Figure 44.) It's coded/tagged in the following manner:

```
<HTML>
<HEAD>
<TITLE>'Zine-Ith</TITLE>
</HEAD>
<BODY BGCOLOR="#000000"
TEXT="#FF0000"LINK="#FFFFFF"><P><P><BR><BR>
```

The colors are a black background and a red text.

```
<BR><BR><BR><BR><BR><BR><BR><BR>
<CENTER>
<!--Open outside Table, no Border, to align half of the title-->
<TABLE BORDER=0><TR><TD ALIGN=RIGHT VALIGN=MIDDLE><FONT
SIZE=+30><P>'Zine</FONT></TD>
<TD>
```

With this code, I placed the word 'Zine to the left side but aligned it to the right of the box of four eyeguys (each of which is a graphic file).

```
<!---Open second outside Table, Border, for four cells of
eyeguy---->
<TABLE BORDER=1><TR>
<TD><IMG BORDER SRC="eyeguy_front2.gif" WIDTH=100
HEIGHT=100>
</TD>
<TD><IMG BORDER SRC="eyeguy2.gif" WIDTH=100 HEIGHT=100>
</TD></TR>
```

```
<TR><TD><IMG BORDER SRC="eyeguy_l22.gif" WIDTH=100
HEIGHT=100>
</TD><TD><IMG BORDER SRC="eyeguy_front2.gif" WIDTH=100
HEIGHT=100>
</TD></TR></TABLE>
<!---Close second outside Table of four cells of eyeguy---->
</TD>
```

I have created four boxes (cells) in one box (Table). In other words, two rows and two columns. So after two <TD>s, i.e., two Table Data (cells), there is a cancellation of the Table Row </TR> and a beginning of a new one with two more <TD>s.

```
<TD VALIGN MIDDLE><FONT SIZE=+30><P>(I_th)</FONT></TD></TR>
</TABLE>
<!---Close outside Table, no Border, to align half of the
title--->
<P>
```

With this code, as with the opening code, I placed the rest of the title (I_th) to the right side but snug left to the box.

```
<!---Signature-------->
E-stablished: June, 1996<br>
E-plugged: July, 1996
<p>
<!---Issue 1.1-------->
<A HREF="ZI1.html"><B>Issue: 1.1</B></A>
<!---Issue 1.2 forthcoming placement-------->
<P>
</CENTER>
</BODY>
</HTML>
```

So when the URL for this 'Zine is typed in and sent searching, we and others will show up at this site first. When we click on Issue 1.1, we then go to that issue (see Fig. 45), which is elaborately tagged in the following way:

```
<HTML>
<HEAD>
<TITLE>'Zine.Ith, Issue: 1.1</TITLE>
</HEAD>
<BODY>
<P><P><BR>
```

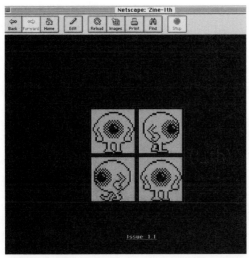

FIGURE 44

This whole site is actually one large table with three columns. Here is the opening of the Table, followed quickly by a Caption tag, which is a mixture of text and a GIF and then the first of the columns.

```
<TABLE CELLPADDING=5>
<CAPTION><FONT SIZE=+18><B>'Zine.<Img
src="eyeguy_front2.gif">.th</B></font></CAPTION>
<TR>

<!----COLUMN ONE--->
<TD VALIGN=TOP WIDTH=150>
<B><FONT SIZE=+4>I</FONT>ssue: 1.1 (1997):</B></CENTER>
<P>
  <A HREF="EDstaff.html">Editors & Staff</A>
```

It is necessary to set the width of the columns, so I decided to set the outside columns at 150 pixels and the inside one at 300 pixels for a total of a 600-pixel width. This tag " " is an ISO-Latin-I character that is called a non-breaking space, or an indentation. It can be also coded " ".

Comment

I repeated the tag " " for the desired indentation. (When I use this tag to indent a paragraph, I will repeat it five times.) It is very important to understand that this kind of tag is never in right/left angles "< >."

```
<P><BR>
  <A HREF="Advisors.html">Faculty Advisors</A>
<P>
  <A HREF="Innagissue.html">Inside this Issue</A>
<P>
<HR NOSHADE>
<P>
<b><FONT SIZE=+4>I</FONT>nvited Inaugural Articles:</B><P>
<P>
  On the Beginning of a Collaborative Student 'Zine!
<P><BR>
<CENTER>
<B>Jane N. Rodriguez</B>, <BR><A HREF="Working.html">Working
with Electricity Collaboratively</A><P>
<B>John R. Jones</B>, <BR><A HREF="View1.html">View I</A><P>
<B>LaKeisha Jefferson</B>, <BR><A HREF="View2.html">View
II</A><P>
<B>Kathy Akcrum</B>, <BR><A HREF="View3.html">View III</A>
</CENTER>
<P>
<HR NOSHADE>
<P>
  "In the spirit of freeware and shareware,
share what you know [about the Web freely]!" <B>Victor J.
Vitanza</B>,
<I>CyberReader</I>
</TD>
```

In this first column, there is:

- Information about the first issue
  Editors and staff
  Faculty advisors
  Inside this issue statement
- Inaugural articles
  One article and three views
- A quotation

These entries are a simple list, but varied by way of spacing. The first grouping is spaced with the " " indentation code, which the second grouping is centered. The names in the second are in bold face (<B>). The quotation is indented as a simple paragraph. Then we come to the end of the first column.

```
<!-----COLUMN TWO--->
<TD VALIGN=TOP WIDTH=300>
<CENTER>
<TABLE BORDER="4">
<TR>
<TD>
<IMG SRC="Zine.jpg" LENGTH=400 WIDTH=250>
</TD>
</TR>
</TABLE>
```

Here we have a Table (for the JPEG) within the larger Table of the middle column.

```
<P>
<FONT SIZE=-1><A HREF="http://contest.html">Join in on the
phun and participate in the Eye-Kon Test</A>.</FONT>
<P><P><BR>
<B><FONT SIZE=+2>I</FONT> &#183; n &#183; t &#183; e &#183;
r &#183; V &#183; i &#183; e &#183; w &#183; S </B>
<P> with . . .
```

Here are more ISO-Latin-I characters, this time representing a single middle dot between the letters. I am using it only for the purpose of variation in design.

```
<P>
The Dean of the School of Communications,<BR><B>Professor
James R. Smith</B><P>
<A HREF="Smith.html"><P>
"Information in 'The Late Age of Print' "</A><BR>
Primary Interviewer:<BR><B>Jessica Noble</B>
<P>
<CENTER> <B>&#167;</B></CENTER>
<P>
and with . . .
<P>
<IMG SRC="iwanna.jpg" ALIGN=CENTER WIDTH=240><P>
<A HREF="http://www.uta.edu/english/mal/iwanna/iwanna.html">...
A Conversation about Music and the Juice; or, Ohhhhh
"NC-Meme" Where Art Thou?</A><BR>
Primary Interviewer: <B>M.a.t.t.h.e.w...A....L.e.v.y</B><BR>
</TD>
```

In this column, following the JPEG, I placed more content, specifically a couple of interviews, both of which I tagged as centered.

Comment

The Important information is placed to the left and works its way to the right. The articles and interviews are spotlighted. This configuration—from top left to right—is typical of print media, and is generally followed in electronic media, though not as religiously.

```
<!----COLUMN THREE--->
<TD ALIGN=LEFT VALIGN=TOP WIDTH=150>
<B><FONT SIZE=+4>WE</FONT>b Presence:<BR></B>
<P>
  <A HREF="PT1Pod.html">E-Mail from our
Readers</A>: Post on HyperNews, an Interactive Website. Rant
on with Us!
<P>
  Want to E-stablish a Web Page?<A HREF="http://
www.uta.edu/english/V/rnftable.html"> Contact Y/Our Staff</A>.
They're Here to Help You.
<P>
  Some Sample WebSites that Our Staff has Helped
with:<P>
<A HREF="http://English/index.html">Department of
English</A><BR>
<A HREF="http://Music/index.html">Department of Music</A>
<BR>  and the <A
HREF="http://Music/Jazz/index.html">Jazz Site</A><BR>
<A HREF="http://Union/Film/index.html">The Creature Features
Site</A>
<P>
<HR NOSHADE>
<P>
  "In the future, everybody will have a Web page.
I mean everybody on Earth."--<B>Douglas Coupland</B>, <I>USA
Weekend</I>
<P>
<HR NOSHADE>
<P>
<b><FONT SIZE=+4>F</FONT>orthComing Issue:</B><BR>
<BR>
```

In the top of this third column, I placed what amounts to a Signature; then in the middle, a quote; and at the bottom, an announcement of the forthcoming issue. The tagging is all pretty much in paragraph form.

```
  <FONT SIZE=+1>I</FONT>n Our Hard Disks, <BR>
   More Articles by Guest Contributors and the
Editors;<BR>
   More Interviews with Experts in Electronic Infor-
mation and Commentators on Music, Plugged and UnPlugged;<BR>
  and a Few Surprises!<P>
</TD>
</TR>
</TABLE>
<!--------Close of large Table------>
```

Here I finally ended the large Table that had three columns.

```
<!--------Signature-------->
<HR NOSHADE><HR NOSHADE>
<BR>
<TABLE WIDTH=100%><TD ALIGN=LEFT VALIGN=TOP>
<FONT SIZE=-1><A HREF="index.html"><B>'Zine-Ith</B></A> is
an electronic publication supported <BR>by the College of
Communication, University of X.<BR> It appears three time a
year during the Fall, Spring and Summer Terms.</TD>
<TD ALIGN=RIGHT VALIGN=TOP>
<FONT SIZE=-1>
Copyright 1997 'Zine-Ith Co-Editors and Authors.
<A HREF="mailto:Zinith@ux.edu">Webmeister</A></FONT>
<BR><P><P><P><BR><BR>
</TD></TABLE>
</BODY>
</HTML>
```

Here we have new Table that is 100 percent in width. Although there is a Signature of sorts in the top third column, there is another, different Signature at the end.

We have traveled a long distance in this chapter in terms of the early personal pages to the collaborative ones. There is so much more to know, however, which will give you still more choices to make. The next is to start adding on to these various pages. What I will do in the forthcoming chapter is what I suggested earlier, namely, to borrow Crystal Waters's page design and redo one of the personal pages and then connect a number of these pages to it. In this way I will be able to demonstrate for you how to situate files with files (pages with pages) and all in a server. Let's take a look.

FIGURE 45

SUGGESTIONS

You might want to begin a collaborative project with your friends and fellow students. Start a 'Zine or a site for your club or whatever. You are limited only by your imagination. I usually ask my own students to do three kinds of assignments: a basic essay that would be done for print medium (and tag it for the Web), a home page, and a collaborative project. Your instructor may want you to do some of these or even other kinds of projects.

If you are going to do a collaborative project, then all those in the group will have to meet and determine what kind of project and how to divide the tasks to be done and the deadlines for completing each task. It is very important that the assignments be distributed equally among those who have decided to collaborate and to help each other.

WEB SITE RESOURCES

Web Site Reviews of On Line Blue Pages, from the magazine *The Net*. (You will find a variety of different genres of Web sites to study, and critiques to accompany them.)

    http://www.thenet-usa.com/blue_pages/bluepage.html

John Labovitz's e-zine-list (This site is the best listing for 'Zines.)
    http://www.meer.net/~johnl/e-zine-list/index.

Beyond the Single Page/File: Disposition of Pages (Directories/Files)

FROM PAGE-TO-PAGE (FILE TO FILE) CONSTRUCTION (CONTINUED)

This chapter, as the main head states, is a continuation of the previous chapters with their templates of *generic first pages* and explorations into "hyper"-text and "hypertext." We will continue learning about connecting pages/files into "hyper"-texts. In other words, we will be learning about and going through a step-by-step process of establishing and revising first pages (Hub or Core pages) and connecting pages/files to them.

Specifically, we will completely redo the last revision of David's home page (either Figures 27 or 32), which I developed and redeveloped in the previous two chapters, and revise it, as I promised, in the light of Crystal

Waters's article: "Steal My Web Page!: A Home Page Template for the Web-o-Rama-Challenged." (Waters tells us that she herself takes her point of imitation from the "Remembering Nagasaki" Web site, http://www.exploratorium.edu/nagasaki/). In redesigning David's home page and making it the first page, we are not, however, going to discard the previous versions. Instead, we are going to incorporate them as links into the overall design. David's new first page will have links to his older efforts at a first page and his other work (e.g., the Jazz site, the Film Series site, the 'Zine site), while simultaneously having links to his new efforts.

In thinking about how these sites can fit together, we will have to develop a flowchart of how the files might be connected and then name them. This step of determining the files is usually done before the files are developed, but can be done at any time. Think of a flowchart as an outline of a paper. Not all writers begin with outlines; some never even think in terms of an outline at all! Some will simply jot down a few ideas or boxes and connect them. I will begin here with jotting down a few ideas in terms of a flowchart, but it has to be remembered that at this point we are not starting from scratch, but we are in midstream. (We must not forget that all this development of a Web site is being done in the context of a textbook on writing for the WWW!) Much of the work already exists in the previous chapters and some new work is to be invented. So it could be that in developing a flowchart a Web designer might be looking for what is missing or what has yet to be invented. A flowchart could possibly demonstrate where the blind spots might be. But again, in developing David's Web site I already have an idea of what I am going to do because, let us not forget, I am in part imitating Waters and am attempting to connect the examples of Chapter 4 with the yet completely developed examples of Chapter 6. With all this mind, I am going to use the flowchart not as a means of discovering connections but as a means of explaining to you the various connections. So first, I am going to develop the new pages based on Waters's imitations of the Nagasaki site and then I am going to illustrate what I have done by way of a flowchart.

After I have developed the various files/pages and given them *Relative* path names (which will be explained in greater detail than in Chapter 2), we will then test them using Netscape. Keep in mind that the files will be in our hard disk and not in a server. It's better to do this kind of work in private space.

When satisfied with our work, I will discuss how to deploy the files to the server by way of FTP (file transfer protocol) programs so that our pages will be available to everyone in the world who has access. I will also discuss the various conventions of the logic of a Web tree, that is, the system of directories, subdirectories, and files. But at first we will simply, since we will have so few files, place all the files into a single directory. Finally I will suggest ways of getting access to a personal account and to Web space if you should need your own access and can afford it.

Just Link: How Your First Page
May Be Virtually All the Above

In more detail now, let's understand by way of summary that a few of the various first pages that we have built in Chapters 4 and 6 will be connected together to make one elaborate personal home page with numerous files linked to and extending from it. Specifically, what we will be doing is connecting first pages and creating some new second-level pages/files, which will be connected to sites on the WWW. In most cases some of the pages such as the 'Zine Web page will not have real files behind the links and generic URLs that we can only suggest are there. I cannot build files for every link, for they would add up to several hundred; there are limits to what I can put in this textbook. The point of this chapter, however, will have been realized by connecting/linking representative files. It is the principle of linking that needs to be understood and illustrated. I am, therefore, extending the *first page templates,* which are for the most part isolated now to a *first page (index.html) template,* which has connections.

Note

A first (Core or Hub) page is usually given the file name of "index.html." The full suffix *-html* is usually done on a Mac. However, if done on a PC/DOS, the suffix is *-htm.* You must be very careful, however, not to mix first pages in the same directory or folder, because there can only be one file/document named "index.html" at one time.

We will reinvent David's home page just as you might reinvent yours. It is common for someone not only to update a Web site but also to redesign it completely anew from time to time. It is, however, not a common practice for Web people to connect the old designs to new ones, thereby leaving a history of the development of their variously changing identities. Whatever you decide, understand that mixing the new with the old is one choice available to you. There is the issue, of course, of how much Web space you have allotted to you. I am, of course, mixing the old with the new for the purpose of illustrating some basic principles of invention and reinvention, design and redesign, in this textbook. Hence my choice. (By the design of the page, I mean the layout, colors, graphics, number of links and quantity of information. The content could remain the same, while the design could change and reshape the way that the viewer perceives and responds to the pages.) So as promised, let's redo David's page in the light of Crystal Waters's suggested design. What is especially interesting about Waters's design is its simplicity and, depending on your sense of esthetics, its beauty. (For the full impact of the design, you of course will have to see it in its virtual environment.)

A New First Page and Building a Sequence of Pages/Files

If you recall (you might want to refresh your memory by looking at Figures 25 and 26) we based the design of David's page on the "Proust Questionnaire" in the magazine *Vanity Fair*. We did this twice. Then we further redesigned David's page as a pictograph essay of sorts (Fig. 30) and then again redesigned it as a multimedia page, with a promise of still further developing it (Fig. 32). Now we are going on to a third redesign but a simpler one with links to the previous designs. Since David is—as you eventually will be—interested in further developing the original sites and pulling them altogether, he will need a file as a starting point. With multiple first pages that constantly get redesigned and added to and that might have changes in file names, David must have a file that will remain as a baseline, so to speak—a file that will act as a *hub* for all his Web works. (Of course, this file too, can be perpetually redesigned if so desired.)

Waters, like the designer of the "Nagasaki" site as well as other Web designers, has created a simple hub page and named the file "index.html." (See Figure 45.) Here is my adaptation of the design, with the difference lying in the change of name. (There is absolutely nothing unique about this design; you can find it all over the Web.) For David's site, I made a JPEG file that simply has David's name on it and then coded it to be the link to his new first page. I followed the basic design, except for the underlining, that my predecessors used and which has become fairly common by now on the Web. (See Appendix B for making graphics.) Here is the tagging for the page/file:

```
<HTML>
<HEAD>
<TITLE>d a v i d v i t a n z a</TITLE>
</HEAD>
<BODY BGCOLOR="#000000" TEXT="#000000" VLINK="#000000">
<P><P><P><BR><BR><BR><BR><BR><BR><BR><BR>
<CENTER>
<A HREF="davida.html"><IMG BORDER=0 SRC="dvbk.jpg" alt="en-
ter here"></A>
</CENTER>
</BODY>
</HTML>
```

As you can see, this page is a simple matter. Notice how not only the background color but also any possible links, if any were to be added, are black

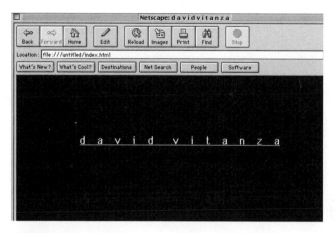

FIGURE 46

("#000000"). The only thing on this page is the JPEG file **"dvbk.jpg"** of David's name and the alt link for people using the text browser Lynx. The URL "davida.html" links this page to one by that name, *davida.html*. To simplify things, I have alphabetized the sequence of the four new pages *davida.html* through *davidd.html*. (So as you can see, without doing a flowchart, I have a plan. Since the set of relationships is fairly simple, I was able to see the connections without having to search them out with pencil and paper. But I will, nonetheless, illustrate the connections later.)

Now let's take a look at what will be David's new home page, *davida.html* (Fig. 47). It, too, is simple in design. On it and on the subsequent three pages that are new with it, I have included, as Waters has, his e-mail address in –1 font size. (Note, however, that the address is up top, whereas in just about all the previous examples in Chapters 4–6, the Signature, which includes the address, was at the bottom.) The background color remains black as it does throughout the four new pages. The text, throughout, is white; the links are a cream color and the visited links are a shade of red. The color combination is pleasant to look at. Notice that there is some preformatting **<PRE>** . . . **</PRE>**, which allows for the arrangement of letters and words on the page in a freer style and which changes the font to courier. And then the main body of the page has the brief announcement about the old and the new. The old home pages and projects can be clicked on and visited or the new work can be followed by clicking on the link called *next*. (In each case, as you progress into the new pages, this Back/Next choice presents itself. However, the Back command in subsequent pages returns the reader to this new first page/file (*davida.html*).

Reminder

As it is with the new files returning to each other, so it must be with the old files. In other words, the older files/ projects (the various home pages, the film page, jazz page, etc.) must be modified with links back to *davida.html*, or wherever you might want to take them to. My intent here is to get everything back to what I see in the design as the pivotal file after the Hub/Core file, *index.html*.

Returning to the overall design of *davida.html*, if you look at the <A HREF> link and anchor </A> you will find something new. Notice the additional code of <TARGET=WINDOW> which is placed into the tag. Hence, <A TARGET=WINDOW HREF=> etc. What this target code accomplishes on Netscape Navigator 2.0 and above is the opening of a new Netscape window. The purpose of this code is to keep your page open and visible to the readers no matter where else they might click themselves to. (This coding is used in subsequent files. This use of a target window has also become fairly common on the Web especially at commercial sites.)

Here is the complete coding for the entire page:

```
<HTML>
<HEAD>
<TITLE>David Vitanza'S HP (new series)</TITLE>
</HEAD>
<BODY BGCOLOR="#000000" TEXT="#FFFFFF" LINK="#FFFF99"
VLINK="#990000">
<PRE>
<FONT SIZE=5>d a v i d   v i t a n z a</FONT>
<HR>
<FONT SIZE=-1>A.K.A.  <A
HREF="MAILTO:.......AOL.COM">DavidV@aol.com</A></FONT><P>
<HR>
<FONT SIZE=4>
... here you will find the old and new together, yet separate.
... just click on the list below for the old.
... just click <STRONG>back</STRONG> or <STRONG>next</STRONG>
to go through my newer site page by page:<P>
...........my <A HREF="david1.html">first home page</A>
...........my <A HREF="david2.html">revised home page</A>
...........a <A HREF="david3.html">pictographic essay</A>
...........my <A HREF="david4.html"> multimedia home page </A>
```

```
...........the <A HREF="david5.html">film club page</A>
...........the <A HREF="david6.html">jazz page</A>
<P>
<HR>
To find out more about my collaborative work on an e-'Zine, go
to <A TARGET=WINDOW HREF="../comm/pubs/Zine-Ith/">'Zine-Ith</A>
<P>
<HR>
<A HREF="index.html"><-- b a c k</A>................ <A
HREF="davidb.html">n e x t --></A>
</FONT>
</PRE>
</BODY>
</HEAD>
```

Tip

About preformatting: You will no doubt notice that some of the spacing of the letters and words, etc. appears irregular here. This is part of the design. But more importantly for the design to appear as I wanted it to on the monitor, it had to take precisely this spacing and shape. In order to discover the necessary spacing and shape, you will find that it is necessary to do the preformatting by trial and error. It is very difficult to tell precisely where the letters and words, etc., should fall on the page to appear on a monitor. And if you are designing a page using this tag, you need to be careful that it will fit on, say, a 15-inch monitor, which is about the standard size. So you might want to check the spacing while developing the site with `<PRE> ... </PRE>` commands. (This is an occasion when viewing your file in your hard disk drive on Netscape will especially come in handy.) I am not suggesting, however, that you must standardize everything you do for a 15-inch monitor; I don't. If I were to follow this suggestion as a rule not to be broken, there would be much that I would not be able to do at all. No Web designer should feel duty bound to follow this or other similar conventions.

When readers click on *next* at the bottom right of the page, they will go to file *davidb.html*, on which they will find a page with a few links to bizarre (comic) Web sites: "The T.W.I.N.K.I.E.S. Project" and "The Pickle Preservation Society" (Fig. 48). There's nothing necessarily new in terms of coding on this page. (See the complete coded page at the end of this chapter.) The link to the Cracker site is on Waters's sample site. Instead of going to the Site and downloading a part of a cracker GIF as Waters did, I got a couple crackers at home, placed them on the dining room table, photographed them and got

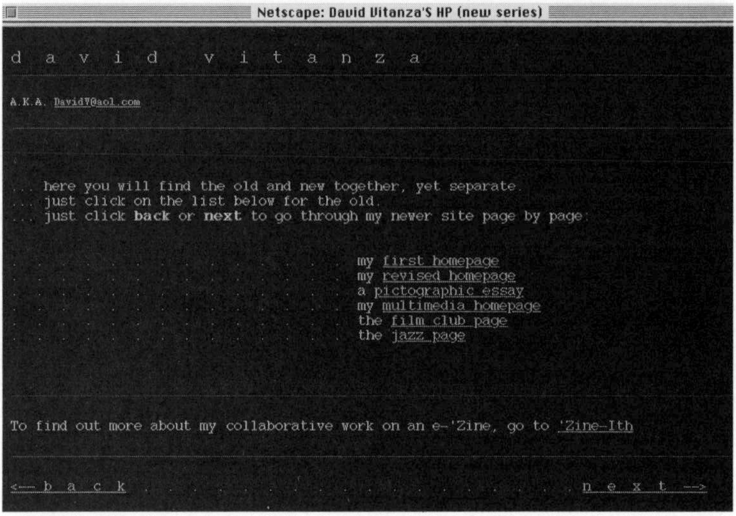

FIGURE 47

them developed so that I could run my photo through a scanner and then PhotoShop in order to make my own graphic. (See Appendix B for instructions.) I aligned the JPEG to be in the middle (i.e., snug left against the text) and then put in horizontal spacing at 5 pixels (so that it would not be too snug against the text!). And again, I used the `<TARGET=WINDOW>` tag.

The next page, *davidc.html*, is coded in a familiar manner with the exception of the JPEG and the text (Fig. 49). Instead of downloading one or

FIGURE 48

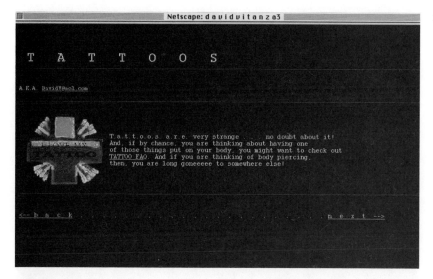

FIGURE 49

two tattoo graphics from the Web—and there are so many available, though not in the public domain—I designed my own in PhotoShop and then made a JPEG of it. I then sized it with width and height tags and put in a horizontal space tag and value of 8 to create space between the image and the text to the right. I could have used a Table tag to control the relationship between the JPEG and the text but I wanted, for this text, to illustrate other means of controlling these pixels electronically. Notice that I simply used paragraph and break tags to work the image down from the top to the middle. Then I typed in the text, with a link to a Tattoo FAQ that Waters herself uses. My text is different from hers: this link is run and included here as a public service. Following the text, I included a horizontal rule. But notice that to keep that rule from electronically floating up to the text, I, like Waters, had to use a tag that I have previously used in this book: **<BR CLEAR=ALL>**. What this tag accomplishes, as the wording might suggest, is the establishment of a clear break between all text and the horizontal rule. The alternative would have been to use a number of consecutive paragraph and break tags. (See the completely tagged pages for Figures 48–49 on pages 156–157.)

In the final page of this set of new links, there is a list of sites from Yahoo considered to be the best of the day, the week, and the month. If you are interested in Web design like David, then you will want to visit links such as these to take a look at what Yahoo or some other major source of information about the Web thinks is worthy of our consideration. The tags here are by now standard. (See fully tagged page for Figure 50 on pages 157–158.) Notice that at the bottom of the page there is no Next link, just the Return.

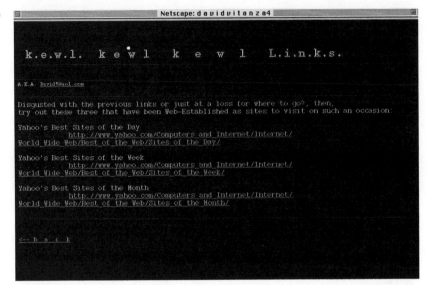

FIGURE 50

These, then, are the new pages. What we need to do now so as to get everything straight and clear in our heads is to draw a flow chart for all the pages determining the names of the files and the relationships among them. (Recall that I said I am doing this after the fact as a means of showing what the connections look like).

Linking the Old to the New Pages: Creating a Flow Chart

What pages and files are we dealing with? Remember that we are concerned with only those files that we have (or David has) created. We don't have to be concerned with the links to sites that we did not create. We already have the URLs in our files and they are all that's necessary. Let's first make a basic list (or inventory) of all the files that we have included or might have included if we had started at this point from near scratch in thinking about our (David's) Web site:

- *index.html* (this is hub site, Fig. 46)
- *davida.html* (Fig. 47)
- *davidb.html* (Fig. 48)
- *davidc.html* (Fig. 49)
- *davidd.html* (Fig. 50)

These are the new pages/hypertext files that we just reviewed. Now what are the other files included from Chapters 4 through 6? If you recall noticing, the names of the files are in the coding of *david*(number).*html*. They are

- *david1.html* (David's first home page, Fig. 26)
- *david2.html* (the second home page, Fig. 27)
- *david3.html* (the pictographic essay, Fig. 30)
- *david4.html* (the multimedia home page, Fig. 32)
- *david5.html* (the film club, Fig. 29)
- *david6.html* (the jazz site, Fig. 42) and
- *../com/pubs/Zine-Ith/* (the 'Zine site, Fig. 43).

This is going to be relatively simple, since the determination has already been made in the various pages/files. Yes, I cannot repeat enough so that you are not misled: I intermittently thought about what the relationships might be and then finally decided—as I am recapitulating in an encapsulated form here—for myself, and now for you, what the relationships among the pages/ files are. This is also for illustrative purposes. (You or another could do otherwise by first sitting down and talking through a set of possible files and then creating and revising an initial flowchart, which would be, of course, open to constant revision while building the Web site.) And so what are the files/pages and their relationships?

Well, if you will recall, the hub is *index.html*, which is linked only to *davida.html*, which, in turn, acts as the central home page; at least, it acts as such for the most recent revision of the home page. From that page there is a forking or branching in two directions. One branch—all of which is visually present as links on that page—is composed of seven coequal files. The second branch begins at the bottom of the page as *next* and moves successively from new page to new page (for a total of four pages/files).

But have we forgotten something? Let's not forget that we redesigned or created a number of JPEGs and GIFs for both the old and the new files, which have to be included here as well:

For the old files
```
alpha_a.gif
alpha_d.gif
alpha_i.gif
alpha_v.gif
angst.gif
critic.good.gif
eyeguy2.gif
eyeguy_front2.fig
eyeguy_122.gif
iconmovie.gif
iconsound.gif
italmanshades.gif
```

```
iwanna.jpg
ligtbold.jpg
music1.gif
mus_not.gif
next_icon.gif
quicktimelgif
return_icon.gif
simp.nerd.gif
surfer.gif
tomatoplant.gif
Zine.jpg
```

For the new files
```
crackers.jpg
dvbk.jpg
tatTWO.jpg
```

When drawn out as a flowchart (without the graphic files, for they are already separated into old and new sites above), the relational chart of the text files (Fig. 51) looks something like this:

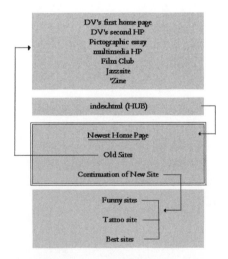

FIGURE 51

Or the relationships can look more informally scribbled or boxed in this fashion (Fig. 52):

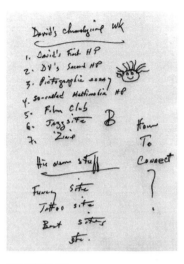

FIGURE 52

What does it matter what variety of representations the relational chart might take, as long as each illustrates the possible connections!

Now with all of these files accounted for, let's put them into one folder in our hard drive. Yes, all of them together as equal. (See Figure 53.) The reason for putting them together is so that we can test them on Netscape 2.0+ before placing them in a server and publishing them for the world. As I stated

FIGURE 53

earlier, these files should be in Text Only format, or what is also called *ascii*. If you have not already done this, you can go to your word processing program menu and pull down File to Save as and designate the file to be saved as Text only, or ascii. In this way, you will have files that are stripped of all hidden-to-your-eyes formatting codes that are encoded by way of a word processing program, and in formats such as boldface, italics, paragraphing, etc.

Testing and Revising the Pages Before Placing in a Server

Once we have gathered all of these into a folder in our hard drive, or as far as that goes in a 1.4MB floppy if it can hold everything, which is the case with all the files that I have developed for these examples, then, we can see what we have done, and if we discover any errors or design flaws we can correct them. I recommend that you use the most recent version of Netscape; in some cases, you might want to use a Beta version, one which is available but is being tested. (In many cases, if you are using the version of Netscape that is in your university's server, you will have what the system operator considers to be the most safe and reliable. By the time this book appears, I suspect that Netscape 2.01+, or comparable for Windows, will be standard. Right now, this is not the case. But since we determine what is in our own hard drive, we can download a copy of the most recent version ourselves. (For instructions on downloading a copy, see the closing section of Chapter 2.) The reason for having Netscape 2.01+ is that it has a drag-and-drop function that speeds up the testing of files. Once the files are in a folder in your hard disk, all you have to do is drag and drop the hub file, *index.html*, into Netscape space. (Or go to File and then Open, locate the folder, and call it up on Netscape.) Then just click and read and be amazed at what you have done. Even better, drag and drop the complete folder onto Netscape. What you will see is an index of all your files as they will appear on Netscape after you have deployed them to your location on a server.

A bit of a digression to explain something: If you noticed, when I named the files, I wrote them all as *relative* links or paths, not *absolute links*. What does this distinction mean? Let me explain it in this manner by starting with what the URL could possibly be for the home page and all the other files.

A URL (Uniform Resource Locator) is composed of, first, the *protocol* (which will be *http//:*, for hypertext transfer protocol), then the *Web location* (which is composed of the domain name and the agency abbreviation [e.g., edu, com, net, gov] which usually, but not always, follows this pattern, *www.address.edu/*), and finally the *file location* (which is a home directory and usually a series of subdirectories that can end in a file).

Hence, a generic URL for our inventory of files might look like this: http://www.univofX.edu/english/student/dmv/ or something along this line. When we get beyond the Web location, beyond the first slash (/), we get into directories such as the *English* (here, signified in lower case *e*) department directory, which has a subdirectory *student,* which has a sub-subdirectory of *dmv/,* which are David's initials and in which we could theoretically place our files in a server. (In our hard disk, there are similar directories, or logic trees.) One thing you must always keep in mind: URLs and directory and file names are case-sensitive. When mistakes are made, it is usually because attention was not paid to this convention. Another thing to keep in mind: while the conventions of directories are set, the names we can give to them are arbitrary but should be recognizable to the people using the accounts.

Now to the point of the digression explaining the difference between *relative* and *absolute* paths/links: A *relative* path/link is only in my example pages/files the name of the file itself. When I type in `<A HREF="davida.html">` this is a relative path. However, if I were to type in a complete URL `<A HREF="http://www.univofX.edu/english/student/dmv/davida.html">`, then we would have an absolute path or link. Hence, again, if you will recall, I gave only the file names (i.e., "davida.html") as links, whereas when I was linking elsewhere to sites done by others, I put in the full URL. David's files are *relative* paths; the others are *absolute* paths. This should be enough at present to explain the difference, but we will definitely have to return to this again in a later section.

Therefore, when we put all the files in one folder/directory in our hard drive, we are creating relative links. When we get to placing the files in a directory in a server, we can do the same to simplify matters, but there are reasons for creating additional directories to simplify matters if there are numerous files for other projects. (Simplification is a double-edged sword.)

Using Netscape, we will revise, revise, revise, making sure we have everything just as we want it and have met the basic conventions of the Web, or if we have gone against convention, then we have done so for good reasons. (Turn to Chapter 9, for a checklist of what you might want to look for in the process of revising.)

SUGGESTIONS

If you have been developing the kinds of pages described in the previous chapters, you might now want to bring them together as multiple files off of one page. It may very well take you a while to figure out how to connect them all by way of a design. Remember to just jot down the file names and then start connecting them in terms of a flowchart. If nothing comes to mind after thinking about connections, spend some time searching the Web for ideas. You definitely will want to take a look at Lynda Weinman's *<deconstructing web graphics>* for ideas about constructing sites. Also see David Siegel's *Creating Killer Websites.* (Full references are below.)

FULLY TAGGED PAGES
(REFERRED TO IN CHAPTER)

HTML tags for Figure 48

```
<HTML>
<HEAD>
<TITLE>d a v i d v i t a n z a</TITLE>
</HEAD>
<BODY BGCOLOR="#000000" TEXT="#FFFFFF" LINK="#FFFF99"
VLINK="#990000">
<P> <P><BR><BR>
<PRE>
<FONT SIZE=6>i'm s-t-i-l-l laughin' about these Sites . . .
<HR>
<FONT SIZE=-1>A.K.A. <A HREF="MAILTO:......AOL.COM">
DavidV@aol.com</A></FONT>
<HR><FONT SIZE=4>
One of the funniest . . . I have bitten into so far is <A
TARGET=WINDOW
HREF="http://www.owlnet.rice.edu/~gouge/twinkies.html">the
T.W.I.N.K.I.E.S. Project</A>.
Some people do not have enough homework to do!
<HR>
And then there is . . . <A TARGET=WINDOW
HREF="http://www.ithaca.edu/orgs/pickle/pickle1/pps.html">
the Pickle Preservation Society</A>.
<HR>
And then (again) . . . because Nobody Else is Perfect, <A
TARGET=WINDOW HREF="http://www.mrmedia.com/mrmedia/">Here's
Mr. Media</A>.
<HR>
. . . Which reMinds me of . . . <P>
the MARX Brothers' film <STRONG>Animal Crackers</STRONG>.
Wanna see some Crackers? <A TARGET=WINDOW HREF="http://
mathlab.mathlab.sunysb.edu/~elijah/cstuff/"><IMG BORDER=0
SRC="crackers.jpg" ALIGN=MIDDLE HSPACE=5 HEIGHT=60
WIDTH=60><BR CLEAR=ALL></A>
<HR>
<A HREF="davida.html"><-- b a c k</A> . . . . . . . . . . .
. . . . . . <A HREF="davidc.html">n e x t--></A>
</PRE>
</BODY>
</HTML>
```

HTML tags for Figure 49

```
<HTML>
<HEAD>
<TITLE>d a v i d v i t a n z a3</TITLE>
</HEAD>
<BODY BGCOLOR="#000000" TEXT="#FFFFFF" LINK="#FFFF99"
VLINK="#990000">
<P> <P><BR><BR>
<PRE>
<FONT SIZE=6> T A T T O O S
<HR>
<FONT SIZE=-1>A.K.A. <A HREF="MAILTO:......AOL.COM">
DavidV@aol.com</A></FONT></PRE>
<HR>
<IMG BORDER=0 SRC="tatTWO.jpg" ALIGN=LEFT WIDTH=150
HEIGHT=150 HSPACE=8>
<P><P><BR><BR><P><P><BR>
T.a.t.t.o.o.s. a.r.e. very strange . . . no doubt about it!
<BR>
And, if by chance, you are thinking about having one <BR> of
those things put on your body, you might want to check out <BR>
<A TARGET=WINDOW HREF="http://www.cis.ohio-state.edu/
hypertext/faq/usenet/bodyart/tattoo-faq/top.html">TATTOO
FAQ</A>. And if you are thinking of body piercing, <BR>
then, you are long goneeeee to somewhere else!<BR CLEAR=ALL>
<P>
<HR><PRE>
<A HREF="davida.html"><-- b a c k</A> . . . . . . . . . . .
. . . . . . . . . . . <A HREF="davidd.html">n e x t -->
</A>
</PRE>
</BODY>
</HTML>
```

HTML tags for Figure 50

```
<HTML>
<HEAD>
<TITLE>d a v i d v i t a n z a4</TITLE>
</HEAD>
<BODY BGCOLOR="#000000" TEXT="#FFFFFF" LINK="#FFFF99"
VLINK="#990000">
<P> <P><BR><BR>
```

```
<PRE>
<FONT SIZE=6> k.e.w.l.   k e w l   k  e  w  l  L.i.n.k.s.
<HR>
<FONT SIZE=-1>A.K.A.  <A
HREF="MAILTO:......AOL.COM">DavidV@aol.com</A></FONT></PRE>
<HR>
<FONT SIZE=4>
Disgusted with the previous links or just at a loss for
where to go?, then,<BR>try out these three that have been
Web-Established as sites to visit on such an occasion:
<P>
Yahoo's Best Sites of the Day<BR>
. . . . . . <A TARGET=WINDOW HREF="http://www.yahoo.com/
Computers_and_Internet/Internet/World_Wide_Web/Best_of_the_Web/
Sites_of_the_Day/">
http://www.yahoo.com/Computers_and_Internet/Internet/
World_Wide_Web/Best_of_the_Web/Sites_of_the_Day/</A><P>
Yahoo's Best Sites of the Week<BR>
. . . . . . <A TARGET=WINDOW HREF="http://www.yahoo.com/
Computers_and_Internet/Internet/World_Wide_Web/Best_of_the_Web/
Sites_of_the_Week/">
http://www.yahoo.com/Computers_and_Internet/Internet/
World_Wide_Web/Best_of_the_Web/Sites_of_the_Week/</A><P>
Yahoo's Best Sites of the Month<BR>
. . . . . . <A TARGET=WINDOW HREF="http://www.yahoo.com/
Computers_and_Internet/Internet/World_Wide_Web/Best_of_the_Web/
Sites_of_the_Month/">
http://www.yahoo.com/Computers_and_Internet/Internet/
World_Wide_Web/Best_of_the_Web/Sites_of_the_Month/</A><P>
</FONT>
<HR><PRE>
<A HREF="davida.html"><-- b a c k</A>
</PRE>
</BODY>
</HTML>
```

REFERENCES (BOOKS) AND WEB SITE RESOURCES

Siegel, David. *Creating Killer Websites Online: The Art of Third-Generation Site Design.*
Indianapolis, Indiana: Hayden Books, 1996. This is an advanced book that distinguishes among first-, second-, and third-generation Web sites. Siegel's Web
site: http://www.killersites.com/.

Weinman, Lynda. *<deconstructing web graphics> Web Design Case Studies and Tutorials.* Indianapolis, IN: New Riders, 1996. As the title suggests, this book is a study of the development of select commercial Web sites such as HotWired and Discovery Channel Online. Weinman's accompanying Web site: http://www.lynda.com/decon

▶ 8

Publishing Your First Web Page: Elementary and Advanced Considerations of Placing Files in Directories

STEPS TOWARD PUBLISHING YOUR FIRST WEB PAGE

Once you are generally satisfied with your Web pages, you may want to publish them or have them published for you. If you have direct access to Web space, then you will do the publishing; if your instructors do, then they will.

If you have neither of these possibilities, you will be limited to publishing your work through a friend who has space or through a publisher, just as you would if you wrote something for print. Let's take a look at what is involved in getting access.

GETTING ACCESS TO WEB SPACE

From what I can tell, I think that it is very difficult for an undergraduate student to get access to university Web space. There are exceptions, of course. Generally, access is limited to administration, faculty, and a few undergraduate and graduate students—undergraduates and graduate students if they are putting up a Web site for a legitimate student organization; graduate students if they are involved in teaching about writing for the Web or involved in a scholarly project that requires a Web site. It may very well be, therefore, that your instructor might post your work for you. I do this for my undergraduates. Many of my graduate students have Web sites.

If you are capable of paying out of your own pocket for an ISP account (Internet service provider account), then this is another alternative for getting access. For what is called a PPP and shell dial-up Internet (e-mail) account you might have to pay anywhere from $10 to $30 a month. The best thing to do is determine if any of your friends have accounts and talk to them; or check for ads, etc. You will want to know several things while shopping around:

- Is there is a flat fee and no additional fees for all the time you want per month?
- Is there sufficient tech support (i.e., help when you need it)?
- Does the company have its own FTP directories from which you can download Netscape and additional freeware and shareware?
- Do you get Web space with the account and, if so, how much do you get?

Usually, it is at least 1 MB, but can go to 5MB or more. You will also want to know how much additional space will cost you if you think you need it. Shop around!

Access has become a big issue for many of us interested in electronic environments. At present, primarily it is people who work in education or for corporations and people with money to spend who have access. Most others are left out. Much work needs to be done to get access for as many people as possible. Some communities are creating a service called FreeNet, which, as the name implies, gives free access to both e-mail and the Web. Check to see if your community has such a service. As I finish this book, I have discovered that there is a company by the name of JUNO that provides free e-mail service, but there are loads of commercials all along the way to reading your mail. Nothing is free! I suspect in time there will be "free" access to the Web as well.

ELEMENTARY: PLACING FILES INTO A SERVER

A year or so ago it was more difficult than today to place files/pages on a Web site. By difficult, I mean that it required numerous steps and lots of typing. Now with new FTP programs (File Transfer Protocol Programs), it is just a matter of clicking your way through the entire process. I could give you the step-by-step long process here, but I see no reason for doing so when there's an easier way. Assuming that you have an account, here are the steps that you must take to publish your work:

- First you must make sure that you have all the necessary text files and graphic files and that your text files have been saved as *text only*. Likewise, you must make sure that the names of your files (those that we have put into the folder in our hard drive) match precisely the lower/upper case construction of the relative file names in the body of your files. People often tend to err by having the same names but not the same upper/lower case construction. In other words if the name of your file is *DAVIDA.HTML* (or any variation with a capital letter) and the file name in the body of your file is *davida.html*, the browser (Netscape or any other browser) will not be able to read the file.
- Second you will want to transfer your files to the server in which you have an account. (As I stated in the preface to this book, my basic assumption here is that you know how to use e-mail and that you do not need an introduction to being on line.) If you are working on a PC, you will use the program WS_FTP; if you are working on a Mac, you will want to use Fetch 3.0.1+. (See Appendix A, p. 212, for instructions on obtaining these freeware/shareware programs.) Both programs are easy to use and are comparable; if you can use one, you can intuitively follow the other. If you are working on a computer in your university lab or classroom, most likely you will have one or the other of these programs already installed with direct access to the server.

Update

As I am making the final revisions of this manuscript, Netscape has released version 3.0 of its browser, which has what is called an *editing* function. Therefore, while you are actually in Netscape, you can edit your pages and transfer the changes directly to the server.

If you are not working on a computer in your university lab or classroom, I am assuming that you have online access by way of an ISP account which you personally pay for. In order to transfer the files, you must be dialed in, that is, connected to the university's or your private account by way of a modem. (Your ISP will give you special software and instructions for dialing in. Do not confuse using your e-mail software for dialing in.) Once connected, then, double click on Fetch to activate the program. You will get a dialogue box asking for your:

- HostName
- User ID
- Password
- Directory (see Figure 54)

You should *already have* this information from the system operator (or possibly your instructor) who has given you an account (i.e., access to the Web tree) at your university, or you will have been given this information from your ISP representative. Understand, however, that simply because you might have what is called a VAX or UNIX e-mail account at your university, you do not necessarily have access to the Web tree or Web site. Such access you must ask for; it's getting another account altogether and in most cases it's a Unix account.

Okay, so you have opened up the program Fetch and are asked for your host name, which for me is *cwis.uta.edu*. You type in whatever it is for you. Then you are asked for your User ID, which again is assigned to you, and you type that in. You are asked for a Password, previously assigned to you; then a Directory, which is also assigned to you and which can vary widely from university to university.

Think of yourself as "David": The Directory that David is going to use is *dmv*. When David asked for an account, he also asked for a directory to be established following the conventions already established for the directory named *student*. Remember that the full URL for David's hypothetical directory is *http://www.univofX.edu/english/student/*. Therefore, when a *directory* was made for him it was placed in the *student directory*. These would be the levels and hierarchy of directories:

```
english
    student
        dmv
```

In this hierarchy of directories and subdirectories, there are, of course, other departments along with English (History, Foreign Languages, etc.), other classifications along with student (e.g., administration, faculty), and other student directories/folders with their initials as IDs.

If you have access from an ISP, however, your Directory is usually *public_html* or */pub* or some other possible variation. And when you use your FTP prgram to open your files, you will go directly to your directory, which is usually identical with your user identification, or *userid*. Sometimes, a tilde (~) is used before the userid. (If you have an ISP, all this will be explained by the company providing the service.)

Okay, let's return: David has opened up the program Fetch and is asked for his host name, which is *cwis.univofX.edu*. (See Figure 54.) He types this in and is then asked for his User ID which, let's say, is *dvitanza*, and he types that in. He is then asked for a Password, previously assigned to him, then a Directory, which is fictionally *dmv*.

However, he cannot simply type this in, but must have the correct series of directories, which can vary greatly from server to server, so David had to get this information from his system operator who gave access or from his instructor. For David, let's say that the series of directories is going to be */infohome/.www/webtree/english/student/dmv*. (Perhaps you notice right away that in this string of directories the last three are recognizable. It's the names of the directories that precede that are new to you. All of the names, when the string is this long, do not show in the allotted space in Fetch, but you can click in the Directory field and "arrow your way" to the right to read what you have typed. Trust me: In Figure 54, . . . *nglish/student/dmv* is there.) David could go to the directory *student* and search for his directory, *dmv*, and then click on it to open it. With this information typed in, David just clicks on OK; a new dialogue box opens. (See Figure 55.) And, poof, like magique, there it is . . . *dmv!*

(Was it necessary for the system operator or instructor to create this directory *dmv* for David? No, David could create the directory himself by simply going to the menu on Fetch when he is in the directory *student*, and pull down Directories and go to Create New Directories. Then he will be asked to name it: *dmv* or whatever is appropriate for you.)

Notice in Figures 54–57, David has his desktop folder open with the files that he wants to transfer. (We previously talked about the creation of this directory/folder.) The *dmv* directory in the new dialogue box (Fig. 55) must be double clicked to open the directory. An empty directory opens, in which David has to transfer both text and graphic files. Notice that the box is set at Automatic, which means that the program Fetch is going to determine most things for us. (There's nothing like sending files on automatic pilot.) To begin transferring files into the empty directory, David just clicks on Put File and then a dialogue box opens and allows him to find in his file folder on his desktop what he wants to FTP to the directory *dmv* (Fig. 56). By double clicking on what he wants to transfer, *alpha_a.gif*, David gets another box from Fetch, requesting additional information about how the file is to be saved and transferred (Fig. 57). Since David set the program to Automatic, he will set the FTP to Raw Data and simply send the file. First, *alpha_a.gif*, then *alpha_d.gif*, then *alpha_i.gif*, and so on, until all the files have been trans-

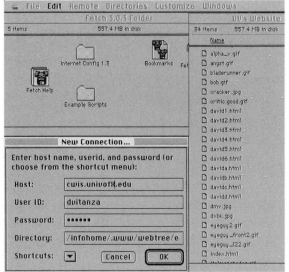

FIGURE 54

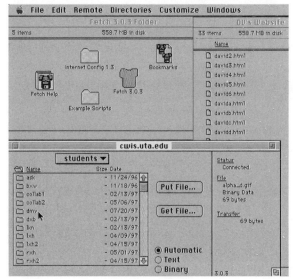

FIGURE 55

ferred. It will take a while for each to reach its destination, depending on the size of the file, the amount of traffic online, etc. David can watch each transfer in progress. (If there are problems, David will get a dialogue box saying that there is a particular problem. If this happens, he will simply try again.) When the file arrives, it will show as part of the inventory, as two already show in Figure 57. If you want to retrieve a file, you simply click on Get File

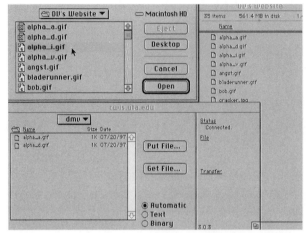

FIGURE 56

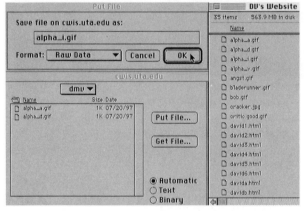

FIGURE 57

and do the same sort of things done to put a file. (Or of course you can retrieve a file by way of Netscape by going to View and pulling down the menu to Source.) There is one more necessary step.

What's that other step? David in many cases will have to set what are called *permissions*. If he does not, his files will not get read by the browser. To set permissions means determining who can *rewrite* or change the contents of the file and who can *read* it. Permissions can be set prior to sending or after sending files. On the recent version of Fetch, you go to Remote on the menu and pull it down to Set Permissions or Set Upload Permissions. (See Figure 58.) The former is to set permissions or reset them after having sent files; the latter is to set them prior to sending. If done after, David would click once on the file, darkening it, and then set permissions. In the dialogue box there is a matrix of squares to check:

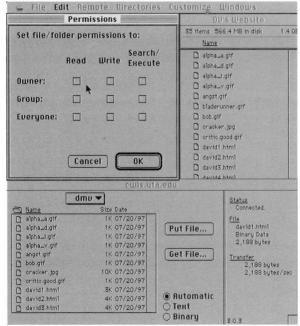

FIGURE 58

- Read (permission to read)
- Write (to rewrite the content)

set across

- Owner (David)
- Group (those who share the server space with him)
- Everyone (in the whole wide world)

If you are setting up your own private files—and you most likely are, except for collaborative projects—you will want to set the Permissions at Owner, read and write; Group, read; Everyone, read.

Congratulations on your (first?) Web publication!

ADVANCED: FURTHER CONSIDERATIONS AND ELABORATIONS

Yes, there's more to know. There's much, much more, given the perpetual development of this technology. And we have yet to get up to date with the old news.

In these final two sections of the chapter, we will generally examine the disposition of additional pages *in a server*—how they are hierarchically arranged in directories. Computational logic trees are very logical in a hierarchical sort of way, with a flowchart configuration holding information and guiding its flow up and down the binary and treelike structures with branches further branching, and then still again further branching. This treelike way of organizing information is often used to structure written prose, and for good reason—it makes it easier for us to process the information.

When we designed David's most recent home page in the previous chapter, we placed the old and the new Web sites in a branching fashion. It's typical to structure the world and our thoughts about it in this fashion. (If you recall, I also explained by way of a flowchart how David's files were connected.) Understand, therefore, that computational machines, computers, and in particular, servers where we store our information are very hierarchical. Consequently, we must understand how that hierarchy works, especially the basic conventions of the codes. (I am not just referring to programming here but to the simple codes and tags that we call HTML, hypertext markup language.)

Disposition of Additional Pages in a Server

In placing the files into one directory in the server, we left much unsaid and not understood. What remains is a more complete understanding of directories and subdirectories and the logic of Web trees and how we can use them for our convenience. Placing all our files into one directory can create a mess of confusion in the long run. There may very well be a point in time when you have so many files that you have to subdivide them just as you do on the desktop of your computer or in your hard disk, with files in folders that in turn may be placed into folders. As a general rule it is considered best—given conventional wisdom—not to go in a server more than three directories deep, starting with your directory, and to keep the names of the directories as brief as possible. If not, then the URLs (with, in this case, the university's directories and your directories and files together) will be exceptionally long. Here is such an example:

```
http://www.uta.edu/english/A/Applications/Undergraduate/
1997/Appli4.html
```

What we are going to take a further look at in this section are some of the basic conventions of setting up directories and getting into them (both of which are easy) and much more about relative paths (which can be easy). Again, instead of discussing and explaining UNIX commands, I am going to insist on the simplicity of using FTP software. All the changes you will want to make at the location in the server where you have your account can be made simply with software.

Arranged Propositionally/Hierarchically: In Directories, Subdirectories, and Sub-Subdirectories, and Files

Let's begin with the example of the text files and graphic files that David (and you) loaded into a university server account. Remember that David first placed the files altogether into a single folder on his desktop (Figure 59), which automatically arranged them alphabetically. Then he transferred these into his student account in a server (Figures 54–58), which was designated by the system operator to be *dmv*, the name of David's directory in the Web tree ../*english/student/dmv/*.

Before starting, let's recall that:

- *text files* have the suffix *.html* or *.htm*
- *graphic files* generally have *jpg* or *gif*
- *directories* have no suffixes at all

What we will do first is look at some conventions of setting up directories and maneuvering our way in a server from one to the next. As an example for establishing directories, we will reconfigure David's files.

If David has to use folders on his desktop and his hard disk so as to organize all of his files, he (and you) will eventually have to do the same in the server. If so, then, what categories should be employed to divide the files? They are fairly commonsensical. Looking at David's files (Figure 59), we should be able to see that there are at least three logical groupings:

- *graphic* files
- *text* files, which are further divided into
- David-*numbered* and David-*alphabetized* files

Since it is a convention to simplify, we will create two new directories for David's files in the server by dividing them into *text* and *graphic* directories and by labeling them as *txfls* and *grffls*, or whatever labels are suitable. If we had done this before we transferred the files to the server, we could easily have grouped them in two folders on the desktop and then sent them to the server. But since files naturally evolve and accumulate and eventually a bundle of them find themselves already in the server, it's good to know how to reconfigure them into these two directories (or whatever number might eventually be necessary).

One other note: David is going to keep his hub/core file, *index.html*, separate from the other files. So what he will have in the directory *dmv* is the hub

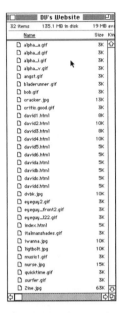

FIGURE 59

file, *index.html,* and the two new directories, *txfls* and *grffls.* Later, David may have to place the hub file into the text directory, especially if he creates a new hub file. Why? Because of the conflict in having two *index.html* files in the same directory, which is not possible. (There are further conventions for getting around this particular problem, but why keep adding more and more to your list of things to know?)

Now we will return to Fetch so that we can create new directories. I am going to suggest how this might be done in one way, but go on to tell you how to do it in the easiest way. What many people do, as I suggested earlier, is to keep all their Web files in a folder in their hard disk. If you do this you will always have copies. David keeps such a folder. Therefore, what he does to make the changes he wants is either to get online on one of the computers in a university computer lab (in this case he would have brought his files with him on a floppy disk) or to dial in from home to his ISP. Once connected, he then opens Fetch and FTPs, as before, into the address that I gave: *cwis.uta.edu.* (As before, you will have your own server address to FTP into.) David then gets connected to the *english* [sic] directory, where he once again finds the directory *student* (Figure 60) and double clicks to open it. Once inside, he finds his directory *dmv,* where all of his files, both text and graphic, are to be found (Figure 61).

Normally, he would not touch these files but simply transfer one or two or more revisions of old files that would rewrite over the old ones or transfer

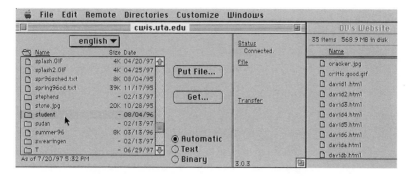

FIGURE 60

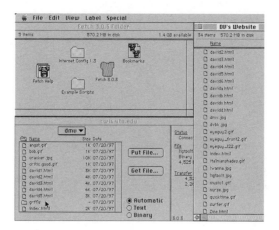

FIGURE 61

altogether new ones; but since he is going to create new directories and generally rearrange everything—his is going to be a major structural revision—he knows that the simplest thing to do is to delete the directory *dmv* and start over. He does this by clicking once on *dmv* and then goes to the menu, selects Remote and pulls it down to Delete Directories and Files. He gets a dialogue box asking him if he really wants to do this, and he clicks Yes. Then the directory and files are wiped out. When this is done he creates a new directory again calling it *dmv*. This is done through the menu item Remote. Once this is created and he has set reading and writing permissions, he begins transferring separately the two folders on his floppy or hard disk, named *txfls* and *grffls*, respectively, that will become new directories with files and then the hub file, *index.html*. This transferring is done, as before, through the Put command (Figures 62–64).

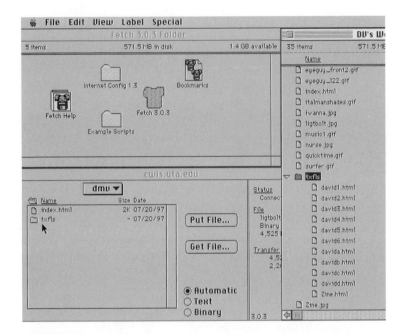

FIGURE 62

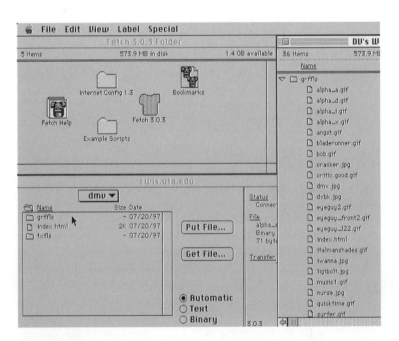

FIGURE 63

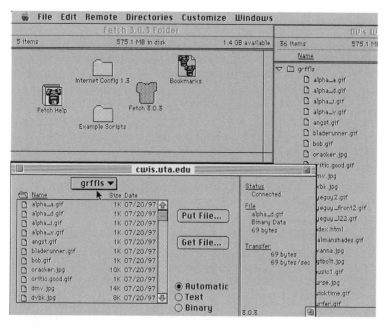

FIGURE 64

Comment

There is a much easier way for David and you to transfer all this, if you have a MAC and operating system 7.5+. All that David has to do is drag and drop the two folders and the hub file from his hard disk into the space in Fetch where they all will reside. He just sits back then and watches how everything is automatically transferred for him! In no time at all, David has a new directory with his hub file and two new subdirectories in it.

Revising URLs

The repositioning of files from one directory to another causes many of the URLs on an entire Web page and associated Web pages to be no longer compatible with the placement (in terms of levels and directories) of the files in the server. This problem exists even if the URLs are in relative paths. Not going back and correcting the URLs would be like moving and not notifying the telephone company, much less your family and friends. If the URLs are not corrected, people browsing the WWW and wanting to call you will not be able to find or read your files. Their call will go to the old directory and not find the file there.

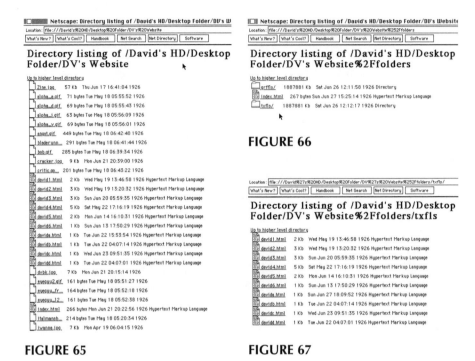

FIGURE 65   **FIGURE 67**

Therefore, let's look in greater detail at the conventions for constructing URLs in *relative* paths. And in surveying the conventions let's take some of the URLs from David's files since they would have to be redone anyway, now that they are in three separate directories, one directory, and two subdirectories, which would look like this:

/dmv/
index.html

/txfls/   /grffls/
files.html   files.jpg, files.gif

Remember that the hub file, *index.html,* is the only file of its kind in the directory */dmv/* along with the two subdirectories.

There's another way to see these logical relationships. Remember that David originally placed all of his single files together—both text and graphic—into a folder on his desktop and then later, in an attempt to organize them as they grew in number, he created two more folders within his first folder and separated out the text and graphic files accordingly into what were subfolders. With that remembered, let's now drag and drop that big folder (pretending it to be a directory) onto Netscape. When done, we will see all the files in a single Directory (Figure 65) just as they will appear through Netscape after the files are all transferred to a server. Now if we take the folder with its two subfolders in it (pretending them to be subdirectories) and drag and drop the folder onto Netscape, we will see what the hub file and the two subdirectories will look like (Figure 66) through Netscape when in a server. If we click on one of the subdirectories, say, the *text* subdirectory, we will get all the text files (Figure 67). This should be getting a little more clear by now.

Revising by Way of Conventions

As promised, let's look more systematically now at the conventions for constructing URLs in *relative* paths. The URL in its absolute form for David's hub file will remain the same: *http://www.univofX.edu/english/student/dmv/*. By convention the directory */dmv/* will automatically open the hub file, *index.html.* (We've explained this point before.) David's hub file, however, has a text and a graphic file in it that must be updated since he moved them to subdirectories. Just about all the files in David's subdirectories will also have to be re-done, which means that subdirectories need to follow sequentially in a URL in this manner */dmv/txfls/* or */dmv/grffls/*. Sounds complicated, right? It can be. But if you notice that all we have done is add a new directory in the sequence, it is not that complicated. And if you understand the following conventions, and think of them as a paradigm, you should not get lost in the process of revising. Think of five possibilities for writing relative (or absolute) path names (URLs):

1. Page (or file) in same directory
2. Page in subdirectory
3. Page in subdirectory relative to another subdirectory (or moving *up* to a directory that shares at least two subdirectories, with one wanting to access a file in the other)
4. Page in another (top level) directory
5. Page elsewhere—in another server on the WWW

(The third one is strange, but it will become more understandable as we proceed, for I will pick it up from time to time by necessity since David has constructed the two subdirectories, thereby forcing me to explain the consequences of his actions.)

The first of these (page in same directory) needs little explanation, for we have been using it throughout our files. It is used when the file to be accessed is in the same directory, so it is tagged as `<A HREF="file.html">`. Prior to David's restructuring his files into subdirectories, all the files were in this relative path form:

```
Relative path:    <A HREF="david1.html">My First Home Page</A>
Absolute path:    <A HREF="http://www.univofX.edu/english/
                  student/dmv/david1.html">My First Home
                  Page</A>
```

The second of these (page in subdirectory) comes in handy now that David has created subdirectories; it is written as <A HREF="subdir/file.html">.

```
Relative path:    <A HREF="txfls/david1.html">My First Home
                  Page</A>
Absolute path:    <A HREF="http://www.univofX.edu/english/
                  student/dmv/txfls/david1.html">My First Home
                  Page</A>
```

Notice that the tag here in its relative form is differentiated by way of *not* having a back slash </> before the URL.

The third of these (page in subdirectory relative to another subdirectory) comes in handy now that David has created subdirectories that are placed in the same directory */dmv/*. Prior to creating subdirectories, David correctly wrote the URL as "tatTWO.jpg." He now has to rewrite the URL so that it can *cross access* what it needs to upload a complete page from the subdirectory for texts, *../txfls/*, which needs a graphic file, to the relative subdirectory for graphic files, *../grffls/*, which has the graphic file, "tatTWO.jpg." Therefore, the rewrite of the URL in *davidc.html* would be:

```
Relative path:    <IMG BORDER=1 SRC="../grffls/tatTWO.jpg">
Absolute path:    <IMG BORDER=1 SRC="www.univofX.edu/english/
                  student/dmv/grffls/tatTWO.jpg">
```

Notice that the tag here is differentiated by way of a *partial ellipsis* and *slash*, <../>. (We will spend some more time on this as we continue.)

The fourth of these (page in another directory) can be illustrated with David's link on his new home page to the collaborative 'Zine; it's written as <A HREF="/directory/file.html">, but can be extended with additional directories as <A HREF="directory/sub-directory/file.html">.

```
Relative path:    <A HREF="/comm/pubs/Zine-Ith/">'Zine-Ith</A>
Absolute path:    <A HREF="http://www.univofX.edu/comm/pubs/
                  Zine-Ith/">'Zine-Ith</A>
```

Notice that the tag here is differentiated by having a *slash* </> *in front* of the directory. This URL reads that the directory is *not* for the English department but the Communications department's publications, one of which is the subdirectory 'Zine, which has a hub file of its own.

So as you can see, you have a choice of either keeping all your files in *one* directory or breaking them up into separate, subdirectories. If the former, then the URLs are simple; if the latter, they can be difficult. You may be thinking, "This is too difficult and I don't need to worry about all this stuff because I will not have so many files that I will have to parcel them out into directories." Well, don't fool yourself! As time and your confidence progress, you will need to divide up your allocated space in the server and you will catch on to what really only appears to be difficult when fairly easy. If you can divide things on your desktop, you can take a step up to dividing them in a server.

For some additional examples, let's take the hub file and rework it and some text and graphic files from *david-alphabetized* and *david-numbered*, one from each of these new and old files, and rework them so that they will be revised to work with the new subdirectories. (These will only be examples of what would have to be done to all the files if they were to work properly.) In doing these revisions/corrections, let's also illustrate the relative paths of subdirectories relative to each other (number 3 of the above paradigm).

If you recall, the contents of the hub file, *index.html*, is very brief. (See Figure 46, Chapter 7.) There is one line that has a graphic file (*dvbk.jpg*), which, when clicked, activates the URL for the text file (*davida.html*) to go to the first page of the new home page:

```
<A HREF="davida.html"><IMG BORDER=0 SRC="dvbk.jpg"
alt="enter here"></A>
```

To revise this string so that it will be in concert with David's restructuring of his directories, David must correct it—as indicated in boldface—to read as follows:

```
<A HREF="../txfls/davida.html"><IMG BORDER=0
SRC="../grffls/dvbk.jpg" alt="enter here"></A>
```

What are the differences here? Only the additions of **../txfls/** and **../grffls/**. But what additions these are in the light of the consequences of not having them in the URL.

Once the hub file is corrected so that all its contents can be accessed, we then need to correct its target file *davida.html*, which has a number of text files with URLs that must acknowledge that they are now in subdirectories. Originally, they were tagged as:

```
my <A HREF="david1.html">first home page</A>
my <A HREF="david2.html">revised home page</A>
a <A HREF="david3.html">pictographic essay</A>
```

```
my <A HREF="david4.html">multimedia home page</A>
the <A HREF="david5.html">film club page</A>
the <A HREF="david6.html">jazz page</A>
```

These will have to be retagged as:

```
my <A HREF="../txfls/david1.html">first home page</A>
my <A HREF="../txfls/david2.html">revised home page</A>
a <A HREF="../txfls/david3.html">pictographic essay</A>
my <A HREF="../txfls/david4.html">multimedia home page</A>
the <A HREF="../txfls/david5.html">film club page</A>
the <A HREF="../txfls/david6.html">jazz page</A>
```

A parallel group of graphic files also will have to be revised. In David's pictographic essay, *david3.html,* he introduces himself with alphabetic blocks:

```
Hello, my name is<P><IMG SRC="alpha_d.gif" WIDTH=30
HEIGHT=30><IMG SRC="alpha_a.gif" WIDTH=30 HEIGHT=30><IMG
SRC="alpha_v.gif" WIDTH=30 HEIGHT=30><IMG SRC="alpha_i.gif"
WIDTH=30 HEIGHT=30><IMG SRC="alpha_d.gif" WIDTH=30
HEIGHT=30>.
```

These will have to be revised thus:

```
Hello, my name is<P><IMG SRC="../grffls/alpha_d.gif"
WIDTH=30 HEIGHT=30><IMG SRC="../grffls/alpha_a.gif" WIDTH=30
HEIGHT=30>
<IMG SRC="../grffls/alpha_v.gif" WIDTH=30 HEIGHT=30>
<IMG SRC="../grffls/alpha_i.gif" WIDTH=30 HEIGHT=30>
<IMG SRC="../grffls/alpha_d.gif" WIDTH=30 HEIGHT=30>
```

▶ 9

Suggestions for Web Writing and for Assessing and Revising Drafts: A Checklist

PREPARATORY COMMENTS

Writing for the World Wide Web

Writing for the Web is a very new craft and art. Our concern with it has arisen in the past three or four years. Within a short period of time, people writing for the Web and commentators on such writing (and designing) have developed some conventions about what information should appear and how it should appear on a viewer's monitor.

Here's a statement to ponder: As in writing for paper, so in writing for monitors. What can this statement possibly mean? I read it and I want to disagree with what I think it says, and yet I want to give assent. Does it mean that writing for paper and a monitor are the same, or does it suggest that there are some similarities? For me, as I have stated throughout directly or indirectly, the answer is no, they are not the same, but sometimes there are similarities. I'm raising this question—as I did in the Introduction—and in passing pondering it again because some of you have already received and practiced from early age the basic conventions of writing on paper, and when you examine the checklist that follows, you will discover that some of those conventions are repeated. However, you will also discover that some conventions are set aside for quite different and contrary ones. If you were to look at other authors' lists of conventions, you would find similar statements in many cases. (How else could it be if I am listing, as I say, what are called "conventions"?) Occasionally, you will also find, however, the opposite said about a particular detail. (How can this be if these are called "conventions"?) My answer is that it's conventional to disagree at times. The basis of the disagreement can be accounted for usually because of the amount of emphasis a writer of *tips and suggestions* might place on the prior conventions of writing for paper and the yet-to-be-"fully" explored ways of writing for electronic environments.

The next chapter is entitled "The Future is the Present." I will talk some about what I mean by that title there; but I can say in reference to the word *conventions,* that I use the word as a *mixture* of the past and the future. When thinking of writing for the World Wide Web, I think in terms of the past (what has been tried and proven to be successful) and of the future (what has yet been tried but will be discovered and become successful and hence conventional). As I suggested in the Introduction, we must be amphibians. We know what our conventional medium of paper is like, and yet we crawl out of it to be in an electronic environment and, as we adapt to our new medium of electricity and pixels, we project what our new conventions of living in this space will be. That we are on the margins and flopping about means that we have at least an intuitive sense of how to survive in our newly found space, and as we learn more and more, we develop conventions for our survival and for those who will follow us.

I have tried to hit a happy balance between ink and pixels. I have tried to communicate the value of being flexible. The technology driving electronic media grows geometrically. Exponentially. Think of the tips and suggestions that I offer, therefore, as only very general, provisional guidelines. As we pile up more and more of the future in our past, be constantly open to revision.

STUDY, STUDY, STUDY THE WORLD WIDE WEB!

Browsers

Differences
Lynx, Netscape, Mosaic, are the lens through which we view what someone has put on the Web. Browsers are different and represent HTML differently. Lynx reads only text and not graphics, whereas Netscape will read both. In some cases, particular browsers that read both text and graphics will not read particular codes such as for a Table. Just because other people are using Netscape, it does not mean that they are using the Netscape designed for

your operating system or that they are using the version you are using. Hence, there can be major differences in what gets represented from monitor to monitor. If at all possible, try to determine what your Web page will look like on a variety of browsers. Look at it on Lynx and you will come to understand the importance of the *ALT=* tag. Look at your page on a variety of browsers that read graphics. These various viewing experiences will teach you more than can be mentioned in this book.

The First Page: General Tips

Title
Make sure you have a Title as part of the HTML tags and that you have a Title on your page that is accurately descriptive of the purpose of your page. The title will in great part be determined by the kind (or genre) of page you have established. If you do not include a title, you will have a title, nonetheless, which will be No Title.

Statement of Purpose
Why this page? Answer this question and be succinct! But avoid saying "The purpose of my Web page is . . . "! The first page should *show* more what it is all about than *tell*.

Shape of Content
Block it out so that it can be easily processed and understood, not just by you, but by your readers. Most sites are expository (i.e., have as their purpose to inform). When you want information, you want it given directly and without complications. Therefore, you yourself, give it that way. (If, however, your genre is an experimental one, which is not at all stressed in this book, then artfully deviate, but remember that this is extremely difficult to do.)

Links
If you have a lot of them on a page, take care to organize them topically and perhaps alphabetically. Also, perhaps you will want to annotate them, especially if you have a lot of them and even type in the URLs so that they, too, will be visible on the page.

Navigational Buttons
Supply and arrange links that will always inform the viewers at a glance where they are in relation to other sections of your Web site and perhaps the relation of your Web site to your institution (department, program, university, business, etc.). If you are using graphical links, be sure to supply *ALT=* tag or simply repeat the navigational scheme as text for users of Lynx.

Signature

Provide a *mailto:* so that people who visit your site can contact you. State when the site was established and last updated. The signature may be at the top or bottom of the page, but is usually at the bottom. The signature should *not* be conspicuous.

Warning Notes

If your site should have particular features that only a particular version of Netscape (PC, Windows, MAC versions) or a special reader or plug-in (RealAudio, QuickTime Video) can display, put a warning note at the beginning of your page. If special software is required, put a link to the site so that it can be downloaded.

In General

Do not write a mystery-novel Web site and, worse, a bad one that never answers the questions Whodunnit? and For What motive?

The First Page: Style Tips

Introducing Yourself

It is remarkable just how common triteness is among newcomers. Often people new to a technology will attempt to be "smart" but come across as being only (not so) "cute." If you wish not to be a "Newbie cliché," avoid announcing: "Well, you have finally made it to God's gift to the WWW," etc. If you insist on doing this kind of thing, we have hope that you will eventually outgrow it; most people eventually do. This phenomenon of "cuteness" seems to be common among adolescent males, not females.

Background Graphics

Avoid these at first. It is a tendency for Newbies (amateurs) to put up a graphic over which it is impossible to read anything at all. Consequently, everything is a loss, and people just click elsewhere. Try to use subtle graphics as background wallpaper or none at all.

Blinking

There is a tag or code for blinking; I've avoided giving it. You can certainly find it, but my advice is to *forget* it, except for once-in-a-life time! It's another sign of a Newbie.

Inline Graphics

Avoid large-K (memory) graphics. (Bandwidth, the amount of information that can pass through a connection, should be taken into consideration.) Try to use GIFs instead of JPEGs, if possible. The former will compress large files into smaller files. Remember that lots of files on a first page can take a long time to load and this can be bothersome to some people who might, therefore, leave and go elsewhere. However, I myself have some first pages that require on an average as much as three to four minutes to load. *You load your page; you take your chances!*

Under Construction 1
Please, for me, don't state that your site is under construction and don't use the available icons to announce this! It is generally understood that . . . all sites are!

Under Construction 2
Please, for me, never construct your site step by step, piece by piece initially *in the server.* It looks terrible when viewed from day to day. Construct your site in your *hard disk* and cross check it on Netscape, revising it as you go. Once your site with all of its files is ready for the public, then FTP your files to your allocated space in the server. (I explain this incrementally in Chapters 7 and 8. See the Index for precise pages.) And after you have transferred your files, continue to work on your Web site but on your hard disk. And then when ready, FTP the new files, etc.

Under Construction 3, or Revision
Work with a repertoire of templates. Once you have templates (preferably in folders) for a number of different occasions, you can easily call them up and work with them by modifying them to suit your revisions.

Also, when in a mode of revising, try to establish the ability to shuttle back and forth from working on your Text Only file (using such programs as NotePad, SimpleText, etc.) and Netscape (or Mosaic, etc.). Remember that you do not need to have Netscape connected online to use it. Simply launch it from your hard drive and stabilize it by clicking on whatever dialogue boxes pop up telling you that Netscape cannot find a socket. Just keep clicking on the Stop graphic at the top right. Once Netscape is stabilized, you can then work on your Text Only files revising them, checking to see if you are coding correctly and how it looks, whether you need to create more or less space between items, increase the width and height of a graphic, etc. Hence you will shuttle from your Text Only document, *to* Netscape, *back to* Text Only for revisions, and *then back to* Netscape to see the revisions, *and so on.*

A typical way of working on a home page or whatever would be to collect your templates, documents/files, and graphics into the *same* appropriately named folder. When you make links among the various files that you yourself are creating, you will construct relative URLs, that is, just the name of the file such as *index.html* or *resume.html* or *crackers.jpg*, etc. (This principle is followed and explained throughout Chapters 4 and 5.) Therefore, when you test a document in Netscape, you will be able to see your graphics and also click on any link that goes to one of your files and see the graphic and read the file. It will be as if your documents/files were virtually in the server and not in your hard disk. You will call up the Text Only files into Netscape by simply going to File and then Open and find the document/file in whatever DOC it is in and click on it. If you are using a MAC with system 7.5+, and Netscape 2+, you will simply drag and drop the document/file onto Netscape and read and see what you have done. It is amazing how fast you can work with this drag and drop routine.

The First and Subsequent Pages: Content

Copyright
Is what you put on your Web site yours, or have you lifted it from someone else, another person's site? If it's not yours, give full citation if it's from a book, and be careful of how much you are using. If it's from a Web page, ask for permission and get it in writing. Not only ask to use something, but also ask how the permissions and acknowledgment statement is to be worded on your Web site.

Study, Study, Study Design

Writing and Designing
The first word of this book's title is "Writing." The word, however, does not mean what it normally means. Writing is closer to *designing* a graphic, closer to composing music, closer to sketching a new (perhaps make-believe) wardrobe for yourself or another; planning the layout of your dream home (or hut, treehouse, space satellite) and decorating the outside and the inside; or doodling, just playing around, whether on paper, a sidewalk, a wall, the sky, or wherever!

Study the Web
To find out what you think is and is not successful in regards to writing (designing), you must study the Web. Listen to your instructor. He or she will guide you through this process of studying the Web. Listen to other instructors and artists and how they talk about looking at a Web site. (Ask for help, and help others.) Search for *web design* (and use similar words) on search engines to find an individual designer's and school's Web sites that discuss the issue and display various techniques on the Web. And as I have suggested in Chapters 3 and 4, look at how people design a page—fill virtual space with pixels—on the Web, but also how they fill space in magazines, on television, films, in CD ROMs and games. Study art and design magazines. (If you cannot afford them like me, go often to a good bookstore

with lots of magazines and flip through the magazines and study them. Study painters, architects, and film directors. Study how people fill space with ink, plaster, oils, glass and iron, grass and trees, clay and bricks; how people conceal and reveal space; how people design windows for both outside and inside views. Study various individual media and multimedia every chance you get. And take risks trying out what you see—a good way to find out what seems to work and does not yet work.

General Writing (Designing)

How to Write
The first word of this book's title is "Writing." The word, however, does not mean what it normally means. (Yes, I am repeating what I said previously.) Writing is closer to designing a graphic, closer to composing music, closer to sketching a new (perhaps make-believe) wardrobe for yourself or another; planning the layout of your dream home (or hut, treehouse, space satellite) and decorating the outside and the inside; or doodling, just playing around whether on paper, a sidewalk, a wall, the sky, your monitor, or wherever.

In general, however, I can say this about writing: Follow the genre and the basic conventions of that genre when you write. (I have suggested several in Chapters 4–6.) Remember that you are in a different medium and that you must write fewer words and include images and sounds (this is multimedia) if technically possible. If you are limited to words, write in the most precise, clipped fashion as possible. There is a real tendency for people not to want to read a lot of words on a monitor. Nevertheless, the Web is a great place to put long essays that can be downloaded and then read on paper. So however you decide to present your material, be sure (again) to follow the basic conventions of writing: Make sure that your prose is mechanically correct, to the point, accurate (be sure to support what you say, and in terms of links, if possible, and be sure that what you cite is worthy of citing as support), and make every attempt to be as cogent as you can when arguing a point.

If you are going to work for a special effect, say, misspelling words, be sure that your reader understands that, in fact, you are conscious of the misspelling and that you are doing it for a particular, acceptable end. In other words, make sure that the misspelling—or whatever the deviation from the norm is—works. If you have not yet developed a sense of how to be effective, study others who seem to be successful at special effects. For the most part, however, play it straight.

Determine Your Audience
It is extremely important that you know precisely for whom you are writing. In one sense, you are writing for everyone who has access to the WWW; in another sense, however, you are writing specifically for those people who

will search you out by way of the powerful search engines on the Web. Once you have determined your audience, you will have a better idea of what needs and does not need to be said on your Web site. But remember: simplify, simplify, simplify. When you have a sense of control over the basic forms of writing (which includes designing a page, etc.), try to find more complicated pages and attempt to imitate them with the purpose of discovering your own sense of "complicated pages."

Shape Your Audience
This is difficult. If you are at a Web site and sense that the person who wrote/designed the site is leading you to see and think in ways that you normally do not, try to figure out how the writer/designer is able to do this. Often it is difficult to determine. Ask your instructor and friends. Study this phenomenon of being manipulated when you see and experience it. (Often when watching a film, you probably have had the experience of being shaped by the director.) Study these occasions and learn from them. And try them on your Web site.

Security and Privacy

Security
Remember to determine permissions (to read and write) when you send files to a server.

Privacy
There is none on the Web. If you attempt to construct privacy, always remember that there are ways around permissions. Don't put anything on the Web that you do not want read by someone else.

Registering your Web sites/URLs
Go to any search engine—whether Yahoo or AltaVista—and you will see instructions for giving your URLs. Remember that whether you register or not, many very powerful search engines enter your university's or ISP's server, read your URL and key terms on your page, and collect and make them all available to anyone who searches for you or any key term that you might use. There is no privacy!

HTML Editors

Help or Hazard?
The bad news: The students whom I have known to use them tend to get in trouble. Besides, HTML Editors are still very limited in what they can do, and even if they can do some commands, they perform them in very mechanical,

stilted ways. It's always a dead giveaway that you have used an editor. If you want that "give away" as part of your image (Web persona), then go for it. The good news is that software developers of HTML editors are beginning to develop better ones. (See Appendix A for freeware and shareware editors.) But a more serious problem is that each HTML Editor uses rather unconventional code for its templates, making it exceptionally difficult for anyone— novice or professional—to edit or revise the code. Use them if you must, but beware of them.

Troubleshooting

Nothing Appears on the Monitor

This can drive you nuts, right? Usually, when this happens, there is a coding error in the tag for Title (i.e., the title that will appear at the top of Netscape), so you should check this out carefully. Sometimes the error will be as simple as not including the `</>` in `</TITLE>`. Or as simple as not closing the angled brackets. Also, sometimes other major sections such as Body are miscoded. As Dave Rieder says, you cannot get hip with your tag names by, instead of typing `<BODY>`, putting in `<BOD>`. It will just *not* work in this case!

If you have checked everything and can find nothing wrong, the next step would be to go to a Weblint site and have the program there check your page to see what might be wrong. But a caveat: Weblint will often find things wrong with your page that are not really wrong. For example, it might point out that you do not have `</P>` at the end of paragraphs. Such a tag is not necessary. But Weblint will find your serious errors. Here is the URL for the Weblint home page: http://www.cre.canon.co.uk/~neilb/weblint/index.html. Here you can find the gateways (sites) to visit and check your coding. If by chance this URL is no longer good, you will find the update at the Web site for this book. Or you can go to AltaVista search engine and search for Weblint. The same holds for the URLs printed here.)

Garbage Appears on the Monitor

When this happens, most likely you did not *save* the file as Text Only or ascii. What is showing as garbage are all the codes used by the word-processing program to format your pages. Remember, therefore, that you need to strip these codes and you do that by saving as Text Only. It's simple to fix this problem.

Tags/Codes Don't Work

From this point on, it might appear superfluous to help you with these problems since you can always go to Weblint. But I would argue that I would want to know—you should want to know—precisely what went wrong and where and would want to discover it myself, using Weblint only as a last resort.

The problem is one of two kinds: either you did not code correctly or you did not nest your tags correctly. *To check on the incorrect codes,* just go through your tags and make sure that you did not leave out necessary units like < >. Check to see if you both opened and closed a string of codes with < and >. Often this mistake will show on your monitor. Also check to see if you left out a slash mark </>. If you tagged a title to be in Bold <B> and then the rest of your text or much of it is in Bold, you obviously left out the slash in the appropriate place where the Bold text is to stop. Just insert </B>. If your Tables are not working as you want them to, especially check the <TR> and <TD> codes. And remember that you must close these also with </> marks. *Either* print out your coded page and mark with a pencil the beginning of a tag and the closing of a tag in order to see if you have opened and closed them properly *or* point with your fingers on the monitor to the opening and closing of tags. As you gain more experience you will make fewer mistakes. Once you have checked the codes, *check whether everything is nested correctly.* First look at the macrolevel to see if you have nested and packaged items like <HTML>, <HEAD>, <TITLE>, and <BODY> correctly; then check the microlevel.

Links Don't Work

There are a number of things that could be incorrectly tagged. Check to see if the URL is accurate and correctly spelled in its entirety, including whether or not you have matching lower- and uppercase letters (not capitalized or CAPITALIZED) for the directory and file names. For example, if you coded the file name as *index.html*, but the file in the server is *INDEX.HTML,* you will get nothing but an error message.

Then look to see if you have spelled out the tags surrounding the URL correctly. Make sure you have typed <A HREF=> in this manner and with a space between the A and the H. Make sure there are double quotes at the beginning and end of the URL. Make sure that you anchored the site you want visited with a name and a closing tag </A>. If you do not have some of these tags, the hotlink will run continuously into line after line until it gets anchored.

Make sure that when you transferred the file by way of Fetch or similar software to your server, you wrote writing and reading permissions. Just because the file has been transferred does not mean that it can then be read. Usually, if the file is in the server and you have not given even private reading permission, you will get an error message saying that there is a problem with permissions.

Graphics Don't Load

There could be, with this problem as well, any number of reasons. For example, sometimes graphics will not load on Netscape because you have run out of memory to load them or have inadvertently turned off the loading of graphics. Assuming that these are not the source of the problem, check to see if the same problems listed in reference to links are the problems with the graphic file. For example, the upper-/lowercase problem with the names of the files or the permission problem not being set for a public reading. It is possible also that your JPEG or GIF is damaged and has to be redone.

If all else fails, try Weblint!

▶ 10

The Future is the Present: From HTML (Hypertext) to Multimedia

Beyond the Basics
   Netscape Frames
   Acrobat
   GifAnimations
   Java Applets
   Virtual Reality Modeling Language (VRML)
   Multimedia
      Netscape Plug-Ins
      Audio
      Video
      Macromedia Flash
      Shockwave

BEYOND THE BASICS

What does the title of this chapter suggest? Why didn't I write, "The Future is Now"? One notion that the chapter title should suggest is the terrible *time lag* that exists between the technology we actually now have and use and the technology that we would have and use if we could only afford it or somehow or other could get access to through our various public institutions. Many of us would like to engage in the virtual task of making "movies," 3-D movies. To be sure, the technology is *there*. But where? I see it in catalogs and in computer stores. But in most cases, it's out of "our" reach. It is, in a phrase,

191

extremely expensive. But like all things related to computers, prices will eventually come down, and for some of us the future-present will be affordable. Or we can hope that our colleges or universities will purchase the future-present, making it accessible to "us."

There is one other thing that I want to say about the future and in particular about out-of-reach software, and that is throughout this book—as stated in the Preface—I have worked with the assumption that because you are most likely at a college or university, you at least have access to an online connection and have the use of Netscape. I have tried to remind you, however, that many people may have access only to the text browser Lynx. Therefore, I have insisted that when you code a page and design it for Netscape, you should include the ALT=" . . . " tag. This code is good, let us understand, not only because people might be limited to Lynx but good also because the sight impaired might have the technology that virtually reads aloud the message embedded in the ALT tag.

My assumptions, therefore, have all been predicated on having access of some kind or other. Having the technology! They are also predicated on your eventually having the technology (software and hardware) that I discuss in this chapter and that it would be good for you now to start learning not only what the basics presently are but also to start hearing about what the present-day basics will have become. Otherwise, there would be no reason for my writing this book. In terms of technology and communication, we appear to live on the cusp of what will be possible.

Three years ago (upon this writing, August, 1996), I did not have access at all; two years ago, I had access to Lynx; a year ago, I got personal access to Netscape; two months ago, I got access to Netscape in my office at the university. (But I am only one of five people in my department who has access. In another year, all of us who want access will have it.) Most of my first book, *CyberReader*, was done using Lynx. At present, I do not have direct access to some of the technology that I am going to discuss in this final chapter because the technology that I have (at home or at work) has not been upgraded enough (e.g., with enough RAM, cache, megahertz).

Still more wants to be said: I . . . "we" (a relatively small group of us) may live in the present-future but not in the present-past. And though we may have only Lynx, there is a high enough probability, as I have indicated, that we will eventually have access and use of some of the best technologies and, in particular, browsers. There are others, however, who will live perpetually in the present-past, *perpetually* because they have no hope of ever getting to use this technology as a means of communicating with others. There are varying degrees of being *out of reach* in terms of technology. Let us not forget any of these widely diverse differences and let us do what we can to improve the equal distribution of this technology.

With all that said as a reminder, let's turn now to the future-present by way of a few advances and new tools that are greatly changing the Web—

and our lives, whether or not we have access. HTML is one thing; what's being developed now, however, is quite another. In introducing very briefly a select number of advances,

- I will describe the purpose of the technology, what it does, and how its language might differ from HTML
- I will provide some URLs to Web sites, from which you can download free viewers or players
- I will suggest Web sites that you can visit to use the viewers and thereby see virtually what each new technology has made possible.

I think that in most cases you will be amazed. And after viewing these few sites, remember that we have just *begun* to enter into whatever this thing called the Web is becoming. Let's begin with the familiar, which is the latest version (during most of this writing) of Netscape.

Netscape/Frames

The technology of building Frames, though perhaps not belonging here, is nonetheless included as a transitional conceptual and technological starting point. Netscape Navigator 2.0 (I am presently using the Mac version 2.01) is a huge leap from earlier versions, for it includes some new HTML tags that give us the capability of constructing Frames, which are quite different from Tables, and it includes the capability of something called "plug-ins," which I will describe in a separate section. (As I write this chapter, there was an announcement from Netscape this morning, August, 12, 1996, that Navigator 3.07b is ready for downloading.) The URL for Netscape is *http://home.netscape.com*. From this site, you should be able to find a number of sites such as those for downloading Netscape software. Remember the browser is free to students enrolled in courses and to educators. (As I proofread this book, Navigator 4.01 is ready for downloading!)

What is interesting about Frames is that they allow for both the *division* and the *concentration* of information on a single monitor. The idea of framing several completely different scenes, or screens, of events within one large frame has been around, although in crude form, for a very long time. It has been used in films and called a split screen. However, it is new to and more innovative in format on television and the Web. (No doubt, you have seen at the end of a television program how the screen splits into two frames, with a promo going on the left side and the credits for the previous show being shown on the right.) The appearance of frames on television and on the Web is due to the development of new software programs, which allow for the display of several files or Web sites—say, two to four—simultaneously.

More specifically, how does this work? When we are in a non-Framed page and we click on a link, we go to another completely new page. The first disappears; the second appears. Or if we target a second window to open when we click on a link, we have two windows open but still one per frame. However, when we enter a site that is tagged with Frames, we enter a space with multiple sites/files. For example, it is possible to have in one frame a table of contents with each chapter heading as a link, which you could activate, and have the particular chapter appear in an adjoining frame; and it is likewise possible to have in that chapter numbers for endnotes as links, which you could activate and have the notes appear in the third frame. All three files/Frames—the table of contents, the single chapter, and the single endnote—would be simultaneously present on your monitor. If you want four Frames, that's possible, for example, the book's logo, but the number can be divided just so many times without losing the effectiveness of such a new technology.

Since Frames on Netscape 2.0+ is done with tags, let's take a brief look at how they work. After giving an example, I will give you the URL to Netscape's Web site for Frames so that you can learn more as well as a few sites to visit for additional examples.

I'm going to construct a four-screen frame, with one two screens on the left and two on the right. Those on the left will respectively show a table of contents and a logo; those on the right will show a Chapter 1 and an endnote. It will be necessary, consequently, to create five files, one for the Frame and four for the contents of the four frames with the Frame.

The Frame File: The tag for a frame is `<FRAMESET>`, which takes the place of the body tag `<BODY>`. (Understand that if you place the tag `<BODY>` before the tag for Frames, the coding for Frames will be ignored by the browser!) Think of the tag `<FRAMESET>` as establishing the conditions for a container with various possible subcontainers, in which you will target particular contents. The tag `<FRAMESET>`, like the tag for Tables, has two features, which determine columns `<COLS>` and rows `<ROWS>`.

At this point the issue can get complicated. To ease matters some, I am going to simplify the possibilities and focus on one way of establishing Frames. (The full, more complicated set of possibilities you can review later at the Netscape Web page for making Frames.) Thus, in describing how columns and rows in Frames work, I will stick exclusively with one approach—referred to as "value%" or "simple percentage value"—to what is called "relative scaling values," which determines the number and size of columns and rows. (The particular approach is considered to be a "safe" approach in that it can avoid problems in how the Frame gets represented.) "Value%" works in terms of dividing up percentages and separating them with commas `<,>`. When establishing the Frame as `<FRAMESET>`, we will need to establish the *columns,* which, following my intended Frame page, will look like and take on these values: `<FRAMESET COLS="33%,66%">`; and establish the *rows,* which will each be `<FRAMESET ROWS="75%,25%">`.

Within each of the <FRAMESET> tags for rows, you will find the tag <FRAME>. Recall that I said it will be necessary to have four files for contents. To establish these within the Frame source page, we will have to use the tag <FRAME> and add the source and the target name. Hence, for the table of contents file, we write under the first <FRAMESET ROWS> tag the following source and target name: <FRAME SRC="toc.html" NAME="toc">. Then it will be necessary to make a file named toc.html, which will have in it the table of contents. This is done with each of the remaining three files, one more that will go under the row to the left; two for the row to the right. When done, the Frame source page will be coded as follows:

```
<HTML>
<HEAD>
<TITLE>A Sample Frames Page</>TITLE>
</>HEAD>
<FRAMESET COLS="33%,66%">
        <FRAMESET ROWS="75%,25%">
                <FRAME SRC="toc.html" NAME="toc">
                <FRAME SRC="logo.html" NAME="logo">
        </>FRAMESET>
        <FRAMESET ROWS="75%,25%">
                <FRAME SRC="chapters.html" NAME="chapters">
                <FRAME SRC="notes.html" NAME="notes">
        </>FRAMESET>
</>FRAMESET>
</>HTML>
```

When all of the four content files are made and properly linked with target names, the framed page will still be only partially done (Fig. 68). What remains? The establishment of links across these four files and in some cases target links with files, say, the endnote file. (We have previously covered how to establish links in Chapters 2 through 4, so there's no reason to extend this example any further.)

For additional information on Frames, visit *http://home.netscape.com/assist/net_sites/frames.html.* I am not going to give you a list of frame other than to tell you to visit one of the most remarkable sites—in Frames—that I have ever visited: *http://www.mkzdk.org.* As you surf, you will find more than enough sites constructed in Frames; such sites are everywhere now.

Acrobat

The purpose of Acrobat (with all of its different programs, which are developed by Adobe, *http://www.adobe.com*) is simple: to take something that has

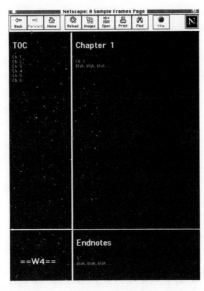

FIGURE 68

been developed on desktop publishing programs, or similar programs, for paper and to translate it as a document in a standard file format (without HTML) for the Web. This does not mean, however, that the designer of a Web page would have to intend to develop a design for paper; instead, what is meant is that when using Acrobat, the results of the technology for developing a file/page for paper is almost perfectly the same for the Web. What we see printed on paper, in other words, is what we will see projected on our screens, as if we had taken a picture of it.

Here's a reverse example of what I am talking about: When I was writing this book and developing example sites, I needed pictures of what the sites looked like on my monitor so that those *pictures* could be included in the book. All I had to do, since I am using a Mac, is to make a picture of the page by striking Shift+Command+3 and a standard *pic.file* was created, which I then turned in with my manuscript. (On other operating systems, all you have to do is strike the picture key.)

Acrobat (which is really a collection of different programs) is often referred to as the technology that produces "electronic paper." Adobe, the company that developed Acrobat, has produced programs for both print on paper and for electronic media. Whereas the program PageMaker is for producing files that can be printed onto paper, Acrobat is for taking those Page-Maker files or other files, created by other means, and imaging them as a Web page to be uploaded on a monitor.

Acrobat (with its various programs) has become more and more sophisticated in mimicking Web sites. It can include links and sound and audio files. It can develop multimedia pages. It can highly compress files which, if done by way of HTML, would be very large and take a long time to load from the Web onto your hard disk drive.

Now here's the downside for most of us. The various programs are expensive. And then don't forget that you *either* would have to develop a page, or what would be your Web page, on a sophisticated word-processing program or on a desktop publishing program such as Adobe's PageMaker or on QuarkExpress and be good at using those programs to design layout, etc.; *or* you would have to use some sort of program that would allow you to design a page, and then translate it through Acrobat into files viewable on the Web. Remember that when you use Acrobat you are not using HTML, which was your former way of establishing and designing a page. So you will have to have some means—hence, I refer to the necessity of using PageMaker, etc.—of developing a site. Not having to use HTML, to be sure, can be liberating, because HTML is not the technology for designing a page. But it's something that all of us can use and do not have to purchase. And it's something that does not automatically require great artistic skill as Acrobat would require.

The programs involved, at present, are Acrobat Exchange, which includes Acrobat Exchange, Acrobat PDF Writer, Acrobat Reader, and Adobe Type Manager; the Pro version of Exchange also includes Acrobat Distiller, which converts documents into what are called *portable document format* (PDF) files. There is also Acrobat Capture, which allows for the conversion of paper into documents viewable on the WWW. It would be possible to work with Acrobat without the latter program, for the Pro version, with Writer and Distiller, will allow you to convert your electronic work into files and place them on the Web. But again, at present it's an expensive way to go, when you consider all the other technology that you need to even get to the point of deciding whether you want to go with Adobe's Acrobat or some other company's approach such as Netscape's or Java's. As I have suggested, however, this decision already may be in the making for us since these different companies are now indicating that they are willing to work closer together in a collaborative manner than solely in a competitive manner against each other. (Upon my writing this chapter, Adobe has announced that it is offering to its registered Acrobat Reader users a copy of Acrobat Pro 2.01 for $99.00, which is a considerable markdown. And it gets better: Adobe will provide a free upgrade to Adobe Acrobat 3.0. By the time this book appears this offer will have passed, but offers of this kind appear from time to time.)

If the technology you have has enough speed (i.e., a Pentium chip or a PowerMac), you can visit the Adobe site, register with them, and then download free of charge the Acrobat Reader: *http://www.adobe.com/Software/Acrobat.* The reader will allow you to view on your monitor *portable document format files,* which means you can see what Acrobat produces, though you will not be able with this program to produce such files. The Reader is available for Windows and Mac and other platforms. You will receive some help notes with it. When you open the program you will be given the opportunity to view Page-only (which is what it says it is.), Bookmarks (which is like Frames), or Thumbnails (small representations of larger ones that are available). In many ways when you're reading, it's like looking at supersophisticated microfilm or microfiche that you have perhaps used in your library. You can find sites to visit from the Adobe HP: *http://www.adobe.com*, but be sure to visit the *New York TimesFax* site: *http://nytimesfax.com*.

GifAnimations

GIFs that are animated are fairly easy to construct. I place this relatively new technology here transitionally between Acrobat and Applets because GIFs as graphics are static except for when they are *laced* or fully animated. (Laced GIFs are animated in that the graphic is designed so that it can change from one to several different colors in sequence.) In the next section, when I discuss Applets, we will see a greater degree of animation. There will be, for the most part, more and more animation as we proceed here.

GifAnimation works on the principle of several GIF files being synchronized into motion. No doubt, you have seen what are called "flip books," which are sheets of animations advancing an image and thereby creating the illusion of movement. GifAnimation works on the same principle. The best way to see GifAnimation is virtually to see it in operation. So I would suggest that you go to a few sites in order to see them. However, you really need Netscape Navigator 2+; without it, the GIFs just look like flat and still graphics.

Part of Netscape Navigator's logo is a navigator's wheel. There's a Gif-Animation of that wheel that virtually turns when placed on a page. There is one of a dog running across a page, one of the earth turning, a compass turning; and the list goes on. You can see a number of these GIFs—at least at this point in time—in action at *http://www.wam.umd.edu/~davewang/animated/animated.html*. It's like walking into a pet store with a bunch of creatures running around and bouncing off the wall! The very best site that I have found, which is done in Frames, is Royal E. Frazier's "First Internet Gallery of GIF Animation" at *http://member.aol.com/royalef/galframe.htm*. Be prepared to spend a lot of time at, and to return many times to this site.

Caveat

Visiting these sites is very dangerous because you are going to want to download these GifAnimations. Remember unless you get written permission from the owner, or unless there is a note that explicitly says you may take them—that they are in the public domain—don't touch them! As you move through and take a look at Frazier's collection of sites you will see on a few occasions some GIFs that you can legally download and use on your own site. For example, if you go to "Animated Pages! The MicroMovie Mini-Multiplex," you will find about a hundred GifAnimations that are placed in the public domain which you can therefore download. Visit *http://www. teleport.com/~cooler/MMMM/index.html.*

For those of you who want to build your own GifAnimations, you will want to download the freeware that allows you to do just that. The Gif Construction Set for Windows can be found, as shareware, at *http://www. mindworkshop. com/alchemy/alchemy.html* and at *http://pandasw.com/gifcon.htm.* The "GifBuilder 0.4" for Mac, by Yves Piguet, is at *http://iawww.epfl.ch/Staff/ Yves.Piguet/clip2gif-home/GifBuilder.html.* At these sites, you will find explanations for how to construct animations. You might also read John Warnock's Adobe tutorial on animations: *http://www.adobe.com/studio/tipstechniques/ GIFanimation/main.html.*

Java Applets

Sun Microsystem's Java (*http://java.sun.com*) has been doing the complete opposite of what Adobe is doing. While Acrobat fixes things and, for its survival, is including animation with a growing degree, Java's initial and continued intent has been to bring things to life by way of animation. (Java goes way beyond the efforts of those people designing GifAnimation.) Java is the name of the programming language, which should not be confused with HTML. Though Acrobat and Java are still different, there's every reason to believe that Adobe and Sun's respective work will become more compatible, if in no other way than through a common browser with necessary plug-ins (See section on plug-ins, this chapter). Acrobat and Java both have their separate, incompatible viewers, but both can be seen in some cases by way of Netscape 2+ and definitely Netscape 3+.

Java is not an easy language to learn. However, to make Java, which is the name of the programming language, less seemingly impossible, Sun Microsystem and Java-teers are at present in the process of making Java more available to prospective users. I did not say more "user-friendly"; again, the programming language is very difficult. I don't mean to scare you away from attempting to learn it; I simply want you to understand it's not HTML, which is fairly simple. By more available, I mean making "applets" themselves available in limited quantity as shareware and I assume eventually for sale.

Let's restart with precisely the question: What is Java and now, more importantly, applets? What are their purposes? The definitions I have read have boggled my mind and may boggle yours. So let's just say (again) that Java is a programming language and that an *applet* (created with Java) is a mini-packaged program that is downloaded onto a hard disk and then written into the HTML code that activates the applet, gives the assigned parameters, and plays it on a Web site.

An applet is not a self-contained program that is a simple GifAnimation graphic and that can be downloaded as you would an image. A Java Applet is composed of several files: Java class file, Java source code, and Data files. You can begin to see what these various files and their purposes are when you visit the Java site: *http://java.sun.com*. While there you should download a copy of the Java Developers Kit (JDK), which is available for both Mac and Windows. In the Applet Viewer, which comes with the JDK, you will be able, as its name states, to view applets or you supposedly can view them locally on Navigator 2.0+, which has not been the case for me or for many other people like me. (By viewing them *locally*, I mean being able from a desktop to drag and drop the Java class file onto Netscape and see the applet in animation.) Navigator 3.7b should work. But the main thing is that the applets do work on the Viewer, and this is all that's necessary now to see them at work.

I want to take you through a few steps, as I did with Frames, that will allow you to see an applet at work and, more importantly, to modify it by adding your own content. We will use the JDK, which you must download; it's exceptionally easy to use. What's nice about some of the applets at JavaSoft (Sun Microsystem Java) is that they are clearly marked as being in the public domain: "Permission to use, copy, modify, and distribute this software and its documentation for non-commercial or commercial purposes and without fee is hereby granted." (You will find the site at *http://java.sun.com/applets/applets.html*. The site is entitled: "Cool applets we've written (beta).") You will find this statement concerning the copyright preceding each applet that the Java team itself developed. Do not think, however, that all the applets at the JavaSoft site are in the public domain; they are not! JavaSoft allows for the modification of these selected applets as well. After you become familiar with the JDK, you will have discovered that many of the applets, developed by the Java team, that are on the JavaSoft Web site are included in the kit. At the site and in the kit, you will mind an applet entitled *NervousText.class*. This is the one that we will work with and modify. All of the applets can be redone and reshaped to fit your own needs for having an applet on your Web site.

It is important to understand (again) that for an applet to work, three files are necessary: The Java class file (which in our case is going to be *NervousText.class*) and a Java source code file and a Java data file, all three of which are supplied by JavaSoft authors and are to be found in the kit. After having looked at the *NervousText.class* file in the viewer, we can easily modify it since it contents is a simple sentence or possibly a set of phrases. But first we need to understand what the basic programming syntax is for an applet. Some parts are required; some are implied or optional:

```
CODEBASE CDATA #IMPLIED -- code base --
CODE CDATA #REQUIRED -- code file --
ALT CDATA #OPTIONAL -- alternate text --
NAME CDATA #IMPLIED -- applet name --
WIDTH NUMBER #REQUIRED
HEIGHT NUMBER #REQUIRED
ALIGN (left|right|top|texttop|middle|absmiddle|baseline|
    bottom|absbottom) baseline #IMPLIED
VSPACE NUMBER #IMPLIED
HSPACE NUMBER #IMPLIED
PARAM NAME #REQUIRED -- The name of the parameter --
VALUE CDATA #IMPLIED -- The value of the parameter --
```

This, again, is the syntax, or paradigm for an applet. It has some similarities with the syntax of a Table and a Frame. Let's take the *NervousText.class* file and place it in this syntax, and while doing that place the whole thing into a HTML file, with an absolute URL, which will call on the class file. (Remember there is more than one file that makes up an applet.) And while constructing this file, I will make some changes in the message:

```
<HTML>
<HEAD>
<TITLE>Nervous text</>TITLE>
</>HEAD>
<APPLET CODEBASE="http://www.javasoft.com/applets/
applets/NervousText" CODE="NervousText.class" width=600
height=150 align=center >
        <PARAM NAME="text" VALUE="Buy, Read, Use . . . W4!
        Make Joe Hoppy!">
        <BLOCKQUOTE>
        <HR>If you were using a Java-enabled browser,
        you would see dancing text instead of this
        paragraph.<hr>
        </>BLOCKQUOTE>

</>APPLET>
</>HTML>
```

In this example, I have added the absolute URL, the name of the code, which is the *NervousText.class,* and the values for width, height, and alignment. The

Param Name is "text" and the value is the content, which will do the nervous (happy) dance. Here I typed "Buy, Read, Use . . . W4! Make Joe Hoppy!" Joe is Joe Opiela, who is the VP for Humanities and my editor at Allyn and Bacon. Also note that I put in a block quote format as an *ALT* message, which will be seen only if a person's browser does not pick up the applet. When this file is dragged and dropped into the applet viewer, you see the letters in the words jumping up and down and sideways. Here is a picture I took (Fig. 69), which of course is a single instance of the dance:

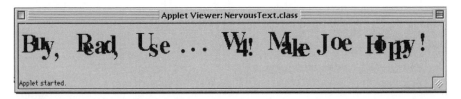

FIGURE 69

This is a start; there's certainly a lot more to know about Java and applets. You will find at the Java site more than adequate explanations for applets, how they work and how already-constructed ones can be modified. And here are some additional sites you can visit, after spending much time studying the Java site:

- Sun Microsystems Java Page at *http://sun.com*
- SunSoft at *http://www.sun.com/sunsoft/index.html*
- Gamelan at *http://www.gamelan.com*
- Silicon Graphics at *http://www.sgi.com*
- The Java Developer (much info here) at *http://www.digitalfocus.com/faq*
- JavaWorld at *http://www.javaworld.com*.

Virtual Reality Modeling Language (VRML)

VRML is a wholly different world! As the animation gets more and more sophisticated from GifAnimation to applets and not to VRML, you will actually have the sense of getting inside the object. This feeling comes with the three-dimensional character and illusion that is created.

The best viewer that I found available for both platforms, Mac and Windows, is Virtus Voyager, made by Virtus Corporation. (There are numerous other companies that have viewers for single platforms or that are in the process of developing for both platforms; I will list their URL after at the end of this section.) Therefore, you should go to Virtus at *http://www.virtus.com* and download their viewer. It took me a while to learn how to use it, but once I discovered that the mouse was just as easy to use as a means of navigating as the controls at the bottom of the viewer, I was well on my way to entering a monitor that became 3-D.

Once you have the viewer, click on the company's 3-D Web site and click on Enter again and thereby download the *homeworld.wrl* file. (3-D files are saved in *.wrl* files.) You read (experience) this file and other files by downloading them and then uploading them into the viewer, the latter of which can be done either by dragging and dropping the file or by going to View on the menu and loading the file. It will take a while for it to load. Once it has, you can advance the image by clicking on the arrow to the left point up. Or you can take your cursor arrow and hold it down on the screen, which will bring the red architectural building to the forefront (Fig. 70). Try to move toward the door and enter it. Once inside you will see the walls in a 360-degree fashion if you maneuver the cursor arrow appropriately (Fig. 71). Keep working with it and you will get the feel of it.

At this writing, the company has listed individuals' prize-winning 3-D files, which can be downloaded and viewed. You will look at them in the same manner as I previously described. Also, while at Virtus, you can download a demo program of 3-D Webmaster Builder 1.0+ or Walk Through Pro 2.0+. (Remember, these are only demos and will not allow you to do much, such as save what you have built, but they do give you a feel of how the programs work.) Here are some additional sites that you might want to visit for 3-D viewers:

- Paper Software, WebFX at *WWW.construct.net/projects/paper/*. At present, this viewer is good for all Windows, although viewers are being developed for Mac and Unix
- Sony, CyberPassage at *http://vs.sony.co.jp/VS-E/vstop.html*, for Windows95
- Microsoft, VRML add-on at *http://www.microsoft.com/windows/ie/vrml.htm*, for Windows95
- Vream, WIRL at *http://www.vream.com*, for Windows95
- Also you will want to go to Netscape's page on 3-D at *http://www.netscape.com/comprod/products/navigator/live3d/vrml-resources.html*

When you visit these pages, you will find their authoring tools (demos) and links to 3-D sites. I would recommend that you visit Cybertown at *http://www.cybertown.com*. Once you get inside 3-D, you will not want to leave. To be sure, it's not anywhere as advanced as what we can get on CD-video games, but it brings the Web to life, which will become more and more alive as we now enter multimedia with streaming audio and video coming together in Shockwave.

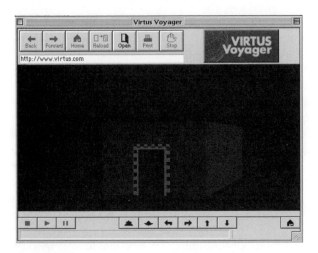

FIGURE 70

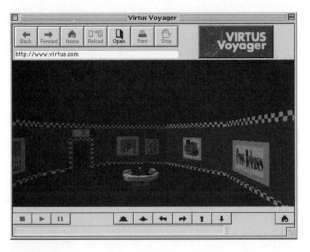

FIGURE 71

Multimedia

Netscape Plug-Ins

Netscape, with its version 2+, has given us, among other advances, *plug-ins*, or what is called plug-in architecture, which allows for third-party software companies to integrate their software directly into Netscape Navigator. With this event, the Web became capable of a multimedia experience. What the plug-ins do is to allow sophisticated sound and video files or both combined to be embedded in the HTML Web page. So when visiting a page that is multimedia, you simple click on the sound or video or combined files or you see a screen appear on your page, which you then activate. The plug-ins allow for one of two possibilities, depending on just how sophisticated the software is: they allow for a sound or video file to be downloaded or they allow for something called continuous *streaming,* which allows your computer to start playing live radio immediately while it is downloading a file.

How do you get these plug-ins? You simply download them from the appropriate Netscape site. They are freeware and there are approximately a hundred plug-in at this writing. When you are surfing the Web and find a Web site that is using audio or video, etc., plug-in(s), you may see a broken plug-in emblem and then get a dialogue box telling you that you do not have the necessary plug-in and that it will give you an opportunity to go to the necessary site to download what you will need to get the full benefit of the site. If you would rather not wait for such a message, you can go directly to the plug-in site at *http://home.netscape.com/comprod/products/navigator/version_2.0/ plugins/index.html* and download what you think you will need. Be careful, however, to check what platforms (Mac, Windows, etc.) the plug-ins are presently available for and be sure to find out what the system and memory requirements are. (If you are using a Mac version of Netscape, go to the Apple menu when you have Netscape launched and pull down "About Plug-Ins" to see what plug-ins you have installed; if a Windows version, go to the Help menu and pull down the same.)

Audio

Let's look specifically now at audio and the Web. (As I have hinted at intermittently, we are moving from stasis to flux, from silence to sound, from pictures to animation to movies, from the flat Web page to multimedia.) If you recall, when David was revising his home page in Chapter 3, he introduced RealAudio and QuickTime links to sites where there were files to be found and downloaded. RealAudio can be found at *http://www.realaudio.com.* If you have not already, you might go there and download the RealAudio Player 2.0 (or the latest version, which is now 4.0), which is freeware. Presently, it exists for several platforms such as Windows95, NT, and Mac. You will most likely be asked to give your name and e-mail address for update messages, and you will be asked what operating system and what your modem speed is, 14,400 or 28,800 or whatever you might have that is faster. If you have anything slower than 14,400, the player will not work for you. Take care to read the tech notes and get the RealAudio plug-in from Netscape. While you are at RA, you might want to download the "RealAudio SDK Beta," which is a kit "for developers who want to create applications such as presentations, games, or educational and training software using archived or live RealAudio content, including synchronized Multimedia files." This kit, however, is available only for Windows OS.

When you are at the RealAudio site, you will see ABC radio and NPR links. Presently, to be able to link to their files and live connections, at least from the RA page, you will have to sign up with RealAudio, which means getting a user's name and password. You definitely will want to go to C|NET radio at *http://www.cnet.com/Content/Radio/index.html*.

Now the question might arrive: Why would I want to listen to the radio on my computer? This is a good question. You may very well have a number of radios, but what you have to understand about Net radio is that you can get stations from all over the world and with good reception, and you can get radio programs, etc., that are primarily designed for the Web and not available elsewhere. And then, if you want to listen to files embedded on multimedia pages, you have to have a player. Be aware, however, that players—and hence, files made by them—are at present incompatible.

Some other players that you might want to check into are:

- Internet Wave at *http://www.vocaltec.com/iwave.htm*
- Toolvox at *http://www.voxware.com/*
- Truespeech Internet at *http://www.dspg.com*

Some sites for radio Web casts:

- National Public Radio (NPR) at *http://www.npr.org/*
- Public Broadcasting System (PBS) at *http://www.pbs.org/*
- Internet Talk Radio at *http://town.hall.org/*
- AudioNet at *http://www.audionet.com/*
- Internet Underground Music Archive: *http://www.iuma.com/*
- and Yahoo's Index of Webstations at *http://www.yahoo.com/Entertainment/ Radio/Internet*

Video
Like audio, you can receive video as files to download and view or you can get them live through view-streaming. Cutting to the chase, let's go to the QuickTime site at *http://quicktime.apple.com/*. There you will find a load of different kinds of software and a new plug-in for Netscape 3.0 to download or you can go directly to QuickTime software at *http://quicktime.apple.com/qt/ sw/sw.html*. For example, you will find at this writing version 2.1.1 of the viewer. The QuickTime VR player can be found at http://qtvr.quicktime. apple.com/. And you can see the archives of QuickTime Live videocasts and, if timely, scheduled live events shown by way of QuickTime streaming.

If you are interested in video files, visit "Video Links" at *http://members. aol.com/videolinks/index.html*. Also, go to CNN's Video Vault at *http://www.*

cnn.com/video_vault/index.html. And be sure to visit and read about "streamed video" at Iterated Systems, *http://www.iterated.com*. You will want to download the ClearFusion plug-in for Netscape and view some of their sample streamed videos. Look, I'm tired of doing all the work for you: If you want to know more about videos, then, get on a search engine like AltaVista (*http://www.altavista.com/*) and start finding material for yourself!

Macromedia Flash

There is a relatively new product that is available on the market at this writing, and that is FutureSplash Animator. It's orginally a product of Future-Wave (*www.futurewave.com/*), but has been purchased by Macromedia (*www.macromedia.com/software/flash/*). When you visit this site, you will be told that you must have the plug-in for Flash. It's a small plug-in for Netscape 2+. Click on the appropriate link and download the plug-in that you will need. Be sure to follow instructions for installing the plug-in, which requires that you restart your computer. When you finally get to the site and see what it looks like, you will notice that you can download a trial version of the Flash to see how it works.

What can Flash do? Just about everything! The present version includes both audio and video capabilities. What's especially nice about the technology is that it is situated, in sophistication, somewhere between GifAnimator and Shockwave. The files, even uncompressed, are smaller than those produced with GifAnimator and therefore will load and recycle at a fast clip. And Flash works across many platforms (Mac and Windows included), it works with movies (QuickTime and many others), and is one of the most versatile programs of its kind of the market. The commercially available program is reasonably priced and has numerous examples of various kinds included and a full book-size manual. When you visit the site, be sure to click on the link to sites with Flash animations.

One thing you need to be aware of concerning this program, unlike Gif-Animation, is that for your animations to work on your server (so that other people with the correct plug-in can virtually see the animations), it will be necessary for your system operator on campus to make a few minor adjustments in the reading protocol. These adjustments, however, should pose no problem, and there is every reason for your SysOp to want to meet your request since he or she wants visitors to the site to get the full impact of your work.

Shockwave

Shockwave, which has been developed by Macromedia (*http://www. macromedia. com/software/director/*), is *the* experience of the Web. It is part of the multimedia program Director. What Shockwave will do is to allow you to view multimedia content. (I am not going to get into a discussion about the authoring program Director, for it is really the subject of another, more advanced book.) For a copy of the player, go to "Macromedia: Shockwave Center" at *http:// www.macromedia.com/shockwave/*. What you will be downloading is a plug-in for your Netscape browser. Shockwave works seamlessly. Be aware, however, that this plug-in takes a lot of memory. Be sure to read the specifications carefully. You will need more than 8MB of RAM.

When you are at the Shockwave Web site, be sure to visit their various links to sites with illustrative work done with Director. At present, the sites at Adobe/Shockwave are called simply "Cool Sites," "Vanguard Gallery," or "Shockzone." You can get lost in these places.

If you have noticed, I have written less and less as we have approached multimedia. I will end here, for Shockwave should not be written about but visited on the Web itself. Enjoy yourself!

APPENDIX **A**

Important Sources on the WWW for Students of the Humanities

The URLs for Web sites are included here are highly selective; they supplement those given in individual chapters. They are given only to suggest further what is available on the Web. The search engines will, no doubt, give you many more comparable sites to visit. Be sure also to check the Web site for this book, *W4*.

Search Engines

Lycos, HP
http://www.lycos.com/

WebCrawler
http://webcrawler.com/

AltaVista
http://altavista.digital.com/

HotBot
http://www.hotbot.com/

Directories and Lists

VVinks, numerous links on numerous topics
http://www.uta.edu/english/V/Rhetoric.html

The English Server-CMU
http://english-www.hss.cmu.edu/

Voice of the Shuttle/Index, a list of lists at UCSB
http://humanitas.ucsb.edu/shuttle/

Yahoo, Directory
http://www.yahoo.com/

Whole Internet Catalog
http://nearnet.gnn.com/gnn/wic/index.html

Copyright Sites

World Wide Web Issues
http://www.benedict.com/webiss.htm

The Copyright Website
http://www.benedict.com/

Copyright, Intellectual Property, and Publishing on the WWW
http://www.pitt.edu/~hypertch/copyright.html

Humanities Sites

Voice of the Shuttle HP
http://humanitas.ucsb.edu/

The WWW Virtual Library: Humanities
http://www.hum.gu.se/w3vl/w3vl.html

Rhetoric and Composition

WWW Resources for Rhetoric and Composition
http://www.ind.net/Internet/comp.html

Rhetoric Links, artifacts, classic texts, debate resources, historic speeches, institutional links, U.S. government speeches, etc.
http://www.bc.edu/bc_org/avp/cas/comm/Rhetoric.html

Writing Process

Ted Nellen's collection of numerous links on the Writing Process
http://mbhs.bergtraum.k12.ny.us/writing.html

Communications

American Communication Association WWW Archives (numerous links)
http://www.uark.edu/depts/comminfo/www/ACA.html

The Media and Communication Studies Site
http://www.aber.ac.uk/~dgc/gen.html

Literature

Literature Links
http://elwing.otago.ac.nz:889/dsouth/links.html

Authors Links and Info, extensive
http://www.empirenet.com/~rdaeley/authors/authors.html

American Literature, Voice of the Shuttle
http://humanitas.ucsb.edu/shuttle/eng-amer.html

Philosophy

Philosophy on the Web
http://www.phil.ruu.nl/philosophy-sites.html

Bjorn Christenson, Philosophers' Guide (Aquinas, Aristotle, Augustine,
Berkeley, Descartes, Hegel, Heidegger, Hobbes, Hume, Kant, Kierkegaard,
Leibniz, Locke, Marx, Mill, Nietzsche, Pascal, Plato, Rousseau, Russell, Sartre,
Schopenhauer, Spinoza, Voltaire, Wittgenstein)
http://www-und.ida.liu.se/~y92bjoch/filosofer/philosophers.html

Women in Philosophy
http://billyboy.ius.indiana.edu/WomenInPhilosophy/WomeninPhilo.html

Criticism (Literary and Cultural)

Gender Studies Page, Voice of the Shuttle
http://humanitas.ucsb.edu/shuttle/gender.html

Literary Theory Page, Voice of the Shuttle
http://humanitas.ucsb.edu/shuttle/theory.html

CTheory
http://english-www.hss.cmu.edu/ctheory/ctheory.html

Online Writing Labs (OWLs)

Purdue University's OWL
http://owl.trc.purdue.edu/

RPI Writing Center + links to other OWLs
http://www.rpi.edu/dept/llc/writecenter/web/net-writing.html

Dakota State U OWL
http://www.dsu.edu:80/departments/liberal/cola/OWL/index.html

Educational MUDs and MOOs

MOO Central, Jeff Galin's links to a variety of MOOs (and MUSHs)
http://www.pitt.edu/~jrgst7/MOOcentral.html

Educational Muds and MOOs
http://www-ts.cs.oberlin.edu/rooms/edmoos.html

Electronic Journals

Computer-Mediated Communication Magazine
http://sunsite.unc.edu/cmc/mag/current/toc.html

CWRL-Computer, Writing, Rhetoric, and Literature-UT/Austin
http://auden.fac.utexas.edu:80/~cwrl/

RhetNet: A CyberJournal
http://www.missouri.edu/~rhetnet/

Kairos: A Journal for Teachers of Writing in Webbed Environments
http://english.ttu.edu/kairos/homepage.html

PRETEXT: Electra(Lite)
http://www.utdallas.edu/pretext/

Fractals

Chaos and Fractals
http://www.dd.chalmers.se/~gu94joli/caf.html

Utilities and Special Freeware and Shareware for Constructing/Accessing Web Sites

ISKM Software Updates (lots of utilities such as NSCA Telnet, UnStuffit, etc., to be donwloaded free here)
http://www.mcp.com/hayden/iskm/iskm-soft.html

For Stuffit Expander
ftp://ftp.ncsa.uiuc.edu/Mosaic/Mac/Helpers/stuffit-expander-352

For Fetch, FTP for Mac
http://www.dartmouth.edu/pages/softdev/fetch.html

For WS_FTP, for Windows
http://www.csra.net/junodj/ws_ftp.htm

Netscape plug-ins
`http://home.netscape.com/comprod/products/navigator/version_2.0/`
`plugins/index.html`

MapEdit, WWW ImagemapEditing Software for Windows, allow you to construct ImageMaps
`http://www.boutell.com/mapedit/`

WebMap for Macintosh, shareware
`http://home.city.net/cnx/software/webmap.html`

Shareware.com, the way to find shareware by way of a search engine
`http://www.dsiegel.com/tips/index.html`

About transparent and interlaced GIFS and tools on several platforms
`http://dragon.jpl.nasa.gov/~adam/transparent.html`

HTML Editors

BBEdit Lite 3.5.1 (freeware version of the commercial Macintosh editor)
`http://www.barebones.com/`

PageSpinner (Macintosh) (shareware)
`http://www.algonet.se/~optima/pagespinner.html`

FlexEd v1.7c (Windows) (shareware)
`http://www.infoflex.com.au/flexed.htm`

Gomer 1.4 (Windows) (shareware)
`http://www.clever.net/gomer/index.html`

Hypertext/Multimedia

Eastgate Systems (Home of "StorySpace"/hypertext)
`http://www.eastgate.com/`

Voice of the Shuttle, Technology of Writing Page
`http://humanitas.ucsb.edu/shuttle/techwrit.html`

Yahoo—Computers and Internet: Multimedia: Hypermedia
`http://www.yahoo.com/Computers/Multimedia/Hypermedia`

Ch. 4, Hypertext & MultiMedia, update to *CyberReader*
`http://www.abacon.com/cyber/public_html/Ch04.html`

VVinks, Hypertext +
`http://www.uta.edu/english/V/writelect.html`

Scanning Images/Pictures and Using PhotoShop

This is just a brief note with a few tips about how to prepare graphics. It will be necessary to look at the manuals that come with the scanning program available to you and especially the manual(s) that come with the program PhotoShop (Adobe, *http://www.adobe.com*). You can learn a lot by just playing around with PhotoShop, so don't rely too heavily on the manual.

Caveat

I have to tell you once again that under no circumstances should you think that you can scan whatever you want and then run it through Photo-Shop, slightly changing it, and then put it out on your Web page. If you do this, you are most likely violating copyright law. Therefore, play it safe and scan only the work that you have personally produced, or the work that another person has done and has given you permission to reproduce.

Basic Tips

First you will scan and then take your file to PhotoShop. All scanners pretty much work on the same principle. The software is intuitive, so you will know where to point and click to get the results that you want. The software will most likely read the item you want scanned and determine whether it is black and white or color, or an ink drawing or a color photo, and hence will automatically establish the correct settings. You can set such features as light, contrast, and the size of the file. Be sure to keep your eyes on the size of the file, the amount of K (memory). You can always change the size later when you take the file to PhotoShop.

You will most likely be given the opportunity to preview the image and make what ever adjustments you want (e.g., deciding what part of the image, if not all, that you want to scan or to zoom in on); then, you will be given the opportunity to make the final shot, which you will save to your desktop or in a Doc. That's about it for scanning.

Launch PhotoShop and then go to File and then to Open. Locate the scanned image and open it into PS. Once this is done, save the file in the format it comes up in. You will resave it later in a more appropriate format. At this point, you can resize, turn, distort, recolorize, crop the file—whatever you want. (Spend some time looking through the menu items.) You will have a tool bar that lets you do any number of things to the image. The large T is for type, the pencil is for inserting a pixel at a time, etc. You will notice at the bottom of the toolbar black and white squares that signify the background and foreground colors. If you double click on these, you will get the color chart that will allow you to change the black and white squares to other colors. Play around with the tools to learn how to use them.

Once you have opened up the scanned image and initially saved it, go to the menu and pull down Image to Image Size. When the dialogue box opens, you will be given an opportunity to resize your file. Make sure that width and height boxes (for pixels or inches) are linked together in proportions. Your resolution should be at 72psi (the Web will not recognize anything greater than this number). Your mode should be set most likely at RGB. At this point simply resize your scanned file. (Do not save yet.) After resizing check to see if you have the size that you want, be sure to check the amount of K (memory). Also look at the top of the box for the file and make sure that it reads "1:1", that is, that the ratio is one to one. If it is "2:1", then your picture is really twice the size that is visibly showing, and will not appear on the Web as you are seeing it. If this happens, go to the menu again and to Window and down to Zoom to find the 1:1 relationship. If you wish to make further changes in size, repeat the process you went through earlier.

When you have found the precise size, you might want to work with the Shade, Contrast, and Sharpness of the file. If so, go to the menu and pull down Filter to Sharpen. Or go to the menu and pull down Image to Adjust and then to Brightness/Contrast or better to Variations, which will give you about eight views of the scanned file to help you make your decisions about all the above features such as contrast, hue, etc.

When you are satisfied with the image size and look, go back to Save As and save this time as a GIF or a JPEG. I would save all nonphotographs in the format of a GIF; and save all photographs as a JPEG. And remember, you want your graphic files to upload fast; therefore, reduce the size (number of K) as much as possible.

If by chance you are working with a lite version of PS, which often comes bundled with a scanner, you will not be able to save your image as a GIF. So I recommend that you get a copy of Kevin A. Mitchell's shareware program, GifConverter 2.1.5+ (*http://www.kamit.com/gifconverter.html*), which does exactly what it says it does. Also you will want to get a copy of the freeware program Transparency 1.0+ (*http://dragon.jpl.nasa.gov/~adam/transparent.html*), which will allow you to convert your GIFs, if the design calls for it, into GIF89a files, which are transparent graphics on your site. Both programs come with explanatory notes.

There is so much more to all this, but you will learn as you proceed.

APPENDIX C

Using the (Re)Search Engines

Many of you probably have a basic understanding of how to do research in the library, how to search for books and articles by way of card catalogs or databanks. If you have a basic understanding of library research, then you are prepared to making word and phrase searches using the powerful search engines that are available now for use on the Web.

If you have access to Netscape (or other graphic browsers), you can get to the search engines very easily. On Netscape, you just click on Net Search and you will get to a page that is filled with the available resources to begin your research. One of the most powerful search engines at present is AltaVista (http://altavista.digital.com/); a rather new engine at this writing is *HotBot* (http://www.hotbot.com), and it appears to be perhaps more thorough in its searches of the Web than any other search engine available. AltaVista and HotBot are not passive search engines: Instead of expecting authors of Web pages to inform them of new Web sites, these engines have what are called Bots (or search agents) that sweep the Internet and Web, that virtually go into every accessible server and read the contents of every file (page, document) and send the data back to its Big Machines. AltaVista claims to be able to make a sweep of the servers every two weeks; HotBot, every three days! These figures are grossly overexaggerated by the companies. Both search engines, however, are excellent and you should have some basic understanding of how they work. The best way is to go to each home page and click on its Help icon and to read the instructions.

Let's take a quick look at the basic instructions at AltaVista. You can make two kinds of searches, Simple and Advanced. Simple is usually enough. When you are ready to search for what is on the Web about a person or a topic, type in the *name* or *phrase* (avoiding punctuation) and see how many "hits" (returns) you get. Usually searches are done at such a high level of generalization that far too much information is listed. Sometimes it can be easily over 100,000 items, which would be ridiculous. Therefore, you really need to learn how to pinpoint what you are looking for.

Here are some strategies to narrow your search: One of the most powerful ways to put together a search is to use *quotes* around the word or phrase. Hence, if you were searching for information on "bell hooks" you would put her name in quotes as I have done here. It is also a good idea to keep all words, including names, in *lowercase.* If you use uppercase (capital letters) the engine is directed to look only for those items in caps. (Since "bell hooks" represents her name in lowercase, you would never find it on the Web unless someone had stuck to the convention of capital letters for proper names when writing about "hooks.") This is a very general way to search for "hooks" but since she is relatively new in the history of literature and criticism, you would be wise to start at a general level.

If you were searching for "William Shakespeare," you might start out by typing in his name in quotes just to see the number of hits you might get. Remember that just because Shakespeare has been read and written about longer than bell hooks has does not mean that on the Web you will find more about Shakespeare than about hooks. The Web, unlike an actual library, is so new to us that it is hard to tell what might be available on it. Therefore, it pays to begin with a general search and then narrow things down. One of the best ways to really get specific is to use the Advanced method of searching. On the AltaVista page, click on Advanced. To make detailed searches, you should use Boolean logic, in other words, use the terms AND, OR, NEAR, and NOT. (These may be used in upper- or lowercase.) What do they mean? AND allows for a combination search; OR for one or the other; NEAR for the two items appearing within ten words of each other; and NOT (always represented as AND NOT and never NOT by itself) an exclusion.

Let's say that you would like to search for any Web pages on Shakespeare's sonnets and not the plays. In order to retrieve such sites (if any are available), you would then type into the search form: *Shakespeare AND sonnet* AND NOT plays.* What does this search for? Well, it searches for any information, if available in the AltaVista databank, on Shakespeare's sonnets and *not* his plays. Note that the symbol * is used. When this is put into the middle of a word or at the end, it allows for the search to find variable spellings or forms of the word, which in this case would be, beside the singular form of *sonnet,* the plural form *sonnets.* It is possible, since the Web often has material on it that is not proofread in any professional way, variations on spellings. In Shakespeare's own day, there were many ways to spell his name! It would be wise, therefore, to add an asterisk to *Shakespear** and not type in *Shakespeare.* It also would be wise to try both spelled differently. The

NEAR command may appear to be puzzling, but what if on a page there is a rendering of our author's name as "Shakespeare, William"? It is possible that a conventional search of "William Shakespeare" (in quotes) might miss "Shakespeare, William." Hence, it would pay to type into the search form: *William NEAR Shakespear* AND sonnet* AND NOT play**.

I will leave you with HotBot and your own resources; it's also a very user-friendly Web site, so give it a try. Besides these two search engines there are many other ways to research the Web.

Other Search Engines and Directories: Global Search

Infoseek
```
http://guide.infoseek.com/
```

Excite ("Excite Live" allows you to set up your own Excite page according to your preferences.)
```
http://www.excite.com/
```

Lycos ("My Yahoo" allows you to set up your own Yahoo page according to your preferences.)
```
http://www.lycos.com/
```

Whole Internet Catalog
```
http://nearnet.gnn.com/gnn/wic/index.html
```

Yahoo, Directory
```
http://www.yahoo.com/
```

Telephone Numbers and Mailing Addresses and Electronic Addresses

For *White Pages*, (helps locate people on the Internet):

Bigfoot, (E-mail forwarding service, good for when you change your number or provider)
```
http://bigfoot.com/
```

Four11 (E-mail, current addresses and telephone numbers)
```
http://www.Four11.com/
```

WhoWhere?, (E-mail addresses, home pages, URLs, internet phone numbers)
```
http://www.whowhere.com/
```

For *Yellow Pages* (locates businesses):

BigBook
```
http://www.bigbook.com/On'Village
```

On'Village
http://www.onvillage.com/

GTE Superpages: Yellow Pages
http://superpages.gte.net/

FAQ: How to Find E-mail Addresses
http://www.cis.ohio-state.edu/hypertext/gaq/usenet/
finding-addresses/faq.html

For UseNet (Newsgroups):

Deja News (Looks where people chat on Newsgroups. Many of the Global
Search Engines give you a choice between searching the Web or Newsgroups.)
http://www.deganews.com/

▶ APPENDIX D

Citing Electronic Discourse

What, in part, contributes to people not citing what they find on the Net or WWW is that there is not yet a standardized (i.e., widely accepted) bibliographical form for citing electronic discourse. The Modern Language Association in the *MLA Handbook for Writers of Research Papers* (4th Edition), recommends several formats (in section 4.9–10, Citing Online Databases). Also, you might want to check the American Psychological Association's (APA) *Publication Manual* (4th Edition). In any case, you should check with your instructor about which style of citing references is to be used.

I will give the following brief outlines and a few examples from the *MLA Handbook.* I have tried to follow the suggested forms for citing electronic discourse; in some cases, however, as you might discover, I have had to modify the forms, or create forms. You, too, may find this a necessity. In any case, here are the general recommendations for citing electronic discourse:

a. An electronic text that has a printed source but is also online (for Work Cited). The concept of "printed source" generally suggests that the discourse is fixed or stable, though of course the text may be corrected by textual scholars. What you have to keep in mind, however, is that prior to being placed in an electronic medium (online or on a CD-ROM), the text was in print. Here is a simple outline to follow for bibliographical references:

1. Name of author (if available)
2. Title of the text (underlined)
3. Publication information for the printed source
4. Publication medium (online)

5. Name of the repository of the electronic text (e.g., Oxford Text Archive, CD-ROM)
6. Name of the computer network (e.g., Internet, Bitnet, America Online, Dow Jones News Retrieval)
7. Date of access
(8. The Electronic Address, or the URL, if available. The address should be preceded by the word *Available.*)

Some examples:

Aristotle. *Rhetoric.* Trans. W. Rhys Roberts. NY: The Modern Library, 1954. Online. The English Server (Carnegie-Mellon Univ.). Internet. 22 August 1995. Available: http://www.rpi.edu/~honeyl/Rhetoric/index.html

Simply skip any of the information that is not available. I think it would be helpful to add another item of information such as a URL, if available, which would serve as simple specific locator. Hence, following date of access, I would include the word "Available" and then the URL.

Hardy, Thomas. *Far from the Madding Crowd.* Ed. Ronald Blythe. Harmondsworth: Penguin, 1978. Online. Oxford Text Archive. Internet. 24 Jan. 1994.

Shakespeare, William. *Hamlet. The Works of William Shakespeare.* Ed. Arthur H. Bullen. Stratford Town Ed. Stratford-on-Avon: Shakespeare Head, 1911. Online. Dartmouth Coll. Lib. Internet. 26 Dec. 1992.

b. Material in general with no printed sources (for Work Cited). This form is for text that have not (yet) been printed.

1. Name of author (if available)
2. Title (in quotations)
3. Date
4. Title of the database (underlined)
5. Publication medium (online)
6. Name of the computer service or provider
7. Date of access
(8. The Electronic Address, or the URL, if available. The address should be preceded by the word *Available.*)

Examples:

Brickman, Gary. "HotWired Interviews Elmer-DeWitt." 7 July1995. *HotWired.* Online. 8 July 1995: Available http://www.hotwired.com/special/pornscare/.

"Middle Ages." *Academic American Encyclopedia.* Online. Prodigy. 30 Mar. 1993.

"Foreign Weather: European Cities." *Accu-Date.* Online. Dow Jones News Retrieval. 20 Aug. 1993.

c. Material specifically from electronic journals, electronic newsletters, and electronic conferences (for Work Cited). This form is for text that have not (yet) been printed.

  1. Name of author
  2. Title of article (in double quotations)
  3. Title of journal, newsletter or conference (underlined)
  4. Volume, issue
  5. Year of publication (parentheses)
  6. Number of pages or paragraphs or n. pag. (no pages)
  7. Publication medium (online)
  8. Name of computer network (Bitnet or Internet)
  9. Date of access
 (10. The Electronic Address, or URL. The address should be preceded by the word *Available.*)

Examples:

Newsletter

Vitanza, Victor J. "Women on the Net." PRETEXT, *The Pretext Conversations News-letter* 1.1 (1995): n. pag. Online. Bitnet. 28 May 1995. Listserv@miamiu.acs.muohio.edu

(Note that there are no pages or URL available, which means that this post has not been put out on a Web site, but note that the Listserv, which serves this academic list PRETEXT is given. What this piece of information tells you is that you could subscribe to this list via the Listserv address.)

Electronic conference

Ulmer, Gregory. "Invention and Heuretics." REINVW, *The Pretext Conversations* (1994): n. pag. Online. Bitnet. 12 Nov. 1994. Available: http://miavx1.muohio.edu/~pretext/.

(Note that the URL is given, which means that the post, along with the rest of the conversation, is available at a Web site.)

Electronic Journal

Moulthrop, Stuart. "You Say You Want a Revolution?: Hypertext and the Laws of Media." *Postmodern Culture.* 1.3 (1991): 53 par. Online. Bitnet. 21 August 1995. Available: http://jefferson.village. virginia.edu/pmc/contents.all.html.

d. E-Mail Communication (for Work Cited): Some suggest that the e-mail address of the sender be included. I usually do not include it if the address is not publicly available on the author's Web site or through other media. Thus, I caution you not to include private addresses just as you would not give out someone's telephone number who does not have it publicly listed.

1. Name of author
2. Subject heading or description of post
3. Date of post

Examples:

Rheingold, Howard. "Permission to reprint." E-Mail to Victor Vitanza. 22 July 1995.

Haynes, Cynthia. "MOO Project." E-Mail to Victor Vitanza. 5 August 1996.

   e. Web site (or home page)

1. Name of author
2. Title
3. Last date modified (if available)
4. Electronic Address, or URL
5. Date accessed

Example:

Rheingold, Howard. "Brainstorms." http://www.well.com/user.hlr/. 6 September 1996.

Parenthetical Citations

To cite the above material within the body of your paper, use parenthetical, short forms including the author's name (if not used in introducing a quote or paraphrase) and a short title and date. For example, when I was editing and writing the book *CyberReader*, I e-mailed Howard Rheingold and he responded ("Permission to reprint," 22 July 1995), granting me permission to reprint a section of his book, *Virtual Reality*. Note that in the previous sentence I referred to the author's name in the text and then parenthetically cited the title of the message and gave the full date; the full reference, as given above would be in a Works Cited page. If I were to include the citation to the printed book, which is not online, then, I would follow standard MLA form for books in print.

    Citations of this sort are simple. The primary reason for the date is that there might be multiple posts back and forth and at times the title (usually taken from the subject heading of the post), might be the same as the posters' replies back and forth. (If there are more than one post and with the same title from one poster, then, I would simply label them "first post," "second post," etc., or whatever is comparable as long as you are consistent with your citations. Just remember that you are abbreviating what will be found as a complete reference in the Works Cited section.

If you are citing parenthetically something from an electronic journal, say, from an article by Moulthrop (as above), you might write something like the following:

> *In speaking about Ted Nelson's Xanadu Project, Moulthrop says: "As Nelson foresees it, Xanadu would embody [a] textual universe. The system would provide a central repository and distribution network for all writing: it would be the publishing house, communications medium, and great hypertextual Library of Babel" ("You say You Want," par. 6).*

Hence, the method of parenthetical citation is comparable to that method for citing published works in print.

However, if you were to limit the citation as such, you would be missing a wonderful opportunity to create a link to the full essay on the Web. Therefore, you might extend the above approach by using the HTML tag for a reference, anchored around the title of the article; in other words, you could tag the parenthetical citation in this manner:

```
(<A HREF="http://jefferson.village.virginia.edu/pmc/
contents.all.html">"You say You Want"</A>, par. 6).
```

When writing an electronic essay, you should attempt, if possible, to integrate the links into the prose without writing awkward cues:

```
("You say You Want"</A>, par. 6). And if you would like to
see this full essay, then, click <A HREF="http://jefferson.
village.virginia.edu/pmc/contents.all.html">HERE</A>.
```

This might look rather silly—and of course it is—but it is not uncommon to find this manner of inserting a link. Again, avoid such an approach.

There are, of course, many variations on citing electronic discourse. You should spend some time reading the MLA and APA guides. One other book that you might want to look at is *Electronic Style: A Guide to Citing Electronic Information* by Xia Li and Nancy B. Crane. Westport: Meckler, 1993. And you should definitely visit these Websites for additional information and suggestions: http://www.uvm.edu/~xli/reference/estyles.html.

Additional Resources for Citing Electronic Discourse

Janice Walker's MLA Style Citations of Electronic Sources
`http://www.cas.usf.edu/english/walker/mla.html`

John E. Goodwin's *Elements of E-Text Style*
`http://wiretap.spies.com/ftp.items/Library/Classic/estyle.txt`

Andrew Harnack and Gene Kleppinger's *Beyond the MLA Handbook*
`http://falcon.eku.edu/honors/beyond-mla`

Melvin E. Page's *A Brief Citation Guide for Internet Sources in History and the Humanities*
`http://h-net.msu.edu/~africa/citation.html`

APPENDIX E

Special Characters, Selected (HTML and ISO-Latin-1)

The symbols and character codes listed are not complete. I have selected these symbols, for they are most likely the ones that you will use. You will find instructions for using these character codes in the discussion on HTML in Chapter 2.

Symbol	Char Code	Entity Name	Symbol	Char Code	Entity Name
indented space			Ã	Ã	Ã
			Ä	Ä	Ä
¢	¢	¢	Å	Å	Å
£	£	£	Æ	Æ	Æ
¥	¥	¥	Ç	Ç	Ç
©	©	©	È	È	È
®	®	®	É	É	É
§	°	§	Ê	Ê	Ê
±	±	±	Ë	Ë	Ë
¶	¶	¶	Ì	Ì	Ì
•	·	·	Í	Í	Í
À	À	À	Î	Î	Î
Á	Á	Á	Ï	Ï	Ï
Â	Â	Â	Ñ	Ñ	Ñ

(continued)

Symbol	Char Code	Entity Name	Symbol	Char Code	Entity Name
Ò	Ò	Ò	é	é	é
Ó	Ó	Ó	ê	ê	ê
Ô	Ô	Ô	ë	ë	ë
Õ	Õ	Õ	ì	ì	ì
Ö	Ö	Ö	í	í	í
×	×	×	î	î	î
Ø	Ø	Ø	ï	ï	ï
Ù	Ù	Ù	ñ	ñ	ñ
Ú	Ú	Ú	ò	ò	ò
Û	Û	Û	ó	ó	ó
Ü	Ü	Ü	ô	ô	ô
Ý	Ý	Ý	õ	õ	õ
à	à	à	ö	ö	ö
á	á	´	÷	÷	÷
â	â	â	ø	ø	ø
ã	ã	ã	ù	ù	ù
ä	ä	ä	ú	ú	ú
å	å	å	û	û	û
æ	æ	æ	ü	ü	ü
ç	ç	ç	ÿ	ÿ	ÿ
è	è	è			

Index

(The following list includes Figures, Projects, and Templates of Full Tags.

(This index includes Names, Topics, and Uniform Resource Locaters [URLs] referred to in the book. This index does not include the URLs in Appendix A, which are easy to locate.)

▶

Credits

Amy Bruckman. "Cyberspace Is Not Disneyland." Reprinted by permission of Amy Bruckman and the Getty Information Institute.

Houghton Mifflin Company. "Composing." Copyright © 1996 by Houghton Mifflin Company. Reproduced by permission from *The American Heritage Dictionary of the English Language, Third Edition*.

Figures 1–7, 10–13, 18, 19, 21–28, 33–50, 65–68, 70, 71: Copyright 1996 Netscape Communications Corp. Used with permission. All rights reserved. The screens may not be reprinted or copied without the express written permission of Netscape. Netscape Communications Corporation has not authorized, sponsored, or endorsed, or approved this publication and is not responsible for its content. Netscape and the Netscape Communications Corporate Logos are trademarks and trade names of Netscape Communications Corporation. All other product names and/or logos are trademarks of their respective owners.

Figure 1: WWW Consortium, MIT lab for Computer Science. Reprinted by permission.

Figure 9: Dartmouth College. Fetch screen reprinted by permission.

Figure 18: Dave Rieder. Reprinted by permission.

Figure 19: C/Net. Reprinted by permission from CNET, copyright 1995–7.

Figure 20: Collin Brooke. Reprinted by permission.

Figure 22: Matthew Levy. Reprinted by permission.

Figure 23: Beth Baldwin and Eric Crump. Reprinted by permission.

Figures 26, 27: David Vitanza. Reprinted by permission.

Figures 70, 71: Virtus Corporation. Screen shots courtesy of Virtus Corporation, http://www.virtus.com.